THE BLOOD COVENANT OF GOD

Second Edition

A Series of Studies Based on Ancient and Biblical Blood Covenant Ceremonies

Denis I. Plant

The Blood Covenant Of God

Second Edition

A Series of Studies Based on Ancient and Biblical Blood Covenant Ceremonies

Denis I Plant

Vision Christian College
P.O. Box 84, Macquarie Fields NSW, 2564, Australia.

Copyright © 2007 By Denis Plant.

ISBN 978-1-61529-192-2

Vision Publishing
P.O. Box 1680
Ramona, CA 92065
1 (760) 789- 4700
www.booksbyvision.org

All rights reserved worldwide. No part of this book may be reproduced in any manner without the written permission of the author except in brief quotations embodied in critical articles of review.

"Scripture quotations taken from the New American Standard Bible®, Copyright © 1960, 1962, 1963, 1968, 1971, 1972, 1973, 1975, 1977, 1995 by The Lockman Foundation. Used by permission." (www.Lockman.org)

Genesis 15:1 (KJV) After these things the word of the LORD came unto Abram in a vision, saying, Fear not, Abram: I am thy shield, and thy exceeding great reward.

Table of Contents

Foreword 5
Introduction 7
Chapter 1: The Human Covenant 9
Chapter 2: The Biblical Covenants 23
Chapter 3: Entering Into The Covenant 41
Chapter 4: The Exchange Of Clothing 69
Chapter 5: The Exchange Of Weapons 91
Chapter 6: The Exchange Of Names 113
Chapter 7: Exchange Of Memorial Gifts 127
Chapter 8: Cutting The Covenant 143
Chapter 9: The Covenant Feast 159
Chapter 10: The Reading Of The Word 177
Chapter 11: The Seal Of The Covenant 189
Chapter 12: The Covenant Lawyer 205
Chapter 13: The Forgiveness Of The Covenant 217
Apendix I: Ramsis II Hattusillis III 229
Appendix II: The Mari Tablets 241
Appendix III: The Sacredness Of The Blood Covenant 245
Appendix IV: Covenants Around The World 249
Bibliography 269

Acknowledgements

I think I have come to the end of my "formal" study of the Blood Covenant and yet I shall continue to be fascinated with its wonders. But I need to take a moment to publicly acknowledge some people. The first is my dear wife Rosalind who has heard me teach and preach this subject with endless patience, she had encouraged and helped and nurtured me through the process. To her I am so grateful.

The Rev. Dr. Ken Chant who is very much a father in the faith and to refer to him as a friend is an honour for me. His encouragement, perhaps more than anyone else has left a deep impression in my life. Without his encouragement, I would probably not have completed this work nor had the opportunity to experience the blood covenant in my life the way I have. It is his example that has pressed me to, at least attempt to make a professional fist of the work.

Dr. Stan DeKoven, whose persistent "have you finished it?" has often refreshed my commitment to get back to reviewing and reworking the book he is endlessly encouraging to me.

The many scholars such as William E. Emmons, and H. Clay Trumbull whose work has given inspiration and made the study a greater and more driving fascination for me.

And finally but not least two dear friends Steve and Trish Hart. They are friends, staff members, colleagues, fellow labourers in the Gospel without whom I could not have completed this work.

To all of you I thank you, deeply, for the various helps to complete this work.

Thank you.

Foreword

If you are reading this foreword then you hold in your hands a book that will open up to you one of the greatest themes in the Bible – the *blood covenant* that God has made with his people. You may at once think that there is nothing remarkable in this, for are there not countless studies available on the subject? As a matter of fact, there are not! I'll warrant that many churchgoers have never heard a sermon or Bible study on this great concept! Yet the Bible knows of no acceptable way to make propitiation for human sin, except by the death of an appointed sacrifice.

Denis Plant has no doubt about the efficacy of the biblical promise, nor of the biblical affirmation that *"without the shedding of blood, there is no remission of sin"*. His approach to the theme is fresh, creative, and covers ground that is often ignored.

Thorough research has enabled him to explore the ramifications of the idea of a covenant sealed by blood, not only in ancient Israel but also in other different cultures. He demonstrates the place of the blood covenant in the history of redemption, in scripture, in apostolic times, and in the modern life of the church. Above all, he shows the power of this God-endorsed covenant in the life of each believer.

Our salvation both begins and continues here! Let us fervently trust in the blood of the everlasting covenant that God has made with us in Christ, by which alone we have open access to the very throne of heaven.

As Denis Plant shows, we should never question the truth of the old gospel song, *"There is power, power, wonder-working power in the precious Blood of the Lamb!"*

Ken Chant

Introduction

This second edition on the Blood Covenant has been a continuous labour of love for me. Since first hearing of the Blood Covenant through a series of tapes by a William E. Emmons in 1989 I determined to write a work for myself that would explain the significance of the Blood Covenant and how it works, why God uses a Blood Covenant and what the benefits of the Blood Covenant are to us as His people. This book unashamedly loosely follows his pattern of lectures.

As I began to search through Encyclopaedias of both a secular and religious nature I became fascinated at the similarity between the Covenants in the Word of God and the ancient secular Covenants dating back before the 2nd millennia B.C.

Many of my questions concerning the God's Word such as, why he had made such wonderful promises to us? Why does God hold such an eternal love for us? Why did God deal as so severely with the Philistines and other O.T. people? The real meaning and significance of these and so many more the scriptural truths unfolded for me as I began to search God's Word with reference to the Blood Covenant. The anomalies that I thought were there were wonderfully cleared up for me as the word of God fitted together in a wonderful picture of God's infinite care for us and His attention to the detail of our lives through His blood covenant is truly marvelous.

Through Jesus God, has established a Blood Covenant with mankind. We have been wonderfully elevated to a rich stature in him who he has committed His very existence and life to us and our welfare. He expects nothing less than this same level of commitment from us to Him. This we know.

The Blood Covenant of God explains to us the how, the why, answering many questions we have concerning God, his word, our relationship with him and so much more. Blood Covenant provides us the confidence in God's ability that we need, and enables him to keep us to himself as we keep our commitment to him.

I pray that as you read this that the Holy Spirit will come alongside you and:

> *That the God of our Lord Jesus Christ, the Father of glory, may give unto you the spirit of wisdom and revelation in the knowledge of him: The eyes of your understanding being enlightened; that ye may know what is the hope of his calling, and what the riches of the glory of his inheritance in the saints, And what is the exceeding greatness of his power to us-ward who believe, according to the working of his mighty power, Which he wrought in Christ, when he raised him from the dead, and set him at his own right hand in the heavenly places, Far above all principality, and power, and might, and dominion, and every name that is named, not only in this world, but also in that which is to come: And hath put all things under his feet, and gave him to be the head over all things to the church, Which is his body, the fullness of him that filleth all in all. Ephesians 1:17-23*

The version of the Bible used throughout this work is the New American Standard Bible unless otherwise noted. However, this work is not version specific. You will find the same rich truths, the same reflections and meaning with almost any version of the Bible you prefer to use.

Chapter 1:

The Human Covenant

Introduction

Throughout our ancient past, until our relatively recent past, the most binding agreement between two nations, peoples, tribes or families was the Blood Covenant.

Blood Covenant was responsible for the establishment and maintenance of peace between warring nations, or for the formalisation of existing peaceful relationships, or for the development of alliances between peoples, and nations, more than any other form of agreement.

Almost every culture in the world has its own style of formal agreement. While they may be referred to as an alliance, a treaty, a confederacy, a compact, or an agreement the most binding is the "Blood Covenant" regardless of what it may be called.

The major difference between a blood covenant and any other kind of agreement was that blood covenant was totally binding on both parties and their families. Under no circumstances could the covenant be terminated unless all of one, or both, of the families' descendants died. As long as a descendant of the families remained, the covenant was active.

These covenants and agreements took various forms and yet there are several common factors among them and, remarkably, the closer they are to Blood Covenant the more similarities there are in them in both their ritual and ceremony.

Much of the historical information we have concerning these blood covenant comes to us from information handed down from generation to generation and from mouth to mouth as fathers taught their sons. This is especially so with tribal treaties and covenants of the Africa, or America, or Far Eastern countries.

Sadly much of the information has been lost over time as cultures changed in countries like Great Britain, the USA, and Canada, much of Europe where changes to philosophy and cultural changes with the development, westernisation and modernisation of nations.

Fortunately, some of the ancient covenants of the Middle and Near Eastern countries were written in stone.

Examples of these are the Hittites treaties, the Esarhaddon[1] treaties and the Aramaean treaty of Sefire. As a result we are reasonably well informed of covenants, the reasons for them, the manner in which they developed, their effectiveness, their political and personal implications of Blood covenants.

Although these covenants are several thousand years old, dating back to over 1500 BC, we have explicit information of them in their original form thanks to the stone tablets they were written on. These stone tablets provide us with a permanent record of those ancient covenants.

The similarity between these Middle Eastern covenants written in stone and those of the African, American and Far Eastern handed down through folklore and local culture is amazing.

---

[1] Esarhaddon, King of Assyria {ee-sahr-had"-uhn} Esarhaddon, king of Assyria (680-69 BC), rose to power after the murder of his father, SENNACHERIB. He seems to have been a good general and administrator. After ensuring the allegiance of Babylonia, conquering Media, and strengthening the frontiers of his empire, Esarhaddon attacked Egypt in 675. Four years later he captured Memphis and established Assyrian rule in Egypt. He died while returning there to suppress a revolt.

In addition to the Hittites, the Esarhaddon and the Aramaean treaties we also have the "Amarna Treaties"[2]. These Covenants were dated during the second millennia BC and were successful in bringing about a peace throughout the nations of the time.

Brother Covenants

There were two kinds of Covenants used in the ancient history of the Eastern countries as seen by a study of the "Mari"[3] tablets. The Mari tablets were letters written around 2000 BC. They showed the life, times, laws, society, and the covenant rites of the people of that time having been written in great detail. Copies of them are kept in various museums around the world.

One covenant type was the covenant between equal partners. It was called the "Brother Covenant." It was so called because the covenant partners considered themselves equal with each other in strength, power, and wealth.

The covenant was used to determine and or formalise the relationship between them. Often it came about as the result of war which

---

[2] In the Ancient Near East, treaties between kings was common. These were treaties drawn up among equals and mostly outlined agreements to honor each other"s boundaries, to maintain trade relations, and return run-away slaves. These treaties are preserved in the Mari Tablets and in the Amarna texts. Also preserved in these collections are treaties drafted between a superior and his inferior. If the relationship was familial or friendly, the parties are referred to as "father" and "son." If the relationship is bereft of kindness and intimacy, the parties are referred to as "lord" and "servant," or "king" and "Vassal," or "greater king" and "lesser king." The greater king is the suzerain and the lesser king is a prince, or a lesser lord in the service of the greater king. The lesser lord is a representative of all the common people who are under the protection of the greater king. He enforces the treaty among the masses. -- "Suzerain Treaties & The Covenant Documents the Bible" Notes from lectures of Dr. Meredith Kline, presented at Westminster Theological Seminary in Escondido, California, Westminster Theological Seminary in Philadelphia, Pennsylvania, and Gordon-Conwell Theological Seminary, in Massachusetts

[3] See Apendix II Mari Tablets.

could not be won, as in the case of Ramsis II of Egypt and Hattusilis III of the Hittite empire.

A short history and a fuller explanation of the treaty between Ramsis II and Hattusilis III can be found in Appendix A, at the end of this book by (*Dr. Sameh M. Arab*).

The covenant decided the boundaries of the countries involved. It outlined the terms upon which they may or may not come to the aid of each other in times of war, and the treatment of runaway slaves, trade and various mutual laws of benefit to both Ramsis II and Hattusilis III[4].

The main purpose of their covenant was to help formalise and maintain the existing relationship between these two kings and their countries.

Vassal Covenant

The other type of covenant was called a "Vassal Covenant". This was the most common form of covenant. It usually came about as the result of the conquest of one king by a more powerful king if the conquering king could see some value or merit in sparing the life of the vanquished king.

A Vassal covenant could also come about as the result of the mutual respect of a greater king by a lesser king. This respect caused the lesser king to desire a strong and lasting alliance with the greater king. The relationship between the kings, and the basis upon which the Covenant was made, determined the way in which each king was addressed in the covenant.

If the covenant was the result of a friendly relationship or mutual respect, but one king was significantly more powerful or richer

---

[4] A treaty between Hattusilis III (r.c. 1289-1265 BC) and Ramsis II insured peace between the Hittites and Egypt on the southern border of the empire.

than the other, then the relationship would be marked by such covenant terms as "Father and Son".

If one King was a conqueror over the king of a smaller kingdom the conquering king would be referred to as the "Lord" and the lesser king would be referred to as the "Servant". The proper name for the servant is a "Vassal", and the name of this covenant was called the Vassal Covenant.

Examples of these covenants are found in the AMARNA TREATIES. They are also called the TELL EL-AMARNA STYLE [5] and date back to the second millennia BC. They were a part of the ancient Middle Eastern culture involving the Philistine, Hittites and Egyptian cultures. These covenants were usually laid out in the following manner.

---

[5] Tell el-Amarna, on the east bank of the Nile about 306 km (190 mi) south of Cairo, was the capital of Egypt under the heretic King AKHENATEN (Amenhotep IV, c.1379-1362 BC). This 18th-dynasty ruler founded the city as the centre of his monotheistic religion dedicated to the worship of the sun god Aten. Tell el-Amarna is a misnomer, combining the name of the village Et-Tell with that of a tribe, the Beni Amran, who settled nearby approximately two centuries ago. Its ancient name was Akhetaten, meaning "horizon of Aten." Akhenaten chose the site for the city and planned its layout, a record of which was carved on 14 stelae marking its boundaries, three west of the Nile. The administrative offices, the chief palace, and the great temple of Aten stood in the centre of the city, flanking the main road. In this region most of the so-called Amarna tablets--diplomatic correspondence in CUNEIFORM script with rulers and Vassals in western Asia--were found by chance in 1887. The site was extensively excavated (1891-92) by Sir Flinders PETRIE and by later British and German expeditions. In the crescent-shaped rocks east of the city, the Egyptians constructed tombs of the courtiers, mostly unfinished, and the tomb of the king. The tombs are famous for their lively wall reliefs, the scenes being executed in the so-called Amarna style, which radically departs from the expressive restraint of most EGYPTIAN ART. Early in his reign Tutankhamen (c.1361-1351 BC) abandoned Tell el-Amarna and restored the capital to Thebes. I. E. S. Edwards

The Covenant Contract

1. First an introduction of the Great King with all his titles and attributes followed by a historical prologue, in which the relationship between the Great King and the Vassal King and their forefathers were outlined. This is an actual history of the benevolence of the greater king to the Vassal and his country.
2. A prohibition of any formal relationship between the Vassal and any other king outside the sphere of the Great King's allies.
3. The prohibition of hostilities between any of the other Vassal Kings in a Covenant relationship with the Great King (often there were several Vassals in covenant with the Great King).
4. The Vassal must provide immediate assistance to the Great King or any of the other Vassals he is in treaty with in times of war or distress.
5. The Vassal must not listen to or give any credence to any slandering of the Great King and must report such slander immediately.
6. The Vassal must not hide nor may any of his people hide any refugees or slaves of the Great King.
7. Once a year the Vassal must appear before the Great King to pay his taxes and renew his treaty.
8. Two copies of the treaty were written. One was kept in the footstool of the Great King and the other was kept in the Vassal's temple. It must be read by the Vassal and to his people at least once a year.
9. A list of gods and goddesses were drawn up and they were called on to witness the covenant. The sun, moon, and stars, the rivers or mountains may be called upon to witness this covenant. The gods of the Great King were given the most prominent position in the document and must be accepted by the Vassal King in preference to his own gods.

10. The Vassal was assured of support in times of war or attack by an enemy and the benefit of any technological progress made by the Great King or any of his allies.
11. A list of blessings were included that were bestowed upon the Vassal King provided that he maintains his part of the covenant. These blessings included the perpetuity of his kingdom, personal wealth, peace and national prosperity.
12. The covenant ended with a list of curses that would befall either king if he broke the covenant. The curse always demanded the death of the covenant breaker regardless of who they were. These curses were of a wide variety and some were reserved for divine judgement.

Once entered into the covenant could not be broken except on pain of death of the covenant breaker, his entire family and sometimes his people.

This description of the AMARNA TREATY is the oldest recorded covenant in its entirety that we know of. It is fascinating that almost all Blood Covenants in almost every culture include most, if not all of the ceremonial aspects of this covenant.

It seems that at sometime in our distant past there was one form of covenant ceremony that was accepted and respected by every nation. Whether this came about as a result of a series of conquests by a superior king or whether it was an "evolutionary" development is now impossible to say with absolute certainty. However we do know that these principles have been adhered to throughout the world. In some countries these covenants were written as part of their religious culture, sometimes enshrined in their laws and sometimes they were simply understood by mutual consent.

In Africa, the Americas, Europe, the Middle or Far Eastern countries these concepts were adhered to and held as sacred by their people as they were by the peoples of Hattusilis III or Ramsis II and their descendants. Even thought their history is found often in folklore, handed down from generation to generation, or recorded in less robust forms than stone, the similarity is amazing.

It is not just the formal contract that is held in common. The covenant ceremony between countries and cultures is also amazingly similar.

Certainly there are some differences between the various kinds of covenant ceremonies. However the differences are more the result of differing cultural values for there are enough similarities to see that there was probably a common form of ceremony that either evolved or was adapted only to suit certain cultural needs and values.

The Covenant Ceremony

A covenant ceremony would incorporate the following points:

1. First there must be a mutual desire[6] on both parties to agree together to the concept of a covenant. This must be mutual for it will be binding on both parties.
2. Once the agreement was reached the terms of the covenant were publicly outlined by both parties. The Great King's scribes drew up the covenant contract as agreed upon.
3. The ceremony commenced with an exchange of weapons and armour by the covenant partners, (usually only from the Great King to the Vassal). This is to show that the Great King is bestowing his power and authority on the Vassal. At this time, and throughout the ceremony, it is the Vassal who will be in receipt of the majority of blessing. This part of the ceremony shows the mutual respect that each member has for each other, although the Great King will now take the predominant role in all the proceedings.

---

[6] The "mutual desire" for the Vassal was often the choice between agreeing to the Blood Covenant or being destroyed along with all family, tribe and sometimes the nation"

Once performed, all the armies of the Great King became the armies of the Vassal King. All the authority of the Great King became the authority of the Vassal King. All the laws of the Great King are the laws of the Vassal King.

It is worth noting that unless stipulated the Vassal King has little to offer the Great King.

4. After the exchange of the weapons came the exchange of clothing. The Great King gave the Vassal at least his cloak although sometimes it may also include fine outer garments as well. These robes were always among the finest robes in the kings respective wardrobes. This was done to show that all the wealth of the Great King became the wealth of the Vassal. All the honour of the Great King is become honour of the Vassal.

As clothing was a major means of identification of rank and authority in those days, the significance of the kings robes were much more important than today. Once given, the Vassal King had every right to wear the garment of the Great King and was entitled to the same respect and honour of the Great King as though he were the Great King himself.

5. Then came the reading of the covenant laws and its terms of reference. Not only was this to be done during this ceremony but also at the covenant feast and at least once a year on a designated day, usually on the first day of the year. The purpose of this was to remind the Vassal and his people of the relationship they were in and of the laws they must follow.

6. After the reading was the sacrifice of the substitute animal. There are many reasons for this which will be dealt with in greater detail later; however, I will touch briefly on some of them at this point.

   a) In coming together in a covenant the two kings have quite literally agreed to die to themselves and to live for each other. From this point on they are to consider themselves dead to themselves and alive for each other.

b) If the Kings literally died they would have been of little value to each other, so a substitute sacrifice had to be offered in their place.

c) This sacrifice usually took the form of a lamb or another domesticated animal such as a bullock, or a goat. It must be provided by the Vassal King as it was his life that was spared at this point. The sacrifice must come from his own herd or he must purchase it himself. This was the only way that the sacrifice could represent his own life. The animal was killed and cut down the spinal cord and lay open in two equal parts.

d) The two kings would then walk between the two pieces of the sacrifice in opposite directions in a large figure eight (8). They would begin and end this part of the ceremony between the two halves of the sacrifice.

e) As they did so they would pronounce the advantages and blessings of the covenant to each other. Each king would try to outdo the other in the pronouncement of blessings.

f) At a predetermined point the terms of the covenant would be outlined and the responsibilities of each covenant head would be pronounced.

g) Again at a predetermined spot the covenant heads would announce the curses that would befall the one who broke the covenant. The two covenant heads would attempt to outdo each other in curses. This would always end with the pronouncement of a horrific death to the covenant-breaker and sometimes his whole family.

7. Each of the kings called on their gods to witness the event, the Great King's gods always take the dominant role.

8. At the conclusion of the ceremony there would always be a ceremonial feast. At some point in the feast, which could last for several days; there would be a "breaking of bread"

ceremony. This ceremony was to be symbolic of the death of the sacrificial animal. In many cultures the flesh of the animal could not be eaten. To represent it they ate a piece of bread and declared that this bread was symbolic of the body that has died for them. They identify with the dead sacrifice and now live for their new covenant partner. In some cultures a piece of the actual carcass could be eaten. Again this would be done with the declaration that this body represented their own lives.

9. They would take a cup and drink some of the blood of the sacrificed animal. As they did so they believed that the life of the animal was in the blood. As this animal represented each covenant head, they believed that the blood of the animal represented their own blood; therefore they believed that as they drank they were drinking each other's blood. As they took the cup they made a declaration that from this time on they would live for each other. Again, they would declare that all that each owned was the property of the other.

10. This breaking of bread must be repeated as often as the kings came together. It must also be taken on feast days that commemorate the covenant with their people and occasionally when the Great King may call the Vassal King to a feast.

11. At sometime during the feast came an exchange of names or an addition of the name of the covenant partner's names to their name. This is perhaps best identified for us by our marriage ceremony when the woman will often take the man's surname as hers. However, as it concerns the covenant we will see that both of the parties take each other's name in a similar fashion.

12. Finally there came the seal of the covenant. This came in two ways;

   First a personal seal. The personal seal of the covenant was performed by the cutting of the individual's flesh, usually on the wrist or arm of both partners. Each partner would then press their open cut to the other's open cut and allow their blood to mingle as it flowed out. The idea was that once this was done the blood of each other would then be flowing through each other's veins. Therefore the life of each other is flowing through their veins. While this concept is often ascribed to the American Indian it is a world wide idea in various forms. However the scar, like any other form of the seal, was to remind the covenant heads of the covenant, its privileges, its rights and responsibilities.

The public seal of the covenant was to remind all their people of their covenant. This came in many forms such as the planting of trees, the building of monuments, or the giving of a herd of sheep or goats or other animal. As long as the monument remained the covenant was to remain and remind the people of the commitment to each other.

Nothing could be more binding on a nation, or as positive for them, than for their king to be in a covenant relationship with a Great King. Security for all was guaranteed, peace and prosperity was to be enjoyed by everyone from the least to the greatest. Justice would be done and be seen to be done. The covenant was practical, dynamic and a reality for everyone and was embraced as often as the opportunity raised itself.

An Application

It is remarkable that this is the avenue through which God has chosen to deal with us. Let there be no doubt that these aspects of the covenant, and many more, are found in our own Blood Covenant relationship with Jesus. This will be shown in great detail as we look to the word of God. Each aspect of the covenant forms an integral part of our Christian experience.

The more we examine the word of God in the light of the covenant the more sense the word of God makes to us and the more real our covenant relationship with him becomes.

As I confronted covenant these issues in the word of God, and studied the historical records I had to ask the question; Did God see fit to present his covenant to his people in a cultural form developed by Near Eastern empires, or did God's original pattern for his covenant in Eden form the cultural pattern of the Ancient Near East?

I will leave you to decide, as you explore this subject with me. As we leave this introductory history lesson and take a journey through time and archaeology, the bible and modern history we will begin to understand that we are united with Jesus as our Great King and with each other as His Vassals through Blood Covenant.

Blood Covenant is the reason for our relationship with Him, the means by which God will respond to us. It is why we must respond to Him and understand our relationship, as the seed of Abraham

> *After these things the word of the LORD came to Abram in a vision, saying, "Do not fear, Abram, I am a shield to you; Your reward shall be very great." Genesis 15:1*

End of Chapter Questions

1. What is the singular most import and difference between a Blood Covenant and any other form of commitment between peoples.
2. Describe the difference between the Brother Covenant and the Vassal Covenant.
3. What are the Mari Tablets and what is there significance to blood covenant.
4. Who were Ramsis II and Hatulsillis III.

Chapter 2:

The Biblical Covenants

Introduction

Blood Covenant is rarely taught or preached about in our churches, Bible Colleges or seminaries today.

It is not spoken of in the main stream of society for purposes other than historical interest or occasional entertainment purposes, and even then it is usually misrepresented as the film and entertainment industries simplify the concepts almost to the point of irrelevance.

As a topic, Blood Covenant is often considered in one or the other the extremes of being barbaric and bloodthirsty or a novelty.

Since the beginning of the 20th century Blood Covenant terminology has gradually disappeared from our everyday vocabulary and our Christian jargon. Disappear from our jargon it may, perhaps our understanding of it will slide into obscurity, but the force and fact of Blood Covenant is not and cannot be diminished. The effectiveness and responsibilities of Blood Covenant agreement are still in force and as powerful today as when the first drop of blood was spilt for the first blood covenant. This creates a problem.

A problem is created in that God deals with us through a blood covenant. Unfortunately we have often entered into this arrangement unwittingly, out of ignorance. We have done so because the purpose, principles and responsibilities of a blood covenant were not explained to us by those who brought us to Christ, for often they did not understand themselves. They did not understand because the principles and concepts have been relegated the obscurity of history.

As a result, without realising the majesty of our relationship, the awesomeness of our responsibilities to the covenant, or the binding effect that it has on us, we are often in violation of our relationship with God. As a result we suffer the consequences of ignorance. Fortunately for us, God deals with us through our heart, His grace and mercy intervene on our behalf, yet we deny ourselves much of the blessing available to us because we remain in ignorance.

I trust that as we peruse through this study together that your spiritual eyes will be opened and you will be as blessed as I have been, coming into a greater understanding of the most important of biblical concepts.

Let us begin our journey by reviewing the biblical facts

There is no single blood covenant agreement mentioned in the bible that demonstrates the whole of the blood covenant ceremony as clearly or completely as is shown in the covenant between Ramsis II and Hatusillis III. However with all of the covenants we will look to there is sufficient information for us to recognize Blood Covenant. God's Blood Covenant predates Ramsis II and Hatusillis III, this we know because Abraham[7] is mentioned in the Mari tablets, (see appendix II). I am convinced that many of the ceremonial rites that are associated with Ramsis II and Hatusillis III were added, in part, because of the typical desire of tyrannical monarchs to embrace pomp and ceremony, not only then but today also. Even so this does not take away from the reality or legitimacy of the ceremony and it does in fact enhance for use the often hidden meanings.

The Blood Covenant of God with Abraham is probably the most complete of the Blood Covenants and it is not surprising that there

---

[7] Throughout the text I have used the name that God gave to Abram, Abraham, in an attempt to reduce confusion. The exception is in the chapter on the exchange of names and the direct insertion of scripture.

is so much more information on the rites with this patriarch than with any other.

> *After these things the word of the LORD came to Abram in a vision, saying, "Do not fear, Abram, I am a shield to you; Your reward shall be very great." Abram said, "O Lord GOD, what will You give me, since I am childless, and the heir of my house is Eliezer of Damascus?" And Abram said, "Since You have given no offspring to me, one born in my house is my heir." Then behold, the word of the LORD came to him, saying, "This man will not be your heir; but one who will come forth from your own body, he shall be your heir." And He took him outside and said, "Now look toward the heavens, and count the stars, if you are able to count them." And He said to him, "So shall your descendants be." Then he believed in the LORD; and He reckoned it to him as righteousness. And He said to him, "I am the LORD who brought you out of Ur of the Chaldeans, to give you this land to possess it." He said, "O Lord GOD, how may I know that I will possess it?" So He said to him, "Bring Me a three year old heifer, and a three year old female goat, and a three year old ram, and a turtledove, and a young pigeon." Then he brought all these to Him and cut them in two, and laid each half opposite the other; but he did not cut the birds. The birds of prey came down upon the carcasses, and Abraham drove them away. Now when the sun was going down, a deep sleep fell upon Abram; and behold, terror and great darkness fell upon him. God said to Abram, "Know for certain that your descendants will be strangers in a land that is not theirs, where they will be enslaved and oppressed four hundred years. "But I will also judge the nation whom they will serve, and afterward they will come out with many possessions. "As for you, you shall go to your fathers in peace; you will be buried at a good old age. "Then in the fourth generation they will return here, for the iniquity of the Amorite is not yet complete." It came about when the sun had set, that it was very dark, and behold, there appeared a smoking oven and a*

flaming torch which passed between these pieces. On that day the LORD made a covenant with Abram, saying, "To your descendants I have given this land, From the river of Egypt as far as the great river, the river Euphrates: the Kenite and the Kenizzite and the Kadmonite and the Hittite and the Perizzite and the Rephaim and the Amorite and the Canaanite and the Girgashite and the Jebusite." Genesis 15:1-21

Biblical Facts

The word Covenant is found in over 400 Bible references in its various forms. The most common word is Covenant. However, we can also look to the word promise, oath, testament and league along with several others. Not all these references relate to the Blood Covenant of God with man, however many of them do.

This study is concerned mainly with those references that relate to the Blood Covenant of God, and other relevant covenants between God and man, or man and man. Each will help us in our understanding of the Blood Covenant of God.

It is particularly important for us to realise that we are dealing with the Blood Covenant of God not a Covenant between man and God. This is a Blood Covenant between God and man and it is God's Covenant. God Himself makes this point no less that 51 times throughout the Bible with the specific term "My Covenant[8]". It is first used with the first detailed reference of the Covenant in Genesis 6:18 in His Covenant with Noah.

---

[8] This is the most common number of times that this phrase is found in English Bibles, the KJV, WEB, Webster's, ASV, HNV, and others. Of course the actual number of times the phrase is used depends on the version of the bible used, the Message uses this phrase 35 times, and some others vary a little also. Where the phrase "My Covenant" is not used a weaker version of the same expression is commonly found. None the less the strength of the statement is clear for us no matter which version is used. It is God's Blood Covenant.

"But I will establish My covenant with you; and you shall enter the ark--you and your sons and your wife, and your sons' wives with you". Genesis 6:18

As God began to outline his Covenant with Abraham the statement "My Covenant" it is seen 9 times, Genesis 17:1-22.

*Now when Abraham was ninety-nine years old, the LORD appeared to Abram and said to him, "I am God Almighty; Walk before Me, and be blameless. " I will establish **My covenant** between Me and you, And I will multiply you exceedingly." Abram fell on his face, and God talked with him, saying, "As for Me, behold, **My covenant** is with you, And you will be the father of a multitude of nations. "No longer shall your name be called Abram, But your name shall be Abram; For I have made you the father of a multitude of nations. "I will make you exceedingly fruitful, and I will make nations of you, and kings will come forth from you. "I will establish **My covenant** between Me and you and your descendants after you throughout their generations for an everlasting covenant, to be God to you and to your descendants after you. "I will give to you and to your descendants after you, the land of your sojournings, all the land of Canaan, for an everlasting possession; and I will be their God." God said further to Abram, "Now as for you, you shall keep **My covenant**, you and your descendants after you throughout their generations. "This is **My covenant**, which you shall keep, between Me and you and your descendants after you: every male among you shall be circumcised. "And you shall be circumcised in the flesh of your foreskin, and it shall be the sign of the covenant between Me and you. "And every male among you who is eight days old shall be circumcised throughout your generations, a servant who is born in the house or who is bought with money from any foreigner, who is not of your descendants. "A servant who is born in your house or who is bought with your money shall surely be circumcised; thus shall **My covenant** be in your flesh* *for an everlasting covenant. "But an uncircumcised male who is not circumcised in the flesh of his foreskin, that person shall be cut off from his people; he has broken **My covenant**." Then God said to Abraham, "As for Sarai your wife, you shall not call her name Sarai, but Sarah shall be her name. "I will bless her, and indeed I will give you a son by her. Then I will bless her, and she shall be a mother of nations; kings of peoples will come from her." Then Abraham fell on his face and laughed, and said in his heart, "Will a child be born to a man one hundred years old? And will Sarah, who is ninety years old, bear a child?" And Abraham said to God, "Oh that Ishmael might live before You!" But God said, "No, but Sarah your wife will bear you a son, and you shall call his name Isaac; and I will establish **My covenant** with him for an everlasting covenant for his descendants after him. "As for Ishmael, I have heard you; behold, I will bless him, and will make him fruitful and will multiply him exceedingly. He shall become the father of twelve princes, and I will make him a great nation. "But **My covenant** I will establish with Isaac, whom Sarah will bear to you at this season next year." Gen 17:1-21*

When God related with Moses He referred to "My Covenant".

*I also established **my covenant** with them, to give them the land of Canaan, the land in which they resided as aliens. I have also heard the groaning of the Israelites whom the Egyptians are holding as slaves, and I have remembered **my Covenant**. Exodus 6:4-5*

*Now therefore, if you obey my voice and keep **my covenant**, you shall be my treasured possession out of all the peoples. Indeed, the whole earth is mine,. Exodus 19:5*

*then will I remember **my covenant** with Jacob; I will remember also **my covenant** with Isaac and also **my covenant** with Abraham, and I will remember the land. Leviticus 26:42*

There are many other references to this expression My Covenant[9], however these are sufficient for us to see that this wonderful concept was entirely God's doing and not mans.

Biblical Covenants

There are several well recognized Covenants also in scripture, these are:

Adamic	Gen. 3:10-21
Noahic	Gen. 6:18 & 9:8-17.
Abrahamic	Gen. ch. 15 & 16.
Mosaic	Exo. chs.19 to 24.
Davidic	2 Sam chs. 7.
New Testament	Mat. 26:17-30 (28).
New Covenant	1 Cor. 11:23-34.
Marriage	Eph. 5:21-33.

The "New Covenant" or "New Testament," while it replacing the existing Blood Covenant, still relates very strongly to and expands the terms of the old Covenant, it also enhances its terms of application. That is to say, it makes eligibility into Blood Covenant with God even easier.

This will be established beyond any doubt as we examine these Covenants a little later in this study.

---

[9] A short list of references of the expression My Covenant . These are but a few of the references available. Gen 6:18, Gen 9:9, Gen 17:2, Gen 17:4, Gen 17:9-10, Gen 17:13-14, Gen 17:19, Exo 6:4-5, Exo 19:5, Lev 26:9, Lev 26:15, Lev 26:25, Lev 26:42, Lev 26:44, Num 25:12, Deu 31:16, Deu 31:20, Josh 7:11, Judg 2:1, Judg 2:20, 1 Ki 11:11, Psa 50:16, Psa 89: 8, Psa 89:34, Psa 132:12, Isa 56:4, Isa 56:6, Isa 59:21, Jer 11:10, Jer 31:32, Jer 33:20-21, Jer 33:25, Jer 34:18, Ezek 16:60, Ezek 16:62, Ezek 17:19, Ezek 44:7, Hosea 8:1, Zec 11:10, Mal 2:4-5, Rom 11:27, Heb 8:9.

It is most important to note that this list of Blood Covenants are the Covenants of God that he makes with man, there is no example of Man making a Covenant with God and indeed he cannot. As man is, and always will be, the weaker of the two it is impossible for man to offer a Blood Covenant contract with God.

Not only are these all blood Covenants established by God as he reaches out to man it is important to realise that they are all eternal in the longevity. Each of the references to the length of the covenant is the same, they are eternal.

Each of these Covenants are called the "Everlasting Covenant[10]."

To see that the Covenant with Noah was an Everlasting Covenant we need to look to the book of Genesis ch 9. This is God's promise not to destroy man by flood.

> *When the bow is in the clouds, I will see it and remember the **everlasting covenant** between God and every living creature of all flesh that is on the earth. Genesis 9:16*

The Abrahamic Covenant was an eternal Covenant of faith and blessing.

> *I will establish my covenant between me and you, and your offspring after you throughout their generations, for an **everlasting covenant**, to be God to you and to your offspring after you. Genesis 17:7*

---

[10] In every reference to the longevity of the Covenant the Hebrew word used is "owlam". I have inserted Strong s definition of the word from the Strong s Concordance. It is clear that although the word is translated into several differing English words they can all be correctly translated as "Eternal" or Everlasting". As far as God is concerned his Covenant is a Covenant without end, - EVERLASTING. 5769. "owlam {o-lawm"}; or "olam {o-lawm"}; from 5956; properly, concealed, i.e. the vanishing point; generally, time out of mind (past or future), i.e. (practically) eternity; frequentatively, adverbial (especially with prepositional prefix) always: -alway(-s), ancient (time), any more, continuance, eternal, (for, [n-])ever(-lasting, -more, of old), lasting, long (time), (of) old (time), perpetual, at any time, (beginning of the) world (+ without end). Compare 5331, 5703.

The Mosaic Covenant, a covenant of God's law and love for his people, was also an eternal Covenant as we can see in Leviticus 24:8

> *Every Sabbath day Aaron shall set them in order before the LORD regularly as a commitment of the people of Israel, as a **covenant forever**. Leviticus 24:8*

The Davidic Covenant, a covenant of rulership, was also eternal as we can see by looking to 2 Samuel 23:5

> *Is not my house like this with God? For he has made with me an **everlasting covenant**, ordered in all things and secure. Will he not cause to prosper all my help and my desire?. 2 Samuel 23:5*

We can also see that the New Covenant, a covenant of salvation and faith to all who believe is also an eternal covenant from Hebrews 13:20

> *Now may the God of peace, who brought back from the dead our Lord Jesus, the great shepherd of the sheep, by the blood of the **eternal covenant**, Hebrews 13:20*

Although there are many other references these help us to see how God views Covenants. These are all considered Everlasting Covenants and yet there can be; by its definition, only one Everlasting Covenant. Therefore they must of necessity all be a part of the same Covenant. How can this be? The bible speaks of the different covenants each of which has its place in the word of God.

This is made possible by the fact that each new covenant embraced, enhanced, and incorporated the preceding Covenant. Each covenant had to be better, bigger, and more effective than its preceding covenant and must embrace those in the preceding covenant and provide for them the blessings of the new covenant; the figure below is an example of the effectiveness of the process.

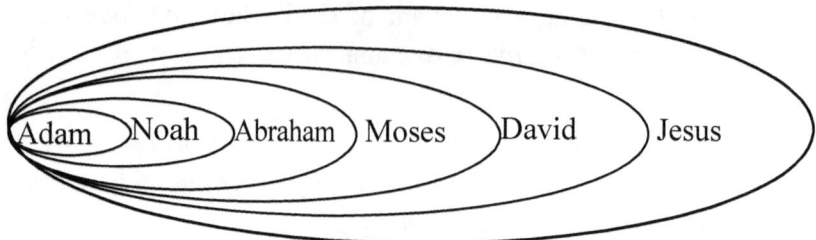

Human (Biblical) Covenants

There are three Covenants between men that we will refer to, as they will help us in our understanding of our Blood Covenant relationship with God. These Covenants are:

    Abraham and Abimelech   Genesis 21:22-34.
    David and Jonathan   1 Samuel 18:1-4.
    The Marriage Covenant   Ephesians 5:21-33.

Throughout secular history, there are many covenants that we can consider as well as those found in Chapter 1, that deals with some of the most notable. Some references to other Blood Covenants are found in Appendix III

The Covenants between Abraham and Abimelech, David and Jonathan will enable us to understand aspects of the New Covenant in day-to-day terms.

The Marriage Covenant is the only "covenant ceremony" left in common usage today. In the covenant of marriage we are able to identify some of the concepts of the Blood Covenant, for it is indeed a blood covenant in itself, even though our perceptions have been that this has been weakened with our moral values.

These three types of Covenants, as we will see, relate to the same principles that God does in His Blood Covenant with us. As such they will enable us to understand the Blood Covenant of God more profoundly.

We will constantly call on references to these and other covenants throughout our study within each of the following chapters.

Thus the focus of this study we will be the Covenants between God and Abraham, God and Moses, and the New Covenant in Jesus Christ.

Why A Blood Covenant?

Modern man and modern Christians tend to shy away from "Blood Religion," it is considered uncivilised, old-fashioned, and often distasteful. However, the truth is that God has not changed his point of view in these matters.

From the time that God first sacrificed a lamb, forgave Adam and Eve in the Garden of Eden, and clothed them with its skin, until this present time He has continued to deal with his people within the confines of a Blood Covenant.

Christianity is a "Blood Religion." While it is true that because of the sacrifice of Jesus we no longer need to kill birds or animals in a blood sacrifice to appease God for our sin. His sacrifice was an once-and-for-all sacrifice, that is to say that his sacrificial offering was sufficient to meet all of the past, present and future sacrificial needs, but it was still a blood sacrifice. We are indeed involved in a blood religion *for without the shedding of blood there is no remission of sins* (Hebrews 9:22) and we cannot enter into relationship with God without that same shedding of blood. This blood religion comes to us in the form of a Blood Covenant.

To understand this in greater depth we will move systematically through the Covenant Ceremony to see how we are affected by these truths

We shall examine why God deals with people in the terms of a Covenant. The answer is very simple. The nature and framework of a blood covenant provides the infrastructure that brings peace and security to the warring factions, whether they are kingdoms, tribes, families or individuals. Peace between such people can only be brought about by a totally binding contract of some form that clearly examines and satisfies all of the issues that are at stake. It is Blood Covenant that provides the totally binding contract.

Three major issues are dealt with through Blood Covenant that cannot be effectively done so in any other way.

1. Unregenerate man and God are at war.

That there is a war between unregenerate man and God is patently obvious. Out inbuilt desire to commit sin, to hold in contempt the word of God and his people, the desire to satisfy self with a total and even wanton disregard for others as well as God is testimony to this warfare.

Our capacity to war with each other to destroy, man's inhumanity to man, our willingness to corrupt and to be corrupted adds to the clear testimony to this warfare.

For all of this we deserve the judgment of God and all that He may choose to give us in punishment. We have earned our place in hell and the punishment of a righteous God.

> *For the wages of sin is death, but the free gift of God is eternal life in Christ Jesus our Lord. Romans 6:23*
>
> *All have sinned and fall short of the glory of God; Romans 3:23*
>
> *For this reason the mind that is set on the flesh is hostile to God; it does not submit to God's law--indeed it cannot. Romans 8:7*

This creates a dilemma. God made man for companionship with himself. He wants to enjoy that relationship with man. He has a purpose[11] and design for us individually, and yet a totally righteous God cannot have fellowship with someone with a sinful nature.

---

[11] For we are His workmanship, created in Christ Jesus for good works, which God prepared beforehand so that we would walk in them. Ephesians 2:10

The difficulty arises because there is a reaction when righteousness and sin come into contact with each other; the result is much the same as turning a light on in a dark room. When the light is turned on the darkness must go. When righteousness and sin meet, the sin must go. Because the nature of man is sinful, the only way that sin can leave is if the nature of the man leaves, in other words he must die. The meeting of sin and righteousness produce death if some form of restitution and reconciliation does not take place. It is through the medium of the Blood Covenant that this reconciliation is made possible. The nature of God can be given to man, as we *put on the new man Eph 4:24.* Because of Blood Covenant, restoration and reconciliation take place.

Some form of compromise between these two parties must be made or man and God cannot meet. It must be a compromise that will be honourable to both and yet totally satisfy all the legal and moral issues involved.

As man, we need to feel, if we are to surrender to God that our surrender is with dignity, while at the same time recognizing the omnipotence of God and the futility of not surrendering to him. At the same time, as God takes his rightful place in the life of man it must be with the sense of honour that come from a righteous and well deserved victory.

2. Only a Blood Covenant could effectively satisfy the legal and moral issues.

    a. It is the only form of agreement that is totally binding on both parties and therefore guarantees peace to all concerned.

    b. It provides forgiveness for all the offences that have been committed, that both restoration and reconciliation is made for both parties. Instead of being enemies, they become friends, and are now totally committed to each other.

    c. All of the legal penalties and moral obligations are completely satisfied for everyone concerned. This is done without trivialising the matter or dismissing the offences; justice will be done and be seen to be done.

Restitution is made where it is required and a new era begins for both God and man. This occurs on two levels:

    a. Effectively for all mankind, Jesus died as the sacrifice and rose again as the King. He provides the opportunity for all mankind to be reconciled to God.

    b. On a personal basis, as an individual chooses to appropriate for themselves the promises of God through Jesus and make his sacrifice effective.

3. A Blood Covenant is totally binding on all parties and therefore guarantees security for all.

As long as there is an heir of the families, the Covenant is effective. The lives of the Covenant Heads and their heirs are the guarantee of the Covenant. In this case, the Covenant Heads are God the Father and Jesus himself. God has committed his very existence to the continuance of the Blood Covenant.

Whilst the penalty for breaching the Covenant is death, the Covenant itself cannot be threatened. The reason for the death penalty is simple. By breaching the Covenant, an individual is declaring that he or she wants no part of the covenant or any of its benefits. The decision of an individual in relation to the covenant is irrelevant to the reality of the covenant itself, and so the covenant continues regardless. It is eternal.

Since the time of Adam and Eve God has chosen to deal with us through the avenue of the Blood Covenant. Each of the preceding forms of the Covenant was unable to fulfil its goal of bringing God and man together, until Jesus came. Only Jesus was able to satisfy all the requirements of the Abrahamic or Mosaic Covenants by his life and sacrifice. In doing so he was able replace the old

Covenants and provides us with a better and more effective Covenant which did all that was expected of it.

Paul discusses this in detail in Galatians 3:6-29 and Galatians 4:22-31. The Covenant given to Abraham was to be fulfilled in Jesus. Faith in Jesus is the key by which we enter into Covenant, just as Abraham received the Blood Covenant through faith in God.

The Covenant given at Sinai (The Law) was ineffective and was only a schoolmaster until Jesus fulfilled it.

> *Wherefore the law was our schoolmaster to bring us unto Christ, that we might be justified by faith. But after that faith is come, we are no longer under a schoolmaster. For ye are all the children of God by faith in Christ Jesus. Galatians 3:24-26 (KJV)*

> *Therefore the law was our disciplinarian until Christ came, so that we might be justified by faith. But now that faith has come, we are no longer subject to a disciplinarian, for in Christ Jesus you are all children of God through faith. Galatians 3:24-26*

The law of Moses could only show us where and how we fail and provide us with examples. The Father then sent Jesus to fulfil the promise given to Jeremiah.

> *The days are surely coming, says the LORD, when I will make a new covenant with the house of Israel and the house of Judah. It will not be like the covenant that I made with their ancestors when I took them by the hand to bring them out of the land of Egypt--a covenant that they broke, though I was their husband, says the LORD. But this is the covenant that I will make with the house of Israel after those days, says the LORD: I will put my law within them, and I will write it on their hearts; and I will be their God, and they shall be my people. No longer shall they teach one another, or say to each other, "Know the LORD," for they shall all know me, from the least of them to the greatest, says the LORD; for I will forgive*

their iniquity, and remember their sin no more. Jeremiah 31:31-34

This familiar passage is quoted by the writer of Hebrews, not as something that God was to do, but as an accomplished fact through Christ. Hebrews 8:6-13 and Hebrews 12:22-25.

An Application

Just as the Jew had to come to God through the mediation of a covenant, so too do we. However, our Covenant is secured, not through bulls, goats, or other sacrificed animals but through the sacrifice of Jesus as the living sacrifice. He is the sacrifice of an everlasting Blood Covenant.

The principles of the Blood Covenant have not changed. It is still as binding on us as it was for Abraham and God or as it was between Ramsis II and Hattusilis III.

Because of unfamiliarity with these concepts, we may have difficulty in understanding covenant principles. They are long since lost to our vocabulary and western culture, thus we do not understand the conditions, promises, benefits and blessings of this Covenant as we should. We fail to take advantage of this wonderful relationship. Even worse, we often find ourselves offending its principles in our ignorance, earning for ourselves the anger of the God we have promised to honour.

The covenant, which we have entered into, is not so much a covenant of laws and rituals or demands and regulations, but this covenant, as all Blood Covenants is a covenant relationship. It is a means of bringing peace and restoring relationships.

We are involved in a Vassal Covenant. God the Father is the Great King and Jesus is the Lesser King or the Vassal. We are entitled to enjoy all that our King enjoys through the relationship we have with him, for he has made us to be Kings and Priests with him. We are a part of a Royal Family with him and as his heirs entitled to all that he possesses in this present time through our Blood Covenant relationship with Him.

End Of Chapter Questions

1. List the various biblical covenants.
2. Describe the manner in which on blood covenant deals with its previous covenant.
3. Discuss the reasons God Chose to deal with us through Blood Covenant.

Chapter 3:

Entering Into The Covenant

Introduction

All forms of agreements, contracts, or relationships must have a beginning.

A friendship usually comes about by a mutual understanding. It may begin spontaneously, or develop over a period of time or out of some other more formal arrangement, but we enjoy being with someone, and our relationship with them develops into friendship. There are no formal rules for friendship. Yet, universally, we understand the need to honour those with whom we are friends. The rules are unspoken, but powerful and universally accepted.

With formal agreements, friendship is not sufficient. If we want a loan from the bank, we will not gain it by being a friend of the bank manager. His friendship may or may not help us a little, but we will still have to be prepared to put up some form of collateral. We will have to show some form of security and a capacity to meet the loan repayment, while understanding and agreeing to the terms of the loan. Only upon the formal acceptance and understanding of the contract can the funds be made available.

In western culture, when entering a marriage we must first get to know our partner, understand him or her, enjoy a mutual relationship with them, and experience a depth of love such that we will wish to be committed to that person for the rest of our lives. This desire must be mutual. The two must take certain vows and commit themselves to each another in some form of ceremony recognized by their peers and the society in which we live. The ceremony becomes a binding contract, a Covenant, that is not easy to break, nor should it be.

Before we enter a business partnership, we should first see a solicitor. A contract should be drawn up clearly defining the role of each partner that shows the benefits and responsibilities to each other. This relationship helps to ensure the success of the enterprise.

These principles, in one form or another, apply to all of us when we enter some form of contractual arrangement with another person. They are necessary for the effective and mutually beneficial continuation of the relationship. Whether those principles are written down, publicly declared, or simply understood by mutual consent is not important. However, in one way or another guidelines will be drawn up and they will be adhered to for the harmony of the relationship.

The same principles apply when we enter the Blood Covenant with God. He has a set of guidelines that we must accept. These guidelines describe the Covenant, its benefits, penalties and responsibilities for all concerned. The purpose of these principles is to prevent any misunderstandings between any of the parties involved and to provide clear and definite guidelines and instructions when required.

To help us to understand how we can enter this relationship we should refer ourselves to those who have entered Covenant with God before us. Abraham as the Covenant Head of the first formal Covenant provides us with a fine example as indeed do all of those who have paved the way to covenant for us. We shall visit them in Old and New Testaments.

Old Testament Examples

Despite a great deal of speculation, little is really known of most of the patriarchs. We have an impression of them that is developed from scripture, our understanding of their times and culture, however our understanding is often warped by our own world view.

The little that we do know of them helps us to understand something of the way we should respond to God. As we learn from the patriarchs how we aught to respond to the Lord we will also find He will respond to us in the same manner that He responded to them.

Noah. Perhaps one of the most remarkable responses to God's call is that of Noah. We know almost nothing of him, other than he was righteous, and had a relationship with God. There was no known formal form of religion, or worship, of Jehovah that we know of in that day. There was no temple for God, no bible, no scripture, no priest, and yet he has a remarkable relationship with God.

> *Then God said to Noah, "The end of all flesh has come before Me; for the earth is filled with violence because of them; and behold, I am about to destroy them with the earth. "Make for yourself an ark of gopher wood; you shall make the ark with rooms, and shall cover it inside and out with pitch. "This is how you shall make it: the length of the ark three hundred cubits, its breadth fifty cubits, and its height thirty cubits. "You shall make a window for the ark, and finish it to a cubit from the top; and set the door of the ark in the side of it; you shall make it with lower, second, and third decks. "Behold, I, even I am bringing the flood of water upon the earth, to destroy all flesh in which is the breath of life, from under heaven; everything that is on the earth shall perish. "But I will establish My covenant with you; and you shall enter the ark-- you and your sons and your wife, and your sons" wives with you. "And of every living thing of all flesh, you shall bring two of every kind into the ark, to keep them alive with you; they shall be male and female. "Of the birds after their kind, and of the animals after their kind, of every creeping thing of the ground after its kind, two of every kind will come to you to keep them alive. "As for you, take for yourself some of all food which is edible, and gather it to yourself; and it shall be for*

food for you and for them." Thus Noah did; according to all that God had commanded him, so he did. Gen 6:13-22

Imagine for a moment... Noah is living in a pleasant enough area. The people are corrupt but he enjoys his life. He has maintained his standard and relationship with God without being affected by the corruption around him. He is probably aware of all that is going on but is unable to do anything about it. He is one man, alone in a world of corruption, living his life getting on with his business when suddenly, for Noah, God decides that he has had enough of the corruption of man. The corruption of the people has been building for years; God had been patient and not willing to destroy man then any more than He is willing to destroy man today. Then finally the day came when God commanded Noah to do something that was unheard of. He must build an ark.

What is an Ark? What is a Flood?

To the best of our knowledge the earth was watered by the dew of heaven, there was no rain, no idea or understanding of what a flood could be. We would have been filled with questions and objections, doubt and scepticism just as the people of Noah's' day were. Perhaps Noah had doubts too, but note his response in vs. 22. *Thus Noah did; according to all that God had commanded him, so he did.* The heart of Noah was to respond to God and accept His instructions; there was enough relationship for him to agree. For us relationship and agreement are also required.

Abram. Abraham's response to God speaks volumes about his personality and life. We can be sure that Abraham already had a relationship with God as he recognized God's voice and he was quick to follow him. We can also note that God spoke with Abraham as with a friend. (James 2:23).

We can also see that his integrity before God was in good standing for God to deal with him in the way that he did. When God spoke to Abraham he responded without question or argument. Willingly he left everything to fulfil God's will and direction for his life.

This instant response is an important key to entering the Covenant for us if we wish to enter Blood Covenant relationship with God.

> *Now the LORD said to Abram, "Go from your country and your kindred and your father's house to the land that I will show you I will make of you a great nation, and I will bless you, and make your name great, so that you will be a blessing. I will bless those who bless you, and the one who curses you I will curse; and in you all the families of the earth shall be blessed." So Abram went, as the LORD had told him; and Lot went with him. Abram was seventy-five years old when he departed from Haran. Abram took his wife Sarai and his brother's son Lot, and all the possessions that they had gathered, and the persons whom they had acquired in Haran; and they set forth to go to the land of Canaan. Genesis 12:1-5*

It would seem that Abraham was accustomed to enjoying his relationship with God. The evidence for that lay in the promises God made to him to provide all he should ask for. These were promises which Abraham was quick to act upon in asking for (a son), promises which foreshadowed, even then, the promises of his Covenant.

> *After these things the word of the LORD came to Abram in a vision, saying, "Do not fear, Abram, I am a shield to you; Your reward shall be very great." Abram said, "O Lord GOD, what will You give me, since I am childless, and the heir of my house is Eliezer of Damascus?" And Abram said, "Since You have given no offspring to me, one born in my house is my heir." Then behold, the word of the LORD came to him, saying, "This man will not be your heir; but one who will come forth from your own body, he shall be your heir." And He took him outside and said, "Now look toward the heavens, and count the stars, if you are able to count them." And He said to him, "So shall your descendants be." Then he believed in the LORD; and He reckoned it to him as righteousness. Gen 15:1-6*

There is no question, no checking in with Sarah, no discussion with the council, no attempt to call a family conference, just a clear faith, and certainty and confidence in God. "If He wants me to go, I will go and you can come if you wish or you can stay."

He is going to a country that is unknown, taking a journey of indeterminate length, to be the father of a multitude of nations that will begin in his and Sarah's old age! He was to be the means of blessing to every person on earth and every nation!

Fantastic promises, yet embraced fully and without qualification – such should be our response to the call of God.

Moses response to God, which leads him to covenant relationship, is also worth looking at:

> *Now Moses was pasturing the flock of Jethro his father-in-law, the priest of Midian; and he led the flock to the west side of the wilderness and came to Horeb, the mountain of God. The angel of the LORD appeared to him in a blazing fire from the midst of a bush; and he looked, and behold, the bush was burning with fire, yet the bush was not consumed. So Moses said, "I must turn aside now and see this marvelous sight, why the bush is not burned up." When the LORD saw that he turned aside to look, God called to him from the midst of the bush and said, "Moses, Moses!" And he said, "Here I am." Then He said, "Do not come near here; remove your sandals from your feet, for the place on which you are standing is holy ground." He said also, "I am the God of your father, the God of Abraham, the God of Isaac, and the God of Jacob." Then Moses hid his face, for he was afraid to look at God. The LORD said, "I have surely seen the affliction of My people who are in Egypt, and have given heed to their cry because of their taskmasters, for I am aware of their sufferings. Exo 3:1-7*

The very notion that after being called aside by a burning bush and told that he, a refugee from Egypt on the run for murder, a shepherd of sheep, and a stammerer should stand against the might and pride of Pharaoh. That he should lead a nation from slavery must have seemed impossible, a task beyond his ability to comprehend. Even so, Moses responds positively and absolutely to God and as a result, the people are set free and a new covenant is established.

There is an abundance of evidence to the truth of the Blood Covenant with Moses, but here are two more.

Blood Covenant ceremony is clearly stated in Exodus 24:1-11. We will look at this in more detail in the chapter on the Feasts; however, here is evidence of the Blood Covenant.

> *Then he said to Moses, "Come up to the LORD, you and Aaron, Nadab, and Abihu, and seventy of the elders of Israel, and worship at a distance. Moses alone shall come near the LORD; but the others shall not come near, and the people shall not come up with him." Moses came and told the people all the words of the LORD and all the ordinances; and all the people answered with one voice, and said, "All the words that the LORD has spoken we will do." And Moses wrote down all the words of the LORD. He rose early in the morning, and built an altar at the foot of the mountain, and set up twelve pillars, corresponding to the twelve tribes of Israel. He sent young men of the people of Israel, who offered burnt offerings and sacrificed oxen as offerings of well-being to the LORD. Moses took half of the blood and put it in basins, and half of the blood he dashed against the altar. Then he took the book of the covenant, and read it in the hearing of the people; and they said, "All that the LORD has spoken we will do, and we will be obedient." Moses took the blood and dashed it on the people, and said, "**See the blood of the covenant that the LORD** has made with you in accordance with all these words." Then Moses and Aaron, Nadab, and Abihu, and seventy of the elders of Israel went up, and they saw the God of Israel. Under his feet there was something like a pavement of sapphire stone, like the very heaven for clearness. God did not lay his hand on the*

> *chief men of the people of Israel; also they beheld God, and they ate and drank. Exodus 24:1-11*

The fact of the covenant is reinforced as God speaks with Jeremiah, reminding him of the fearful consequences of breaking the covenant.

> *And those who transgressed my covenant and did not keep the **terms of the covenant** that they made before me, I will make like the calf when they cut it in two and passed between its parts: the officials of Judah, the officials of Jerusalem, the eunuchs, the priests, and all the people of the land who passed between the parts of the calf. Jeremiah 34:18-19*

Moses response to God was similar to that of Noah and Abraham. Once God had his attention, he was quick to respond. Moses was not instantly willing to do whatever he is asked without argument but certainly he responds quickly and intelligently to God. It is only his self consciousness of his own inadequacy that holds him back. Nevertheless, note that he is quick to become engaged in God's call to him.

Noah, Abraham, Moses, the patriarchs of the Old Testament lend to us an example of the kind of response that God is looking for, an intelligent swift response to an undeniable God. Note that there is no false humility, no pious bowing or scraping, no fear of wrath, but rather a willingness to do and be as God has called.

God calls few men or women to achieve such great things as they did but we should realise that we are all created, formed and born for a purpose and for some it is to greatness as these men were. Yet Noah, Abraham, and Moses could not have known the magnitude of their calling and without minimising or trivialising the destiny God had called them to, it is not their calling that is important to us, it is their response.

New Testament Examples

The disciples. In the same way that the Patriarchs left everything for God and His will, the disciples responded. The response of the disciples to Jesus call appears to be instant, and without question.

> *As Jesus passed along the Sea of Galilee, he saw Simon and his brother Andrew casting a net into the sea--for they were fishermen. And Jesus said to them, "Follow me and I will make you fish for people." And immediately they left their nets and followed him. As he went a little farther, he saw James son of Zebedee and his brother John, who were in their boat mending the nets. Immediately he called them; and they left their father Zebedee in the boat with the hired men, and followed him. Mark 1:16-20 (Compare Matthew 4:18-22, and Luke 5:1-11.)*

As we compare the Gospel stories, something also becomes apparent. The story relayed in Mark 1:16-20 could indicate that this is the first time they saw Jesus. However when we compare with Matthew 4:18-22 and Luke 5:1-11 we see that Jesus was already established in His earthy ministry. Yes it is early but by now he is known as he is teaching and preaching in the synagogues of Galilee, not just his home town but the entire district.

In His day, the fame of Jesus was "Spread abroad." He was not a stranger who "happened by" and "hypnotised" them with his personality.

> *And Jesus returned to Galilee in the power of the Spirit, and news about Him spread through all the surrounding district. And He began teaching in their synagogues and was praised by all. And He came to Nazareth, where He had been brought up; and as was His custom, He entered the synagogue on the Sabbath, and stood up to read. Luke 4:14-16.*

> *And the report about Him was spreading into every locality in the surrounding district. Then He got up and left the synagogue, and entered Simon's home. Now Simon's mother-in-law*

> *was suffering from a high fever, and they asked Him to help her. And standing over her, He rebuked the fever, and it left her; and she immediately got up and waited on them. Luke 4:37-3*

Even before this meeting took place Jesus and Simon, (later called Peter), knew each other. For it was in Simon's home that Jesus made his first "house call" and healed his mother in law.

His spectacular instructions to Simon to launch out and catch fish and Simon's response "even though we have caught nothing we will do as you say" indicate enough relationship between then to be prepared for the next step. *"leave it all and follow me"*

> *As He passed by, He saw Levi the son of Alphaeus sitting in the tax booth, and He said to him, "Follow Me!" And he got up and followed Him. Mark 2:14*

Philip and Nathaniel also responded in a similar manner as do so many others. When Jesus calls them is a response from the heart to follow.

> *The next day He purposed to go into Galilee, and He found Philip. And Jesus said to him, "Follow Me." Now Philip was from Bethsaida, of the city of Andrew and Peter. Philip found Nathanael and said to him, "We have found Him of whom Moses in the Law and also the Prophets wrote -- Jesus of Nazareth, the son of Joseph." Nathanael said to him, "Can any good thing come out of Nazareth?" Philip said to him, "Come and see." Jesus saw Nathanael coming to Him, and said of him, "Behold, an Israelite indeed, in whom there is no deceit!" Nathanael said to Him, "How do You know me?" Jesus answered and said to him, "Before Philip called you, when you were under the fig tree, I saw you." John 1:43-48*

None of the patriarchs, the disciples or any other follower of Jesus can lay claim to the idea that they knew and understood all that was to be required of them. This call was made without a job description, no union rules, no contract, no guidelines, no instruction except "Follow me"

Yet it is no different for them than it was for Jesus.

Jesus responded to his heavenly Father in the same manner. He was consistent and instant in his response to his Father

> *And the one who sent me is with me; he has not left me alone, for I always do what is pleasing to him. John 8:29*

Without a promise of comfort, Jesus was prepared to do what was required of him.

> *Jesus said to him, "The foxes have holes and the birds of the air have nests, but the Son of Man has nowhere to lay His head." Matthew 8:20*

He left all the glory of heaven, the majesty of being God to become a man for our sake. Not enough to leave all of heaven, he also became subservient for a season to His Father for our sake, that he should be an example for us. From the commander in chief, He became the commanded!

Despite the personal pain and anguish, the will of his father was more important to Jesus than anything else.

> *looking to Jesus the pioneer and perfecter of our faith, who for the sake of the joy that was set before him endured the cross, disregarding its shame, and has taken his seat at the right hand of the throne of God. Hebrews 12:2*

For us. Jesus expects no less of a response from us, Matthew 16:24-25, Luke 14:25-27

> *Then Jesus told his disciples, "If any want to become my followers, let them deny themselves and take up their cross and follow me. For those who want to save their life will lose it, and those who lose their life for my sake will find it." Matthew 16:24-25*

> *Now large crowds were travelling with him; and he turned and said to them, "Whoever comes to me and does not hate father and mother, wife and children, brothers and sisters, yes, and even life itself, cannot be my disciple. Whoever does not carry the cross and follow me cannot be my disciple." Luke 14:25-27*

In this statement Jesus is using an idiom that is better translated: "you must love me more than your mother, father, brother, sister, or anything else and be prepared to do whatever I ask you to do".

Perhaps it is worth making a statement at this point. We are all invited into this covenant by the grace of God to grow in Him. Our growth and development is a gradual process for all of us, and it is as individual as we are. However proper understanding of blood covenant will help us to enter much more fully into the blessing of God much more quickly.

One of the first requirements for entering this relationship with God is a willingness to do so regardless of what it may cost us personally. We must be prepared to follow Jesus without reservation, just as Abraham, Moses, or David followed God's call, just as any of the disciples were prepared to follow Jesus.

This is the same way that the Vassal King must surrender to the Great King and accept his life-style, his laws, his protection, and his authority. We must also surrender to God and for the same reasons. We are not presented with a simplistic, "surrender to me and do as I say," and concept. God presents us with a choice, we choose to live with and for him, or we choose not to live for him. Just as He places certain conditions on us if we wish to be a part of His life he also offers us certain promises. Paraphrased they could read, "live for me and I will live for you, I will meet all your needs, protect and keep you from all forms of danger or harm."

> *After these things the word of the LORD came to Abram in a vision, "Do not be afraid, Abram, I am your shield; your reward shall be very great." Genesis 15:1*

These promises are nothing less than what we should be prepared to expect from an almighty God.

It is important to realize that although following Jesus may cost us dearly it is not without reward. Living for God may cost us everything that we have in the short term but he will give us more in return, and the more that he gives will be better.

> *Peter began to say to him, "Look, we have left everything and followed you." Jesus said, "Truly I tell you, there is no one who has left house or brothers or sisters or mother or father or children or fields, for my sake and for the sake of the good news, who will not receive a hundredfold now in this age--houses, brothers and sisters, mothers and children, and fields with persecutions--and in the age to come eternal life." Mark 10:28-30 (See also John 15:7-12 and Mark 11:22-24.)*

The response is never mindless, nor is it expected to be, but rather with the firm conviction that God has called. This is the element of which we must be certain. That God has called, and that it is to Him that we are responding. Such was the conviction of the patriarchs, the disciples, and of those who have decided before us.

However, there is an important element. Until our relatively recent past, everyone understood blood covenant. If we have a shortcoming, it is in this alone, that we do not understand the nature of this essential agreement we enter into.

The Blood Covenant

It is imperative that we understand what we are getting into. God expects us to examine and understand His Covenant and our own common sense should demand it. In Leviticus 26 we find the most concise details of his Covenant, not only in the Old Testament but also in the whole of the Bible.

One word of caution. We are not about to revert to the Old Testament Law for our relationship with God. We already know that the Law was unable to change man. Let us make no mistake.

The law is now and always was a schoolmaster, given to help us with examples and provide us with the principles that help us to understand God and His requirements of us for a sound relationship with Him.

As each new covenant embraced the old one, its principles applied just as powerfully as its predecessor. Therefore, we find that the changes in the New Covenant are better, making it a better covenant and our access to the covenant is now easier, but just as binding.

Perhaps it was because Blood Covenant was understood so well that it is was not so clearly laid out in single passage that causes us today to miss the full meaning and value of our relationship. So we turn to a passage in the Old Testament as our schoolmaster, not as a matter of law as did the Jew, but we look to it for guidance.

So what are we getting into? Just as God outlined the details of the Blood Covenant for Abraham in Genesis ch. 12, ch. 15, and ch. 17, he has also outlined the Blood Covenant for Israel in Leviticus Ch. 26. Not surprisingly, this pattern follows closely the pattern of the Amarna Style treaties.

Before reading this passage, it is important to realise that this covenant is given as a part of the law, "Old Testament stuff" one might cry. We are promised a new and better covenant in the New Testament, and so it is. However we aught, to stand amazed in the promise of a new and better covenant, for this one is most splendid indeed.

I have divided this passage is broken into five parts for simplicity and understanding and it shows an amazing similarity between the covenant between Ramsis II and Hattusillis III and the Blood Covenant of God.

1. Verses 1-3. Recognition of God

Recognition of God and total acceptance of all his laws. As with the human covenants, this one begins with recognition of God as

God and none other beside him. He is absolute and there is to be no argument on the matter. While we may not like this idea put so bluntly, nothing less that total acceptance of His supremacy is required.

> *'You shall not make for yourselves idols, nor shall you set up for yourselves an image or a sacred pillar, nor shall you place a figured stone in your land to bow down to it; for I am the LORD your God. 'You shall keep My sabbaths and reverence My sanctuary; I am the LORD. 'If you walk in My statutes and keep My commandments so as to carry them out, Leviticus 26:1-3*

2. Verses 4-13. The Blessings of the Covenant

There were blessings of the Covenant to all the people and to their land. Blessings of peace, prosperity, and health, protection from invaders and success in defence, bountiful crops and the presence of God among them. All of the benefits of the covenant are outlined. That this is a part of the Old Testament Law should cause us to stand in awe! These are the benefits under the Old Testament. What then are the better promises of the New Testament?

> *then I shall give you rains in their season, so that the land will yield its produce and the trees of the field will bear their fruit. 'Indeed, your threshing will last for you until grape gathering, and grape gathering will last until sowing time. You will thus eat your food to the full and live securely in your land. 'I shall also grant peace in the land, so that you may lie down with no one making you tremble. I shall also eliminate harmful beasts from the land, and no sword will pass through your land. 'But you will chase your enemies and they will fall before you by the sword; five of you will chase a hundred, and a hundred of you will chase ten thousand, and your enemies will fall before you by the sword. 'So I will turn toward you and make you fruitful and multiply you, and I will confirm My covenant with you. 'You will eat the old supply and clear out the old because of*

the new. 'Moreover, I will make My dwelling among you, and My soul will not reject you. 'I will also walk among you and be your God, and you shall be My people. 'I am the LORD your God, who brought you out of the land of Egypt so that you would not be their slaves, and I broke the bars of your yoke and made you walk erect. Leviticus 26:4-13

3. Verses 14-17. The Penalty of Breaking the Covenant

There is a penalty for breaking the covenant, ultimately it can cost you your life. However as with Ramsis II and Hattusilis III, the penalty had to be outlined and understood. The Penalty NEVER includes the dissolution of the covenant. It is eternal. It must continue. The penalties include Physical sickness, disease, famine, poverty invasion and captivity.

'But if you do not obey Me and do not carry out all these commandments, if, instead, you reject My statutes, and if your soul abhors My ordinances so as not to carry out all My commandments, and so break My covenant, I, in turn, will do this to you: I will appoint over you a sudden terror, consumption and fever that will waste away the eyes and cause the soul to pine away; also, you will sow your seed uselessly, for your enemies will eat it up. 'I will set My face against you so that you will be struck down before your enemies; and those who hate you will rule over you, and you will flee when no one is pursuing you. Leviticus 26:14-17

4. Verses 18-39. The discipline of the Covenant

The discipline of the Covenant applied continued pressure, as in the penalty, but multiplied up to seven times until the personal and national pride of Israel is broken. They will experience further famine, sickness, disease until they yield. Wild animals will attack the children and cattle; they will experience famine to the point of cannibalism.

In all this God refuses to hear their prayers until they surrender to him. It is a picture of absolute desolation in an attempt to bring the children of Israel back to Him.

> *'If also after these things you do not obey Me, then I will punish you seven times more for your sins. 'I will also break down your pride of power; I will also make your sky like iron and your earth like bronze. 'Your strength will be spent uselessly, for your land will not yield its produce and the trees of the land will not yield their fruit. 'If then, you act with hostility against Me and are unwilling to obey Me, I will increase the plague on you seven times according to your sins. 'I will let loose among you the beasts of the field, which will bereave you of your children and destroy your cattle and reduce your number so that your roads lie deserted. 'And if by these things you are not turned to Me, but act with hostility against Me, then I will act with hostility against you; and I, even I, will strike you seven times for your sins. 'I will also bring upon you a sword which will execute vengeance for the covenant; and when you gather together into your cities, I will send pestilence among you, so that you shall be delivered into enemy hands. 'When I break your staff of bread, ten women will bake your bread in one oven, and they will bring back your bread in rationed amounts, so that you will eat and not be satisfied. 'Yet if in spite of this you do not obey Me, but act with hostility against Me, then I will act with wrathful hostility against you, and I, even I, will punish you seven times for your sins. 'Further, you will eat the flesh of your sons and the flesh of your daughters you will eat. 'I then will destroy your high places, and cut down your incense altars, and heap your remains on the remains of your idols, for My soul shall abhor you. 'I will lay waste your cities as well and will make your sanctuaries desolate, and I will not smell your soothing aromas. 'I will make the land desolate so that your enemies who settle in it will be appalled over it. 'You, however, I will scatter among the nations and will draw out a sword after you,*

> *as your land becomes desolate and your cities become waste. 'Then the land will enjoy its sabbaths all the days of the desolation, while you are in your enemies' land; then the land will rest and enjoy its sabbaths. 'All the days of its desolation it will observe the rest which it did not observe on your sabbaths, while you were living on it. 'As for those of you who may be left, I will also bring weakness into their hearts in the lands of their enemies. And the sound of a driven leaf will chase them, and even when no one is pursuing they will flee as though from the sword, and they will fall. 'They will therefore stumble over each other as if running from the sword, although no one is pursuing; and you will have no strength to stand up before your enemies. 'But you will perish among the nations, and your enemies' land will consume you. 'So those of you who may be left will rot away because of their iniquity in the lands of your enemies; and also because of the iniquities of their forefathers they will rot away with them. Leviticus 26:18-39*[12]

5. Verses 40-45. Forgiveness of the Covenant

God is a forgiving God and if the people will turn to him in repentance he will and does offer the Forgiveness of the Covenant. The promises a total and complete restoration of the blessings of the Covenant.

> *'If they confess their iniquity and the iniquity of their forefathers, in their unfaithfulness which they committed against Me, and also in their acting with hostility against Me-- I also was acting with hostility against them, to bring them into the land of their enemies--or if their uncircumcised heart becomes humbled so that they then make amends for their*

---

[12] Some might argue that these are hyperbolic statements rather than actual statements of discipline. If one looks to the history of Israel one must come to the conclusion that this was very much actual for throughout the history of Israel every statement of disciple has been exacted. It is also worth asking the questions, 'Why would God make such threats in a legally binding contract, one in which His own existence depended if it were mere rhetoric?'

iniquity, then I will remember My covenant with Jacob, and I will remember also My covenant with Isaac, and My covenant with Abraham as well, and I will remember the land. 'For the land will be abandoned by them, and will make up for its sabbaths while it is made desolate without them. They, meanwhile, will be making amends for their iniquity, because they rejected My ordinances and their soul abhorred My statutes. 'Yet in spite of this, when they are in the land of their enemies, I will not reject them, nor will I so abhor them as to destroy them, breaking My covenant with them; for I am the LORD their God. 'But I will remember for them the covenant with their ancestors, whom I brought out of the land of Egypt in the sight of the nations, that I might be their God. I am the LORD.'" These are the statutes and ordinances and laws which the LORD established between Himself and the sons of Israel through Moses at Mount Sinai. Leviticus 26:40-46

As we examine these scriptures, we find that God has established a mechanism for dealing with man regardless of his standing in the covenant. Each stage of the Covenant arrangement provides for a way for God to deal with His people in order to bless them and help them and to keep them in the Covenant. Never does God threaten to do away with the Covenant. He has built into his Covenant the provisions required for dealing with and restoring this wayward people rather than for dispensing with the covenant, for the covenant is eternal.

Startlingly it only requires a cursory examination of the Old Testament and a simple knowledge of the history of Israel to shows how exactingly God has dealt with his people in light of this Covenant. Every part of this Covenant has been activated at sometime in the history of the people of Israel, sometimes with fearful accuracy.

Their success in battle and conquests in good times, the defeats, desolation and captivity in times of rebellion, followed by restoration after repentance over the centuries have shown clear evidence that God means business in His dealings with us and that he is intent on keeping covenant with his people.

New Testament Covenant

Unfortunately, the Old Covenant was ineffective, as it could not deal with the sinful nature of man and his failure before God. Fortunately, He understood that the old covenant was, and would be ineffective. Indeed even in the Old Testament the Lord spoke of the new covenant to come, Jeremiah 31:31-3.

He has given us a new and better Covenant capable of dealing with the issues of life and relationship with God, again in terms of a Blood Covenant.

> *For if that first covenant had been faultless, there would have been no occasion sought for a second. For finding fault with them, He says, "BEHOLD, DAYS ARE COMING, SAYS THE LORD, WHEN I WILL EFFECT A NEW COVENANT WITH THE HOUSE OF ISRAEL AND WITH THE HOUSE OF JUDAH; NOT LIKE THE COVENANT WHICH I MADE WITH THEIR FATHERS ON THE DAY WHEN I TOOK THEM BY THE HAND TO LEAD THEM OUT OF THE LAND OF EGYPT; FOR THEY DID NOT CONTINUE IN MY COVENANT, AND I DID NOT CARE FOR THEM, SAYS THE LORD. "FOR THIS IS THE COVENANT THAT I WILL MAKE WITH THE HOUSE OF ISRAEL AFTER THOSE DAYS, SAYS THE LORD: I WILL PUT MY LAWS INTO THEIR MINDS, AND I WILL WRITE THEM ON THEIR HEARTS. AND I WILL BE THEIR GOD, AND THEY SHALL BE MY PEOPLE. "AND THEY SHALL NOT TEACH EVERYONE HIS FELLOW CITIZEN, AND EVERYONE HIS BROTHER, SAYING, 'KNOW THE LORD,' FOR ALL WILL KNOW ME, FROM THE LEAST TO THE GREATEST OF THEM. "FOR I WILL BE MERCIFUL TO THEIR INIQUITIES, AND I WILL REMEMBER THEIR SINS NO MORE." When He said, "A new covenant," He has made the first obsolete. But whatever is*

becoming obsolete and growing old is ready to disappear. Hebrews 8:7-13

The promises of this New Covenant are better than those of the Old Covenant,

> *so much the more also Jesus has become the guarantee of a better covenant. Hebrews 7:22*
>
> *But now He has obtained a more excellent ministry, by as much as He is also the mediator of a better covenant, which has been enacted on better promises. Hebrews 8:6*

The differences in these Covenants lies primarily, but not only, in the in the effectiveness of the sacrifice of Jesus.

Instead of the annual national sin sacrifice and the individual periodical and daily personal sin offering, Jesus sacrifice was an once-and-for-all sacrifice for all sin for all man for all time.

The New Covenant also provided for something not seen since the days of the patriarchs and on a much larger scale. That is a very personal and direct relationship between the individual and God. Even with the patriarchs it seemed to be only certain individuals who had a relationship with Him.

Through the benefit of this new Blood Covenant anyone and everyone can and should have a personal relationship with God.

The Old Covenant was "effective[13]" only through the observance of laws and rituals and all dealings with God came through the office of the priesthood.

All the benefits of the Old Covenant and much more are ours as we enter the New Blood Covenant. The penalties of not embracing the

---

[13] By effective I do not mean that the ceremonial laws brought about salvation or personal relationship or healing or any other such personal benefit between man and God, indeed they were not effective or there would be no need for the New Covenant. It was effective as a national religion; it was effective in making a way for the people of God to worship Him and maintain a relationship.

Covenant wholeheartedly are more severe under the New Covenant than they were under the Old Covenant. The reason is certain, our entrance into covenant now is a matter of faith in the work of Jesus rather than trust in ceremonial rightness.

God leaves the decision to us and gives us the whole of our lifetime to decide what we want to do. Should we decide to enter into this Blood Covenant then there are only three "laws" we need to consider. As Jesus said by the fulfilment of these "laws" we fulfil all the law of God, we then meet all of His requirements of us.

> *And he answered, "YOU SHALL LOVE THE LORD YOUR GOD WITH ALL YOUR HEART, AND WITH ALL YOUR SOUL, AND WITH ALL YOUR STRENGTH, AND WITH ALL YOUR MIND; AND YOUR NEIGHBOR AS YOURSELF." Luke 10:27*

1. Love the Lord your God,
2. Love your neighbour,
3. Love yourself,

The blessings of the Blood Covenant are outlined for us in simple yet very profound terms. We have forgiveness for sin and of our offences; we enjoy the physical healing of our bodies from any form of sickness or disease,

> *and He Himself bore our sins in His body on the cross, so that we might die to sin and live to righteousness; for by His wounds you were healed. 1 Peter 2:24*

In addition, he has promised to provide us with everything we have need of, especially with regard to life and Godliness.

> *And Jesus answered saying to them, "Have faith in God. "Truly I say to you, whoever says to this mountain, 'Be taken up and cast into the sea,' and does not doubt in his heart, but believes that what he says is going to happen, it will be granted*

> him. *"Therefore I say to you, all things for which you pray and ask, believe that you have received them, and they will be granted you. Mark 11:22-24*

This provision is extended to all the things we have need of, in the context of living in his Covenant. These promises are the same as the Promise of God to Abraham and Sarah in Genesis 15:1.

> *After these things the word of the LORD came to Abram in a vision, saying, "Do not fear, Abram, I am a shield to you; Your reward shall be very great." Genesis 15:1*

Access to these promises from God come to us as we enter into Blood Covenant relationship. Entrance to this relationship requires a change in our beings that allows us to live for God. Without this transformation, a life for God is not possible. This change begins with the transformation from "sinner" to "saint." We cannot perform this change in our own ability. It is Peter, on the day of Pentecost, who tells us clearly what is required of us

> *Repent[14] therefore, and turn to God so that your sins may be wiped out, Acts 3:19 KJV.*
>
> *"Therefore repent and return, so that your sins may be wiped away, in order that times of refreshing may come from the presence of the Lord; Acts 3:19*

By repenting we are acting on the words of Jesus to Nicodemus You must be born again in John ch. 3. The very essence of being born again is to die to your self and to live as and for someone else,

> *Even so consider yourselves to be dead to sin, but alive to God in Christ Jesus. Romans 6:11*

---

[14] Repentance: A change of thinking that leads to a conscious decision to change your life. To allow Godly sorrow to become an active part of your life and to choose to live for God and accept his will for your life. To Let the Lord of Heaven and Earth be your personal Lord and decision maker.

This is the nature of repentance, commitment to Jesus and his will for your life, and it is the first principle for entering the Blood Covenant of God.

The decision to repent, the decision to enter into Covenant Relationship with God is a decision that I can make as an individual. I cannot make the changes that are required, that is the work of God the Holy Spirit. As I choose to live for him he makes the necessary changes in my life that I cannot make. The Church and several versions of the Bible call this transformation "conversion" or the more modern word, "changed" Matthew 18:3

> *Matthew 18:3 and said, "Truly I tell you, unless you **change** and become like children, you will never enter the kingdom of heaven." (NRSV).*
>
> *and said, "Truly I say to you, unless you are converted and become like children, you will not enter the kingdom of heaven. Matthew 18:3*

God does not expect us to make a rash, uninformed decision. He expects us to examine the issues, to consider the facts and commit our lives to him and receive all that he is offering us.

This is not emotional blackmail, nor psychological pressure, nor is there any messing with our thinking. It is as clear for us as it was for Noah, Abraham, Moses, or the disciples. It is as clear for us as it was for Elijah as he commanded the children of Israel to "choose ye this day"

> *Elijah came near to all the people and said, "How long will you hesitate between two opinions? If the LORD is God, follow Him; but if Baal, follow him." But the people did not answer him a word. 1 Kings 18:21*

A Thought on Revelation

The scene is in heaven itself. John has heard the message to the churches to bring themselves back to their rightful state in God, Jesus has praised and cautioned all seven of them.

Whatever your interpretation of these events I am reminded that Jesus is the Blood covenant sacrifice. Notice that no-one is worthy to open the book with seven seals until:

> *and in the midst of the elders, stood a Lamb as it had been slain, having seven horns and seven eyes, which are the seven Spirits of God sent forth into all the earth.*

The next chapters of the book of Revelation speak of the awful consequences of the judgment of God, of the anger of Satan and of the consequences of that anger, and of the fear of man against man in that dreadful time.

I am caused to remember that He said He will punish 7 times more, and 7 times more and 7 times more... if we will not repent.

The finality of Blood Covenant is being played out before our very eyes as the end of the ages us rushing toward us. Blood covenant must be played out, and here is a chilling reminder that there is a time when grace runs out...

> *And I saw in the right hand of him that sat on the throne a book written within and on the backside, sealed with seven seals. And I saw a strong angel proclaiming with a loud voice, Who is worthy to open the book, and to loose the seals thereof? And no man in heaven, nor in earth, neither under the earth, was able to open the book, neither to look thereon. And I wept much, because no man was found worthy to open and to read the book, neither to look thereon. And one of the elders saith unto me, Weep not: behold, the Lion of the tribe of Judah, the Root of David, hath prevailed to open the book, and to loose the seven seals thereof. And I beheld, and, lo, in the midst of the throne and of the four beasts, and in the midst of the elders, stood a Lamb as it had been slain, having seven horns and seven eyes, which are the seven Spirits of God sent forth into all the earth. And he came and took the book out of the right hand of him that sat upon the throne. And when he had taken the book, the four beasts and four and twenty elders fell down*

before the Lamb, having every one of them harps, and golden vials full of odors, which are the prayers of saints. And they sung a new song, saying, Thou art worthy to take the book, and to open the seals thereof: for thou wast slain, and hast redeemed us to God by thy blood out of every kindred, and tongue, and people, and nation; And hast made us unto our God kings and priests: and we shall reign on the earth. Revelation 5:1-10

An Application

Entering the Blood Covenant of God requires a decision, a willing commitment to be whatever Jesus wants us to be, whatever he created us to be, that means recognizing His Lordship over our lives.

This is being born again, repenting and being converted. It is the first step of entering into the Covenant.

Unfortunately many of us have make an emotional decision without properly understanding what we are dong. We tend to work through our salvation piecemeal. Sometimes we do well, enjoy blessings, and rejoice in them and sometimes we stagger through from day to day, pleading for forgiveness and just plain trying hard to get it or keep it right.

To solve this we need to understand this covenant, what it is, how it works and respond intelligently. Then our relationship with God, and our salvation will be so much easier for us all.

We will become equipped with the knowledge we need, and enter more richly, into blessing and promises and find it so much easier to walk with God, as He wants us to. Somehow, the right information removes fear, doubt, and confusion and at the same time empowers us to be that which we were called to be. As Jesus said, truth sets free:

Then said Jesus to those Jews which believed on him, If ye continue in my word, then are ye my disciples indeed; And ye shall know the truth, and the truth shall make you free. John 8:31-32

This concept of Blood Covenant does seem daunting at first, but we are opening a way to blessing, relationship, and responsibility that will more than meet every hope we have had or will have since we made our first commitment.

End of Chapter Questions

1. Discuss the value of a blood covenant contract.
2. What are the major differences between the covenants with Noah, Abraham, Moses and God.
3. Explain the value to us today of covenant responses of the disciples to Jesus.
4. What are the "divisions" of the blood covenant?
5. What old testament scripture is quoted in Hebrews 8:7-13.
6. Discuss how we enter into blood covenant.

Chapter 4:

The Exchange Of Clothing

Historical

Once the decision is made to enter into Blood Covenant, a Covenant Ceremony must take place to ratify the agreement legally. This ceremony will involve several elements as outlined in Chapter 1.

A part of the ceremony includes certain exchanges each of which has their own specific significance with many hidden but vital meanings.

The order of the exchanges does not seem to be of particular importance. It is also true that not all of the ceremonies incorporate all of the elements outlined in our study. In some cultures some elements may not make sense at all, but the similarity in the types of exchanges in blood covenant ceremonies is important for they show a universal acceptance of the covenant.

One of the first exchanges to be made is the exchange of clothing. As the two Covenant Heads came together, the Great King would give at least his outer coat, or cloak, sometimes an entire outfit, or even a whole wardrobe, to the Vassal King.

The statement that accompanies the exchange of clothing is so important. *"All that I possess is yours. You are my family, I am your family, I am one with you, you are one with me"*. However it is the hidden meaning that is so profound.

Once the clothing was given the Vassal was entitled to receive the same respect as though he were the Great King himself. From this time on he should be treated as if he were the Great King.

Any blessing given to the Vassal is given with the respect due to him as if he were the Great King and receives due blessing in return. Any offence to him is an offence to the Great King as if given to the Great King directly and attracts due penalty.

Although entitled to wear the clothing the Vassal usually hung the clothing in the Great Hall of the Vassal as a reminder of the Covenant.

This exchange of clothing signified the total acceptance of the individual and his family or tribe, into the family or tribe of the other Covenant partner. All the family rights and obligations are then transferred to each other.

All the wealth and the possessions of each of the Covenant partners becomes the possession of the other.

In modern terms this the equivalent of the richest man on earth declaring to you, "here is my Platinum[15] Amex card, go and use it, buy anything you wish, and I shall be pleased to pay the bill". I am sure that there are many of us who would like to make him a very happy man!

In some communities this bond was held to the point that, if a man's wife dies childless then his covenant partner's[16] wife can bear him children. It is a concept of giving absolutely all that you own to your partner as if your partner is yourself!

---

[15] With the Platinum card you can purchase anything. The holder of such a card has totally unrestricted credit and the right to purchase anything from a bar of chocolate to a mansion or an island. The credit card company has total confidence in the person holding the card. This really is how we should see our relationship with God, after all his line of credit is far superior to any credit card company.

[16] A similar principle is expressed in Deuteronomy 25:5, such customs were not uncommon in the middle east, and have also been reported among Eskimos.

Clothing is important. Perhaps clothing is less important today than in the times of Jesus or the Old Testament. In those days a person and their station in life was identified by the clothing and the colours of their clothing.

To a lesser measure, we see this today, usually in a more formal sense. We recognize a police officer by his uniform as we do a member of military forces. We take confidence in a nurse, not because of their knowledge but because of their uniform. The Uniform speaks of their ability. So it is for so many different peoples. Socially we assume that the well dressed are "better off" in so many ways.

Being able to wear the clothing of the Great King, to be recognized by him and have his influence attributed to the Vassal was a matter of significance advantage and prestige.

Old Testament Examples

One of the best examples of this exchange found in the Bible concerns the Covenant between David and Jonathan. As these men enter a Covenant relationship with each other, they exchange clothing and weapons to signify their relationship with each other. Each exchange has a hidden meaning that we need to understand.

> *And it came to pass, when he had made an end of speaking unto Saul, that the soul of Jonathan was knit with the soul of David, and Jonathan loved him as his own soul. And Saul took him that day, and would let him go no more home to his father's house. Then Jonathan and David made a covenant, because he loved him as his own soul. And Jonathan stripped himself of the robe that was upon him, and gave it to David, and his garments, even to his sword, and to his bow, and to his girdle. 1 Samuel 18:1-4*

Although little is said at this point the fact is that the exchange of clothing and weapons accompanied by the statement that they "made a covenant" make it clear they entered into a blood covenant. This is further strengthened by the statements made by David later in his reign as King that for "covenant sake"[17] he wanted to bless Jonathans house.

> *Then David said, "Is there yet anyone left of the house of Saul, that I may show him kindness for Jonathan's sake?" 2 Samuel 9:1*

This was not the first exchange of clothing.

> *The LORD God made garments of skin for Adam and his wife, and clothed them. Genesis 3:21*

When God sought to re-establish his relationship with Adam and Eve he sealed it with a Covenant. This is evidenced by the fact that He actually clothed both Adam and Eve himself. He clothes them with the skins of animals, to provide the skin of an animal which had to die for them.

This was the first Blood Covenant, and it is significant to us for in this blood covenant all of the principles of blood covenant are found, the subservience of the Vassal, the supremacy of the Great King – God, the sacrificial beast, protection, blessing, responsibility. All are found in the first blood covenant. It will be developed and affirmed, but the all of the required elements are found in this first blood covenant.

Adam and Eve are evicted from the Garden of Eden and forced to work for their living. Eve is to give birth in great pain. They are given authority over the Devil because they are restored into right relationship with God but he has permission to hurt them and their offspring.

The clothing was not to simply cover their nakedness; it was to restore righteousness and relationship. He has given them clothing

---

[17] I deal with this in some detail in the last chapter, the Forgiveness of the Covenant.

and at the time, unbeknown to Adam and Eve, He has embodied[18] all future blood covering in the typology of the first gift of clothing, a sheepskin, also a type of salvation – of Jesus himself.

The was the first physical death[19] recorded in the bible. This sacrifice provided a covering for sinful man in both the physical and a spiritual sense, showing that from the beginning the blessing of God is designed to reach the whole of man, body, soul, and spirit. God provided a sacrifice, he made the sacrifice. He taught Adam and Eve the meaning of physical death and the awesome consequences of sin, and He provided protection for them, showing the level of blessing He was extending to them.

Another example of the exchange of clothing as a result of covenant is seen in the life of Joshua in Zechariah 3:3-5.

The high priest stood before the angel of the Lord in filthy clothes. These filthy clothes are not just dirty clothing; they represent the sinful life of Joshua and show us how God saw him in his sin. In spite of the sinfulness of the High Priest God orders a change of garments for him. He is given garments of regal finery showing his new standing in the presence of God as his filthy rags are exchanged for the finest of robes.

> *Now Joshua was clothed with filthy garments and standing before the angel. He spoke and said to those who were standing before him, saying, "Remove the filthy garments from him." Again he said to him, "See, I have taken your iniquity*

---

[18] Just as each new Blood Covenant must embrace the old, effectively looking backwards, the existing Blood Covenant must also look forward embracing all who will enter in until it is replaced by the new, see the diagram on page 18.

[19] As this was the first death it served to teach both Adam and Eve of the meaning of death, something of which they had no real concept. They came to realise the awesome price of their sin. Although God had told them that if they sinned they would surely die, we can assume they had no knowledge of what death meant

away from you and will clothe you with festal robes." Then I said, "Let them put a clean turban on his head." So they put a clean turban on his head and clothed him with garments, while the angel of the LORD was standing by. Zechariah 3:3-5

Prophetic Symbolism

Through Ezekiel God prophecies to the nation of Israel. As He does He uses clothing as a type of His care for the people and of his love for them. He reminds Israel that he has clothed them as his bride. He cares for his people as passionately as groom cares for his bride.

"Then I passed by you and saw you, and behold, you were at the time for love; so I spread My skirt over you and covered your nakedness. I also swore to you and entered into a covenant with you so that you became Mine," declares the Lord GOD. "Then I bathed you with water, washed off your blood from you and anointed you with oil. "I also clothed you with embroidered cloth and put sandals of porpoise skin on your feet; and I wrapped you with fine linen and covered you with silk. "I adorned you with ornaments, put bracelets on your hands and a necklace around your neck. "I also put a ring in your nostril, earrings in your ears and a beautiful crown on your head. "Thus you were adorned with gold and silver, and your dress was of fine linen, silk and embroidered cloth. You ate fine flour, honey and oil; so you were exceedingly beautiful and advanced to royalty. "Then your fame went forth among the nations on account of your beauty, for it was perfect because of My splendor which I bestowed on you," declares the Lord GOD. Ezekiel 16:8-14

Israel, God's "Covenant Nation" is told again that God has clothed them with Robes of Righteousness (v 10), as he speaks to them of their restoration as a nation and His love for them as His chosen people.

Isaiah 61:10 I will greatly rejoice in the LORD, my soul shall be joyful in my God; for he hath clothed me with the garments of salvation, he hath covered me with the robe of righteousness, as a bridegroom decketh himself with ornaments, and as a bride adorneth herself with her jewels.

This exquisite picture has been painted of Israel as the people of God, a people in authority with God, a people that he has chosen as his bride and upon whom He has showered lavish gifts. In spite of the many failings of this nation, God continues to see them as his own peculiar people and treats them as such at every turn. They are to be successful in all they turn their hand to even as their God is successful. They exercise authority in their land. Even today, the Jews have turned wilderness into flourishing bountiful land in spite of the many difficulties they face. As a nation and as individuals they are recognized as the people of God. Sometimes persecuted, sometimes blessed but always seen as the chosen people.

As well as the prophetic symbolism there is also the typological clothing of which the word of God speaks:

A garment of salvation.

> *"Her priests also I will clothe with salvation, And her godly ones will sing aloud for joy. Psalms 132:16*

Or the garment of praise:

> *To grant those who mourn in Zion, Giving them a garland instead of ashes, The oil of gladness instead of mourning, The mantle of praise instead of a spirit of fainting. So they will be called oaks of righteousness, The planting of the LORD, that He may be glorified. Isaiah 61:3*

These references to clothing, and many others, speak to us of the attributes or characteristics of God, they speak to us of His dealings with us as his people and His goodness and care for us. The statements of clothing reveal to us what God has done for us for they show us that we wear these attributes as clothing. Wear them as our own clothing in just the same way that the Vassal King could wear the clothing of the Great King as though it were his own clothing. He makes this exchange with us when we accept Jesus as our saviour.

The New Testament

The Jews are no longer the only people of God. The Jews were God's chosen nation, and salvation and blessing will always be to the Jew first and then to the Gentile, and indeed salvation was offered first to the Jew in every form, but there has been a shift in who God now sees as his people. Christians are now the people of God from every nation and people and walk of life.

> *For I am not ashamed of the gospel, for it is the power of God for salvation to everyone who believes, to the Jew first and also to the Greek. Romans 1:16*
>
> *For the Scripture says, "WHOEVER BELIEVES IN HIM WILL NOT BE DISAPPOINTED." For there is no distinction between Jew and Greek; for the same Lord is Lord of all, abounding in riches for all who call on Him; for "WHOEVER WILL CALL ON THE NAME OF THE LORD WILL BE SAVED." Romans 10:11-13*
>
> *There is neither Jew nor Greek, there is neither slave nor free man, there is neither male nor female; for you are all one in Christ Jesus. Galatians 3:28*
>
> *There is neither Jew nor Greek, there is neither slave nor free man, there is neither male nor female; for you are all one in Christ Jesus. Galatians 3:28*

It is not simply that God has embraced men and women of all nations who call on him. It is much more, He has totally received and accepted us as a diverse race of people who were once not only far removed from Him, but were His enemy also, and he has brought under both one banner as one nation in Him.

> For if while we were enemies we were reconciled to God through the death of His Son, much more, having been reconciled, we shall be saved by His life. And not only this, but we also exult in God through our Lord Jesus Christ, through whom we have now received the reconciliation. Romans 5:10-11

> But you are A CHOSEN RACE, A royal PRIESTHOOD, A HOLY NATION, A PEOPLE FOR God's OWN POSSESSION, so that you may proclaim the excellencies of Him who has called you out of darkness into His marvelous light; for you once were NOT A PEOPLE, but now you are THE PEOPLE OF GOD; you had NOT RECEIVED MERCY, but now you have RECEIVED MERCY. 1 Peter 2:9-10

That God has chosen to clothe Christians too is clear from the word of God. He has chosen to clothe his chosen generation, his holy Nation with the same clothing he gave his nation the Jews.

Although there is plenty of scripture to prove the exchange or gift of clothing, it is not always so easily apparent to us, largely because of our use of the English language and the many translations of the word of God that we use.

Presented below are seven scriptures, note that the word "PUT ON" and "CLOTHED" have been highlighted. In every case, and there are many other expression you will be familiar with, the words put on or clothed come from the same Greek word which is never translated in any other way. It is the word "enduō" which is pronounced en-doo-o. The Strong's reference is below[20]

> But put on the Lord Jesus Christ, and make no provision for the flesh in regard to its lusts. Romans 13:14

---

[20] **G1746,** Greek ἐνδύω English enduō pronounced "*en-doo*"-*o:* From G1722 and G1416 (in the senese of *sinking* into a garment); to *invest* with clothing (literally or figuratively): - array, clothe (with), endue, have (put) on.

> *For this perishable must put on the imperishable, and this mortal must put on immortality. But when this perishable will have put on the imperishable, and this mortal will have put on immortality, then will come about the saying that is written, "DEATH IS SWALLOWED UP in victory. 1 Corinthians 15:53-54*

> *For all of you who were baptized into Christ have clothed yourselves with Christ. Galatians 3:27*

> *and put on the new self, which in the likeness of God has been created in righteousness and holiness of the truth. Ephesians 4:24*

> *and have put on the new self who is being renewed to a true knowledge according to the image of the One who created him- - Colossians 3:10*

> *'He who overcomes will thus be clothed in white garments; and I will not erase his name from the book of life, and I will confess his name before My Father and before His angels. Revelation 3:5*

> *and the seven angels who had the seven plagues came out of the temple, clothed in linen, clean and bright, and girded around their chests with golden sashes. Revelation 15:6*

> *And the armies which are in heaven, clothed in fine linen, white and clean, were following Him on white horses. Revelation 19:14*

He "clothes" Christians with many robes; I have separated these from the passages above, we are clothed with the:

> *Lord Jesus Christ, imperishable, immortality, Christ, new self, righteousness holiness truth, white raiment; linen, clean and bright, fine linen, white and clean.*

All of these "clothes" are symbolic of the nature and person of Christ. The word of God declares that we are already clothed with them. We have already put on Christ; we are already clothed with his image. In Blood covenant terms we are as he is because, we are clothed with him.

> *By this, love is perfected with us, so that we may have confidence in the day of judgment; because as He is, so also are we in this world. 1 John 4:17*

Curiously, these expressions are often seen as symbols of something that will happen in the future. For some, they are surrealistic rather than factual. For others there is a danger of reducing these "clothes" to little more than a Christian "lucky charm" that we mystically clothe ourselves with in our prayer closet before we go out on an endeavour for Christ or if when we feel we are in peril!

Sometimes we imagine that in some way God sends us to an enormous wardrobe and selects a range of clothing for us, perhaps a white righteous suit or gown, but no, this is not a suit or a robe of woven fabric nor is it spun magically by angels singing rapturously of the greatness of God. This clothing is more wonderful than any such garment.

These garments are Jesus Himself as He gives Himself to us when we accept Him as our saviour.

When we wear these clothes we are wearing Jesus. Your heavenly Father sees you as He sees Jesus, and the spiritual realm sees you as they see Jesus. We have his victory, we have his wealth, and we have his rights, because we have put on Christ in union with Him.

These robes are given to those saints who will come through the tribulation period as well as to all the saints of God, Jew, and Gentile alike. All of the saints will be clothed in *white raiment* symbolic in scripture of the *Robes of righteousness.* When Jesus comes in his glory to claim this earth as his he will come with armies of Christians and they will be wearing the white robes of righteousness too.

The tribulation saints will also be given White Robes indicating their right standing in the presence of God while they wait for those who must yet join them. Notice that while they are waiting they are given these white robes.

> *And there was given to each of them a white robe; and they were told that they should rest for a little while longer, until the number of their fellow servants and their brethren who were to be killed even as they had been, would be completed also. Revelation 6:11*
>
> *After these things I looked, and behold, a great multitude which no one could count, from every nation and all tribes and peoples and tongues, standing before the throne and before the Lamb, clothed in white robes, and palm branches were in their hands; and they cry out with a loud voice, saying, "Salvation to our God who sits on the throne, and to the Lamb." And all the angels were standing around the throne and around the elders and the four living creatures; and they fell on their faces before the throne and worshiped God, saying, "Amen, blessing and glory and wisdom and thanksgiving and honor and power and might, be to our God forever and ever. Amen." Then one of the elders answered, saying to me, "These who are clothed in the white robes, who are they, and where have they come from?" I said to him, "My lord, you know." And he said to me, "These are the ones who come out of the great tribulation, and they have washed their robes and made them white in the blood of the Lamb. Revelation 7:9-14*

These robes of righteousness are not simply the righteousness of God they are God Himself. We possess the righteousness of God as our own. Our Father God no longer sees us as unrighteous, sinful man, but as family with all of the benefits, graces, and privileges that belong to the members of family of God.

Typological Clothing

As well as the literal mention of clothing, there is the typological clothing that the word of God speaks of such as:

A Garment of Salvation.

> *"Her priests also I will clothe with salvation, And her godly ones will sing aloud for joy. Psalms 132:16*

Or Garment of Praise:

> *To grant those who mourn in Zion, Giving them a garland instead of ashes, The oil of gladness instead of mourning, The mantle of praise instead of a spirit of fainting. So they will be called oaks of righteousness, The planting of the LORD, that He may be glorified. Isaiah 61:3*

As already stated, these references to clothing and many others, speak to us of the attributes or characteristics of God. They speak to us of His dealings with us as his people, and his goodness. The statements of clothing reveal to us what God has done for us for they show us that we wear these attributes as clothing. We wear them as our own clothing in just the same way that the Vassal King could wear the clothing of the Great King, as though it were his own. He makes this exchange with us when we accept Jesus as our saviour.

This concept goes much further for us than mere clothing. The typology is vitally important to our understanding of what God has done for us, He has clothed us not only with clothing of a spiritual nature but also with an immortal and incorruptible nature, indicating to us that we are a part of Him.

> *But when this perishable will have put on the imperishable, and this mortal will have put on immortality, then will come about the saying that is written, "DEATH IS SWALLOWED UP in victory. "O DEATH, WHERE IS YOUR VICTORY? O DEATH, WHERE IS YOUR STING?" 1 Corinthians 15:54-55*

We become new people in him; we are completely new creations without a past. With God we have a brand new start.

> *and put on the new self, which in the likeness of God has been created in righteousness and holiness of the truth. Ephesians 4:24*

In Galatians we read that we have become Christ like because we have put on Christ, we put him on in place of ourselves, in a sense as we would put on a garment. We have exchanged ourselves for himself.

> *For all of you who were baptized into Christ have clothed yourselves with Christ. Galatians 3:27*

Also in Colossians we are reminded to maintain this high standard of life and principle because we have clothed ourselves with Jesus, we have a new self,

> *and have put on the new self who is being renewed to a true knowledge according to the image of the One who created him - a renewal in which there is no distinction between Greek and Jew, circumcised and uncircumcised, barbarian, Scythian, slave and freeman, but Christ is all, and in all. So, as those who have been chosen of God, holy and beloved, put on a heart of compassion, kindness, humility, gentleness and patience; Colossians 3:10-12*

It is not simply that God has clothed us with these garments. These Garments represent wealth, station, office, or rank. They represent what Jesus has done for us, and therefore our relationship with him. He tells us WHAT this clothing represents. We are clothed with immortality; we are new beings of righteousness and holiness. We are clothed with Jesus Christ Himself; we wear his compassion, kindness, humility, gentleness, and patience as He does. This list is almost endless for it is a list of the characteristics of God Himself.

From the time an individual decides to become a Christian they enter a Covenant relationship with God. As such he gives us all this "clothing" and so much more. All that He is, is ours. All that we were is his to deal with, and so our sin is dealt with.

> *As far as the east is from the west, So far has He removed our transgressions from us. Psalms 103:12*
>
> *Therefore if anyone is in Christ, he is a new creature; the old things passed away; behold, new things have come. 2 Corinthians 5:17*

It is left to us to appropriate these truths and believe them. That is we must accept that Jesus is our Covenant sacrifice for sin. Our response to his grace is to believe in and trust him. Each one of us needs to fully comprehend what God has given us in this exchange of clothing and then live out the fact. It is not a matter of putting on Jesus or the new man, it is a matter or realising that He has clothed us.

It is not the secret of instant godliness, but it is a matter of allowing ourselves to receive what Jesus has given us, and at the same time realise that if we accept what we have we will not continue to struggle to be what we already are.

An Application

Everything that we require as a Christian to maintain our relationship with God is already in our possession. He gave us everything that He is and simply expects us to continue in this life in Him. It is not something we can attain to. This standard is already entrusted to us.

Yes we must grow, mature and develop. Yes, we must "work out our own salvation with fear and trembling". But we do so from a position of an accepted family member, not as an outsider trying to earn our right of entrance.

Ramsis II and Hattusilis III understood the rights, responsibilities, authority and relationship of blood covenant family.

How do we make this work for us?

Firstly, by properly understanding what we are getting into. When we accept Jesus as saviour we entered into blood covenant. As the King of Kings and Lord of Lords He gave us His clothing. We fully represent Him as though we are Himself, it is implicit that we should therefore act accordingly.

It is akin to a Police officer donning his uniform, walking out into the street and raising his hand to halt the traffic. The biggest truck to the smallest bicycle, pedestrian or any other road user must respond the authority vested in the uniform and in the man. That authority is vested in both the uniform and the man. Every driver or road user must respond to the signal or suffer the consequence.

So it is for us. When we accept Christ as our saviour we enter into a relationship with God that releases his blessing and authority into our lives for our blessing and for the blessing of those we are in contact with, for the development and furtherance of the Kingdom of God.

If we do not recognize that we have put on Christ, we will be like the policeman who steps into the busy street without his uniform and tries to exercise his authority. He will be ignored to the point of personal peril. Christians who fail to recognize who and what they are also ignored because we have disregarded who and what we are.

If we do not recognize who and what we are then many our prayers will be unanswered, we will live in defeat, we will be ignored by Satan and demons.

Because we disregard our relationship with God we are out of His favour and risk being cast aside and disregarded because we chose to disregard, or do not understand who and what we are in God.

We fail to live and walk in God. God has does not disregard us but we have chosen not to enter the life and authority and responsibility and blessing that God has provided for us.

When we realise that we have put on Christ the authority will being to flow, Satan and his demons will tremble, sickness and disease will be removed, The financial sources will be flowing to accomplish his will.

There are two differences between us and the policeman.

The first is that he must take off his uniform at the end of his shift. He ceases to be on duty. He becomes a civilian. For us there is no reference to taking off the clothing. We are "on duty" 24 hours a day, seven days a week, 52 weeks a year.

The second is that the policeman must learn the law, his rights and responsibility, his role in the community and so on. For us when we accept Jesus we are clothed with Him and grace takes effect immediately for us, filling the gap of ignorance while the Holy Spirit leads us into truth. Yes we will learn, yes we will grow in maturity and understanding, but in the meantime these things, according to Jeremiah, are written on our heart.

Ah, there is a third difference. The policeman cannot act until he has completed his course, while the marvellous work of grace in our conversion releases us immediately, under the watchful "eye" of the Holy Spirit as God's representatives in fullness.

Abraham understood, Moses understood, and David understood that they were family with all the rights of family.

Satan also understands. He understands that our rights in Christ are birthed in God's Blood Covenant promise to look after you. All he can do to deceive us into believing we are paupers, and we will be "blessed in the great beyond for our suffering in the now". He will easily convince us of what do we do not have if we do not understand how this relationship works.

Our authority in Christ is not birthed in knowledge, it is birthed in relationship. Demons do not flee because we shout aloud in the name of Jesus, they do not tremble because we wave our arms, perform or scream out in tongues or get excited, it is not the "power of the anointing" nor our raw adrenalin, and it is the result of relationship with Jesus.

> *And the evil spirit answered and said to them, "I recognize Jesus, and I know about Paul, but who are you?" Act 19:15*

Satan and his demons understand because when they look at us they see someone clothed with Blood Covenant clothing, someone with the wealth and presence of God, for it is God who is our Clothing for we have put on Christ.

We do not have to prove ourselves to God, He has already accepted us. Once we realise that we are right in his sight we can spend more effort and energy in what he wants us to do instead of what we think he wants us to be,

> *For we are His workmanship, created in Christ Jesus for good works, which God prepared beforehand so that we would walk in them. Ephesians 2:10*

To use a simple colloquialism, we are "his kid's," and much more.

The Clothing speaks to us much more of recognition and provision. Whatever it is that we need, he has supplied. His promise is clear in so many passages

> *Simon Peter, a bond-servant and apostle of Jesus Christ, To those who have received a faith of the same kind as ours, by the righteousness of our God and Savior, Jesus Christ: Grace and peace be multiplied to you in the knowledge of God and of Jesus our Lord; seeing that His divine power has granted to us everything pertaining to life and godliness, through the true knowledge of Him who called us by His own glory and excellence. For by these He has granted to us His precious and magnificent promises, so that by them you may become partakers of the divine nature, having escaped the corruption that is in the world by lust. 2 Peter 1:1-4*

Let me introduce a word of caution here. Note the words "*seeing that His divine power has granted to us everything pertaining to life and godliness"*. I am concerned with those who think that the Gospel is the key to wealth, it is not. The gospel is the key to gaining all that we **need** for life and Godliness together. I have no dispute with the ability to provide all that I need for the ministry and for my well being, but it is a matter of meeting need, not greed. With this in mind, let us continue

He urges us to ask him to supply our need and every verse, every scripture, that speaks of clothing should remind us of our relationship with him and our guaranteed supply.

Why does God do so much for us? Is it simply that He loves us? No, He loves His whole creation, He loves every man woman and child, but not all are in receipt of His blessing.

Does he "do for us to honour His word" as some will tell us?

To quote to the occasional evangelist, "God has said it, I believe it, that settles it! He is bound by His word." No, that would place God in an untenable position of honouring the dishonourable for not every quotation of scripture is by every man or woman is in context or in line with His will.

He does for us because of our blood covenant relationship. The many scriptures in the word of God of promises to supply and help, to redeem and to bless are not given to bind God to His word.

These scriptures are given to us to inform, educate, and encourage us, so that we know where we stand, so we can understand how to relate to God, so we can know what we can claim, how we can respond to Him and his promises.

He loves us so much that he chose to enter into a Covenant with Abraham and then with Jesus to make a relationship between Himself and ourselves possible. As long as there is God and man, this Covenant must continue. This fact is as simple as the words of Jesus to Nicodemus

> *"For God so loved the world, that He gave His only begotten Son, that whoever believes in Him shall not perish, but have*

eternal life. *"For God did not send the Son into the world to judge the world, but that the world might be saved through Him. John 3:16-17*

A Testimony

I came out of the mission-field in Papua New Guinea with a burden to place a Bible College on the internet. It had to be a God given desire for I knew nothing of the Internet. I had not so much as sent or received an email at that stage, yet I knew what God wanted of me.

My wife and I arrived home with no money, no job, no ministry and the denomination we were involved in did not have a situation for us. We had done nothing wrong, our time in Papua New Guinea had come to and end and God had a new job for me.

Within three months or returning home I had mastered sufficient basic skill to develop the pages and establish the site. I had spoken with a good friend and father in the faith, Dr Ken Chant, who invited me to use his materials from Vision Christian College, and his permission, the subjects were converted into a format that was useful for the Internet.

Without asking, we were provided with the finance that was needed to purchase programs, establish the site, and do all that was needed, and the Internet Bible College was born www.internetbiblecollege.com.

We already had many, many experiences of God's great provision but this was the grandest example to my thinking. From nothing to a full-blown college on the internet with a steadily growing student body! It was, and is, a miracle.

God provided what was needed. Knowledge and confidence on the internet to the point that I could create a site, the provision of the material, the acceptance by Vision Christian College, the finance – all came from the heart of God. It came because of the principle of blood covenant.

God had clothed me in His care, and in so doing offered all his wealth to achieve whatever was required to accomplish his will.

All the accusation of Satan, the ridicule of men, the impossibility of the task could not stand against the simple will of God working in one of his people who had determined to understand his covenant relationship.

Some say to me "when my ship comes in..." To such people all I can say is, it has, not only had your ship come in, it is waiting for you to board and see what God will do with you.

End of Chapter Questions

1. What is the significance of the exchange of Clothing?
2. Explain the exchange of clothing between Jonathan and David in the light of their individual family relationships.
3. Show three OT examples of and exchange.
4. What is meant by the prophetic symbolism.
5. Discuss two examples of New Testament clothing exchanges.
6. What is meant by a "Type of clothing"?

Chapter 5:

The Exchange Of Weapons

Historical

An exchange of weapons usually followed the exchange of clothing. The particular significance of this exchange lay in the significance of weapons.

Weapons speak of strength, authority, protection, defence.

By making this exchange, which more often than not is a one-sided gift, the Great King is offering all his strength, authority, and armies to the Vassal King. From the moment that the Covenant was entered into, both parties could be sure that if they were attacked or invaded by a foreign power, their Covenant partner would come to their assistance.

These principles are typical of the type of allegiance we find today between countries when they enter a treaty or alliance. The allegiance between Britain and Australia at the time of the Second World War is a fine example.

Britain and Australia were, and still are, in an allegiance, or Covenant, with each other. When Britain declared war on Germany because of the German invasion of Poland, Australia was automatically drawn into that war because of the allegiance between them. The same is true in any such treaty between any two countries.

This kind of response is expected of those who are bound by Blood Covenants and it is a formal part of the Blood Covenant agreement.

Old Testament

As the agreement stood between Britain and her allies so it stands between God and man, yet the veracity of God to the covenant is far stronger than it ever could be between human relationships. When someone decides to go to war against the people of God without good cause, His promise is that He will defend his people. As our Covenant partner, He is our protection, our defence and our shield, as we will see. It is the first part of the first promise of the Covenant with Abraham.

> *After these things the word of the LORD came to Abram in a vision, saying, "Do not fear, Abram, I am a shield to you; Your reward shall be very great." Genesis 15:1*

Blood Covenant agreement commits God to fighting for us against whoever and whatever comes against us. There is no better illustration in the Bible of God's protection that the "Exodus Event" (Exodus 5:1 to 14:31).

Moses was called to lead the children of Israel, the Covenant people of God, out of Egypt. It seems to us sometimes that God is slow to deal with a situation, perhaps for us He is, but he does everything for the best for everyone. He is not willing for anyone to perish, even though the Egyptians were an idolatrous nation who had cruelly treated the Israelites, God wanted to give them every opportunity to recognize him for who he is.

Ten times Moses went before Pharaoh, ten times Pharaoh rejected him, and each time a plague came upon the nation.

- Exodus 7: The river is turned into blood,
- Exodus 8: The plague of frogs, The plague of lice, The plague of flies.

- Exodus 9: The plague and death of livestock, The plague of boils and blains[21]. The plague of hail.
- Exodus 10: The plague of locusts. The plague of thick darkness.
- Exodus 12: The death of the first-born of the Egyptians
- Exodus 14: The parting of the Red Sea and drowning of the Egyptians

Extraordinarily, none of these plagues affected the children of Israel who were living in Goshen, a district in Egypt. Finally, Pharaoh sent Moses and the children of Israel away. Even then, he changed his mind and sent his army after the Israelites and eventually the army of Pharaoh, their horses and chariots, were drowned during the crossing of the Red Sea.

National Victories

The taking of the land of Canaan, or Israel, as told in the book of Joshua illustrates the care of God for his people. It shows how he will fight for them in their battles.

---

[21] **Shall be a boil** - שחין shechin. This word is generally expounded, an inflammatory swelling, a burning boil; one of the most poignant afflictions, not immediately mortal, that can well affect the surface of the human body. If a single boil on any part of the body throws the whole system into a fever, what anguish must a multitude of them on the body at the same time occasion!

Breaking forth with blains - אבעבעת ababuoth, supposed to come from בעה baah, to swell, bulge out; any inflammatory swelling, node, or pustule, in any part of the body, but more especially in the more glandular parts, the neck, arm-pits, groin, etc. The Septuagint translate it thus: Και εσται ελκη φλυκτιδες αναζεουσαι· And it shalt be an ulcer with burning pustules. It seems to have been a disorder of an uncommon kind, and hence it is called by way of distinction, the botch of Egypt, Deu 28:27, perhaps never known before in that or any other country. Orosius says that in the sixth plague "all the people were blistered, that the blisters burst with tormenting pain, and that worms issued out of them." Alfred's Oros., lib. i., c. vii. Adam Clarke's Commentary on the Bible Adam Clarke, LL.D., F.S.A., (1715-1832)

The battle for Ai brings our new dimensions of this relationship. It shows that a people our of relationship will suffer defeat but upon their repentance[22] the past is forgotten and dealt with and the Blood Covenant promise is restored along with the protection of the covenant.

Time and time again God shows his ability against the Philistines, the Amalekites, the Jebusites and the Syrians and all the nations that would oppose the Israelites in Canaan.

Battle for Jericho	Jos 5:13-6:27
Taking of Ai	Jos 7:1 to 8:35
Conquest of Sth Canaan	Jos Chapter 1
Conquest of Nth Canaan	Jos Chapter 11
List of Conquered Kings	Jos chapter 12.

Apart from the military victories, above, won through the protection of God, His supernatural help is demonstrated as He rains down great stones or hailstones, He causes the sun to stand still, and gives advice and strategy that will guarantee victory for his people against their enemies.

However whenever the armies of Israel went to war under the direction of God, they were under his protection. Whenever they were attacked because they were God's people or because ungodly nations wanted to expand their territory God Himself came to their aid, it is often reported they did not lose a single soldier and always won their battle.

Whenever they were the aggressor or acted out of their own will, they suffered heavy casualties.

---

[22] Defeated at Ai, Joshua seeks God who tells him of the sin if Achan. It was his sin that prevented covenant blessing not the covenant, so when the people repented God restored blessing. Joshua Ch.7

Individual Victories

David knew from experience the protection of God as he had faced lions and bears as a shepherd boy. He knew the same God would protect him as he faced the giant Goliath (1 Samuel 17) and killed him with a single slingshot. The tone of his language, born out of the confidence that comes from experience, shows that David expected nothing less than God's protection.

> *When the Philistine looked and saw David, he disdained him; for he was but a youth, and ruddy, with a handsome appearance. The Philistine said to David, "Am I a dog, that you come to me with sticks?" And the Philistine cursed David by his gods. The Philistine also said to David, "Come to me, and I will give your flesh to the birds of the sky and the beasts of the field." Then David said to the Philistine, "You come to me with a sword, a spear, and a javelin, but I come to you in the name of the LORD of hosts, the God of the armies of Israel, whom you have taunted. "This day the LORD will deliver you up into my hands, and I will strike you down and remove your head from you. And I will give the dead bodies of the army of the Philistines this day to the birds of the sky and the wild beasts of the earth, that all the earth may know that there is a God in Israel, 1 Samuel 17:42-46*

It was Blood covenant that protected Shadrach, Meshach, and Abednego in the fiery furnace, their confidence in God was absolute, and there knowledge of who and how they should worship attracted their protection (Daniel ch 3). Not even their clothes were singed. They were aware of their Covenant promises and they were prepared to trust God to protect them.

Daniel knew, as he faced the prospect of the lions den, that his God would protect him and God did (Daniel ch 6). The lions did not so much as touch him as angels stopped their mouths. Perhaps it is more astonishing that it is the King[23] who makes the statement that the God he serves will preserve Daniel. It is Daniel who shows cool-headed confidence in God.

New Testament

This protection of God is not unique to the Old Testament. The power and protection of God is demonstrated for us throughout the New Testament. Throughout the ages, since the last word of the New Testament was penned, Christians have seen and known the protection of God. His protection is for those who walk with Him in purpose, to those who are commissioned to His will; to these people this protection particularly stands.

The Disciples

While the disciples were in their small boat, a storm came and buffeted their tiny vessel. It is to Jesus that they cried out, and as their protector, He stills the storm that threatened their lives, Matthew Ch. 8:23-27.

When Peter was walking on water toward Jesus his attention was turned to the storm and he began to sink. As he did so, he called on Jesus to help him and Jesus lifted Peter out of the water

> *But seeing the wind, he became frightened, and beginning to sink, he cried out, "Lord, save me!" Immediately Jesus stretched out His hand and took hold of him, and said to him, "You of little faith, why did you doubt?" When they got into the boat, the wind stopped. Matthew 14:30-32*

Throughout the Gospels Jesus repeatedly proves his authority and power over Satan's attacks on people in the form of sickness or

---

[23] When he had come near the den to Daniel, he cried out with a troubled voice. The king spoke and said to Daniel, "Daniel, servant of the living God, has your God, whom you constantly serve, been able to deliver you from the lions?" Daniel 6:20

demonization or death. Nothing is too powerful for Jesus. As their Covenant partner and defender Jesus comes to the aid of His people, proving over and over again the promises to Abraham are real to them as much as they were to the patriarch himself.

> *After these things the word of the LORD came to Abram in a vision, saying, "Do not fear, Abram, I am a shield to you; Your reward shall be very great." Genesis 15:1*

His authority extends over natural laws as he feeds the multitudes (Matthew 14), as He walks on water with Peter, raises Lazarus to life (John ch 11), or stills the storms (Matthew 8). These examples not only show us the power of God, they also show us his care and protection for his people. This care has not changed today for Jesus is the same yesterday today and forever, He is the unchanging God (Hebrews 13:8).

The Multitude

Jesus was not only concerned for those who were His disciples. During His ministry He demonstrated the power of Blood Covenant on a daily basis. Jesus came to the defense of all who trusted Him.

There is an abundance of evidence in scripture for this Matthew Ch. 8 provides a wonderful example of the diversity of Christ's power and authority over anything that was to hurt a human being. In this single chapter the power of Blood Covenant authority is so clearly demonstrated and the miracle message of the gospels is encapsulated.

Matthew chapter 8

1-4	Jesus Cleanses leprosy
5-13	heals a paralyzed man
14-15	heals Peter's mother
16	Cast our demons and healed all who were ill
23-27	Calmed the storm

28   Delivered the demoniacs of the Gadarenes

Matthew explains to us what is happening In Verse 17, he states:

> *This was to fulfill what was spoken through Isaiah the prophet: "HE HIMSELF TOOK OUR INFIRMITIES AND CARRIED AWAY OUR DISEASES." Matthew 8:17*

The clear demonstration of Jesus words in Luke are:

> *And the book of the prophet Isaiah was handed to Him. And He opened the book and found the place where it was written, "THE SPIRIT OF THE LORD IS UPON ME, BECAUSE HE ANOINTED ME TO PREACH THE GOSPEL TO THE POOR. HE HAS SENT ME TO PROCLAIM RELEASE TO THE CAPTIVES, AND RECOVERY OF SIGHT TO THE BLIND, TO SET FREE THOSE WHO ARE OPPRESSED, TO PROCLAIM THE FAVORABLE YEAR OF THE LORD." And He closed the book, gave it back to the attendant and sat down; and the eyes of all in the synagogue were fixed on Him. And He began to say to them, "Today this Scripture has been fulfilled in your hearing." Luke 4:17-21*

Throughout His ministry Jesus continued to demonstrate Authority, the authority of Blood covenant relationship and showed the disciples their authority and in so doing has shown us our authority as well.

Jesus Is Protected

Jesus was protected by Blood Covenant, this is amply demonstrated throughout the Gospels, in the Book of Luke, upon Jesus announcement of His ministry His life is threatened the angry crown attempt to throw him over a cliff. Amazingly, He simply walks through the maddened crowd as if they are not there. So often God demonstrates His care and protection for Jesus as he threatened with stoning.

> *And all the people in the synagogue were filled with rage as they heard these things; and they got up and drove Him out of*

the city, and led Him to the brow of the hill on which their city had been built, in order to throw Him down the cliff. But passing through their midst, He went His way. Luke 4:28-30

"Your father Abraham rejoiced to see My day, and he saw it and was glad." So the Jews said to Him, "You are not yet fifty years old, and have You seen Abraham?" Jesus said to them, "Truly, truly, I say to you, before Abraham was born, I am." Therefore they picked up stones to throw at Him, but Jesus hid Himself and went out of the temple. John 8:56-59

"I and the Father are one." The Jews picked up stones again to stone Him. Jesus answered them, "I showed you many good works from the Father; for which of them are you stoning Me?" The Jews answered Him, "For a good work we do not stone You, but for blasphemy; and because You, being a man, make Yourself out to be God." Jesus answered them, "Has it not been written in your Law, 'I SAID, YOU ARE GODS'? "If he called them gods, to whom the word of God came (and the Scripture cannot be broken), do you say of Him, whom the Father sanctified and sent into the world, 'You are blaspheming,' because I said, 'I am the Son of God'? "If I do not do the works of My Father, do not believe Me; but if I do them, though you do not believe Me, believe the works, so that you may know and understand that the Father is in Me, and I in the Father." Therefore they were seeking again to seize Him, and He eluded their grasp. John 10:30-39

The disciples said to Him, "Rabbi, the Jews were just now seeking to stone You, and are You going there again?" Jesus answered, "Are there not twelve hours in the day? If anyone walks in the day, he does not stumble, because he sees the light of this world. "But if anyone walks in the night, he stumbles, because the light is not in him." This He said, and after that He *said to them, "Our friend Lazarus has fallen asleep; but I go, so that I may awaken him out of sleep." The disciples then said to Him, "Lord, if he has fallen asleep, he will recover." Now

> *Jesus had spoken of his death, but they thought that He was speaking of literal sleep. So Jesus then said to them plainly, "Lazarus is dead, and I am glad for your sakes that I was not there, so that you may believe; but let us go to him." John 11:8-15*
>
> *John 5:8-14 Jesus said to him, "Get up, pick up your pallet and walk." Immediately the man became well, and picked up his pallet and began to walk. Now it was the Sabbath on that day. So the Jews were saying to the man who was cured, "It is the Sabbath, and it is not permissible for you to carry your pallet." But he answered them, "He who made me well was the one who said to me, "Pick up your pallet and walk."" They asked him, "Who is the man who said to you, "Pick up your pallet and walk"?" But the man who was healed did not know who it was, for Jesus had slipped away while there was a crowd in that place. Afterward Jesus found him in the temple and said to him, "Behold, you have become well; do not sin anymore, so that nothing worse happens to you."*

It is important to recognize that Jesus did not foolishly put himself at risk. For this same Jesus who saw such wonderful protection over and over again, also saw the need to withdraw and not foolishly provoke, a theme I shall look to further in this chapter.

> *So from that day on they planned together to kill Him. Therefore Jesus no longer continued to walk publicly among the Jews, but went away from there to the country near the wilderness, into a city called Ephraim; and there He stayed with the disciples. John 11:53-54*

Protection For Us

God is no less interested in protecting us today. These principles have not changed. As we look at the armour that God has given to us, we will see that it has not changed. We are told to walk in this same covenant blessing that Jesus and the Disciples walked in, demonstrate and receive the same Blood Covenant promise that they enjoyed.

> *Afterward He appeared to the eleven themselves as they were reclining at the table; and He reproached them for their unbelief and hardness of heart, because they had not believed those who had seen Him after He had risen. And He said to them, "Go into all the world and preach the gospel to all creation. "He who has believed and has been baptized shall be saved; but he who has disbelieved shall be condemned. "These signs will accompany those who have believed: in My name they will cast out demons, they will speak with new tongues; they will pick up serpents, and if they drink any deadly poison, it will not hurt them; they will lay hands on the sick, and they will recover." So then, when the Lord Jesus had spoken to them, He was received up into heaven and sat down at the right hand of God. And they went out and preached everywhere, while the Lord worked with them, and confirmed the word by the signs that followed.] [And they promptly reported all these instructions to Peter and his companions. And after that, Jesus Himself sent out through them from east to west the sacred and imperishable proclamation of eternal salvation.] Mark 16:14-20*

> *Gathering them together, He commanded them not to leave Jerusalem, but to wait for what the Father had promised, "Which," He said, "you heard of from Me; for John baptized with water, but you will be baptized with the Holy Spirit not many days from now." So when they had come together, they were asking Him, saying, "Lord, is it at this time You are restoring the kingdom to Israel?" He said to them, "It is not for you to know times or epochs which the Father has fixed by His own authority; but you will receive power when the Holy Spirit has come upon you; and you shall be My witnesses both in Jerusalem, and in all Judea and Samaria, and even to the remotest part of the earth." Acts 1:4-8*

The great Commission as given through Mark and reinforced in Acts illustrates so clearly that the weapons, the authority and the power that Jesus walked with we are expected to walk with also. Not only to defend, release and empower others, but for our protection too.

Paul identifies this for us in Ephesians as he begins to discuss the Armour or God

> *Therefore, take up the full armor of God, so that you will be able to resist in the evil day, and having done everything, to stand firm. Stand firm therefore, HAVING GIRDED YOUR LOINS WITH TRUTH, and HAVING PUT ON THE BREASTPLATE OF RIGHTEOUSNESS, and having shod YOUR FEET WITH THE PREPARATION OF THE GOSPEL OF PEACE; in addition to all, taking up the shield of faith with which you will be able to extinguish all the flaming arrows of the evil one. And take THE HELMET OF SALVATION, and the sword of the Spirit, which is the word of God. With all prayer and petition pray at all times in the Spirit, and with this in view, be on the alert with all perseverance and petition for all the saints, Ephesians 6:13-18*

This is not only a New Testament concept, we can find the armour of God in the Old Testament as well.

> *He put on righteousness like a breastplate, And a helmet of salvation on His head; And He put on garments of vengeance for clothing And wrapped Himself with zeal as a mantle. Isaiah 59:17*

When we enter Blood Covenant with God, there is an exchange of weapons and armour. As we look to this armour, we see that it is not armour of iron or brass or chain mail. This armour of God is in fact God HIMSELF. God is declaring that when we put on his armour we put him on. When someone, or something comes against the Christian they war, not with the Christian, but they come against God himself. This is especially true in the spiritual realm.

It is no wonder that God declares he will protect us and deal with the issues and attacks that come against us. He is declaring that he is going to stand between us, as a shield, and everything that comes against us, physically, spiritually, materially, whether it is real or imagined. This was the first promise of the Covenant.

> *After these things the word of the LORD came to Abram in a vision, saying, "Do not fear, Abram, I am a shield to you; Your reward shall be very great." Genesis 15:1*

At the very inception of the Covenant relationship God has set down this promise. "Regardless of what is happening to you, I will protect you, I will stand between you and your attacker."

Again and again we read in the Bible of God's promises to protect us in our difficulties, to assure us of His ability to more than cope with our situation. There are innumerable examples of how He has solved similar problems for other people as they trust God and take Him at his word.

> *The LORD is my strength and my shield; My heart trusts in Him, and I am helped; Therefore my heart exults, And with my song I shall thank Him. The LORD is their strength, And He is a saving defense to His anointed. Save Your people and bless Your inheritance; Be their shepherd also, and carry them forever. Psalms 28:7-9*

For further confirmation, we can also look to Isaiah.

> *According to their deeds, so He will repay, Wrath to His adversaries, recompense to His enemies; To the coastlands He will make recompense. Isaiah 59:18*

A Caution

Because of this level of protection that God has given us, he calls on us not to take vengeance into our own hands against those who have harmed us or who wish to hurt us. His constant message to us is to love people and leave the issue of vengeance to him, if they must be taken,

> *Never take your own revenge, beloved, but leave room for the wrath of God, for it is written, "VENGEANCE IS MINE, I WILL REPAY," says the Lord. "BUT IF YOUR ENEMY IS HUNGRY, FEED HIM, AND IF HE IS THIRSTY, GIVE HIM A DRINK; FOR IN SO DOING YOU WILL HEAP BURNING COALS ON HIS HEAD." Do not be overcome by evil, but overcome evil with good. Romans 12:19-21*

Too often we choose to take matters into our own hands. We forget, or fail to recognize, that our enemies are God's enemies. If someone is set upon hurting us, they are effectively, set upon hurting God.

Our response aught to be to forgive, let go, and let God deal with the issue. No matter how difficult that may be for us God is still calling on us to forgive. He will protect us and more importantly He will turn the event into our benefit.

> *And we know that God causes all things to work together for good to those who love God, to those who are called according to His purpose. Romans 8:28*

He is our protector. We need to turn to him and let him take care of the issue. He will attempt to bring about reconciliation if possible but if that fails, he will bring about judgment.

No matter what the circumstances are, no matter how difficult the situation may be, we must learn to take hold of the word of God, and God himself. We must allow him to do what he has promised. He has promised us protection and victory. We should learn from the great men of God such as Elisha in 2 Kings 6:17-22, to see things through our spiritual eyes. We cannot afford to look on the outward appearance of things, for if we do we will not see how God is working on our behalf for our benefit and his glory!

Then Elisha prayed and said, "O LORD, I pray, open his eyes that he may see." And the LORD opened the servant's eyes and he saw; and behold, the mountain was full of horses and chariots of fire all around Elisha. When they came down to him, Elisha prayed to the LORD and said, "Strike this people with blindness, I pray." So He struck them with blindness according to the word of Elisha. Then Elisha said to them, "This is not the way, nor is this the city; follow me and I will bring you to the man whom you seek." And he brought them to Samaria. When they had come into Samaria, Elisha said, "O LORD, open the eyes of these men, that they may see." So the LORD opened their eyes and they saw; and behold, they were in the midst of Samaria. Then the king of Israel when he saw them, said to Elisha, "My father, shall I kill them? Shall I kill them?" He answered, "You shall not kill them. Would you kill those you have taken captive with your sword and with your bow? Set bread and water before them, that they may eat and drink and go to their master." 2 Kings 6:17-22

When surrounded by the enemy Elisha could see that the angels of the Lord protected him. They were camped around him and there were more of God's angels than there were the enemy.

This protection is not just for the astoundingly miraculous situation or the missionary or apostle on the job, but in the humdrum of our daily life the protection of God is real. Countless numbers of Christians have testified of being protected from harm or death as they walk the streets, drive their car, plug in the microwave or TV.

We are at risk constantly and in our world increasingly so. On a daily basis, angels and the Holy Spirit are at work, perhaps even overtime, to keep our lives, our health, and our sanity.

A Note of Warning

Even though Jesus knew that He was protected by Blood Covenant he also knew when to pull away from the crowd. He did not foolishly expose himself.

> So from that day on they planned together to kill Him. Therefore Jesus no longer continued to walk publicly among the Jews, but went away from there to the country near the wilderness, into a city called Ephraim; and there He stayed with the disciples. John 11:53-54

Paul also recognized that he could not go just anywhere he wanted to, on one occasion the Holy Spirit forbade him to go into Asia

> They passed through the Phrygian and Galatian region, having been forbidden by the Holy Spirit to speak the word in Asia; Acts 16:6

To go where we are forbidden is to depart from the protection of the Blood Covenant of God and expose ourselves to great risk.

There is something in a zealous spirit that seeks out martyrdom. This was noted in the early church, as it is today, to the point that early church pastors[24] commanded the Christians to depart from Jerusalem and not to offer themselves up as martyrs as the cause of Christ would be harmed. There came a point where their sacrifice was to no benefit. Self-inflicted martyrdom serves no-one.

---

[24] The persecution faced by the early church, then, did not hinder its growth, but rather strengthened it. Enough people suffered to deter easy conversions and to keep the church alert and pure; but the great majority of Christians lived without peril or harm.

The church leaders also acted wisely, and prevented much harm by discouraging the urge for martyrdom. Wherever possible, people at risk of persecution were encouraged to flee, and to return to their homes only after the fury had abated. Those who deliberately sought martyrdom were rebuked.

Tens of thousands heeded the advice of their pastors, and escaped before they could be arrested. Many of them lost all their possessions, but their lives, and those of their families, were preserved, and their witness for Christ was able to continue. Quoted from The World's Greatest Story, Rev. Dr. Ken Chant. pp 39 Vision Publishing.

Wisdom is still preferred to rushing headlong into a situation, because the "cause is just" or "we are children of God therefore who can stand against us?" mentality.

When Jesus, the disciples, Paul, the saints of the Old and New Testament, and believers down through the centuries have placed themselves at risk it is with the knowledge that they are doing what God wants them to do.

In such cases, the protection of God is a reality. Occasionally God will be glorified through the sacrifice of one of His own, but the decision should be boldly left to Him, so that we may, under his authority, go where angels fear to tread in authority and power, not presumption.

An Application

Paul learnt the secret of successfully trusting God in difficult times. No matter what was happening, no matter how difficult the situation or how bad the outlook Paul knew that his God would take care of him.

> *What then shall we say to these things? If God is for us, who is against us? He who did not spare His own Son, but delivered Him over for us all, how will He not also with Him freely give us all things? Who will bring a charge against God's elect? God is the one who justifies; who is the one who condemns? Christ Jesus is He who died, yes, rather who was raised, who is at the right hand of God, who also intercedes for us. Who will separate us from the love of Christ? Will tribulation, or distress, or persecution, or famine, or nakedness, or peril, or sword? Just as it is written, "FOR YOUR SAKE WE ARE BEING PUT TO DEATH ALL DAY LONG; WE WERE CONSIDERED AS SHEEP TO BE SLAUGHTERED." But in all these things we overwhelmingly conquer through Him who loved us. For I am convinced that neither death, nor life, nor angels, nor principalities, nor things present, nor things to*

> *come, nor powers, nor height, nor depth, nor any other created thing, will be able to separate us from the love of God, which is in Christ Jesus our Lord. Romans 8:31-39*

If we believe that this is the truth of the matter then we should rest in this knowledge. There is no greater object lesson for us than the very existence of the church itself, not the denominational church but the ecclesia or the body of believers, the saints. Since the time that Jesus ascended back to heaven this church has been persecuted, ridiculed, blasphemed against, and betrayed. The Bible has been burnt and buried, kept from the believers themselves by various means and all kinds of groups.

Tyrants have tried to crush the church; laws have been passed to outlaw it. Individual Christians have been persecuted, fed to lions, crucified, burnt at the stake and boiled in oil and cannibalised. They have been shot, murdered for their faith, tortured, put into prison and lunatic asylums and yet the church has and will continue to grow and to grow from strength to strength.

No other faith has been scrutinised and survived as the church of Jesus and yet it still continues. Sometimes wounded, sometimes discouraged, and often with differences of opinion or purpose but the church still continues. The church continues not because of its institutions or doctrines but because of the mass of individuals called Christians who dare to believe, even against belief itself, for only when we stop believing can the church itself cease to exist.

Jesus has given us his armour. It will protect us as certainly as it has protected Him. He is our protection. As He has promised He will protect us from sickness, disease, poisons, failure, poverty, distress, witchcraft, evil spirits, human enemies, ourselves and even Satan himself, it is the first promise of the Covenant.

> *After these things the word of the LORD came to Abram in a vision, saying, "Do not fear, Abram, I am a shield to you; Your reward shall be very great." Genesis 15:1*

Two Testimonies

In Kenya

While on a ministry trip to Kenya we were travelling late at night in a vehicle that was, to say the least, un-roadworthy. The beam from one headlight struck the treetops while the other beam shone off into the left of the road making travel difficult. To add to the visibility problems it was raining quite heavily.

The driver could hardly see the road and what he could see was wet. Potholes were filled to the brim with mud and rainwater making them invisible.

Suddenly the vehicle stopped in its tracks with a shudder. The drive shaft had come out of its socket, and the car should have rolled, at least. It was as if the hand of God held the car in place and He said "no further."

I knew our situation was precarious, our lights were dim, and other vehicles could run into us before they saw us. I decided we should get out of the car and our friends told us we should stay. They said it is a dangerous place and there were many bandits and we were at greater risk by moving away. I knew God's urging enough to insist on getting out of the car with my wife and our friend's wife.

We stood by the side of the road and after some minutes, a car came down the road. It stopped a few metres from us. The full beam of their headlights blinded us, but we heard two doors open and two men get out, and the ominous sound of automatic shotguns being cocked.

The men stepped forward and then spoke, and addressed us. They identified themselves as police officers. They told us that they were sure we were bandits preparing a car jacking, something the area was well known for, but when they saw me, a white man, and my wife who is Chinese and they realised that we were in some kind of distress. We were told that if they had not seen us they would have shot all of us and ask questions later.

We were doubly protected. The area is well known for car jackings and I had read only two nights before of a man and his wife held up, as it turned out, in that same area. He had been beaten and bound to a tree with wire, his wife beaten and raped in front of him and then petrol poured over them both and lit. They were found alive with dreadful injuries and died later.

The Policemen told us that a few kilometres back they came to a "T" junction in the road, they should have turned left, back to Kissumu, but were compelled to turn right to Kissi, a town where they had no right or reason to be. Because they turned right they came upon us. Doubtless, we were preserved from being shot by the police; we were saved from attack by bandits by the same policemen.

The police then towed our vehicle into Kissi and to safety.

The word of God says that angels are ministering spirits for His people and that we should entertain strangers for often we entertain angels unawares. That night, I am convinced; we were entertained by and ministered to, by angels from God. Our Blood Covenant contract was operating.

Back Home in Sydney

Not every story has so good an ending. Having returned to Australia from Papua New Guinea where I had spent two years as a missionary, I had to find employment. I obtained a job in the city of Sydney.

To get home I had to travel by train. There are two routes to Central station I could take. One a short cut, the other would take me 15 minutes. It was late and I was tired. I began to take the short cut.

Just a few steps and the Holy Spirit (retrospectively, as I now understand) spoke to me. "Go the other way." I stopped turned around and walked back. After a few steps I reasoned, "this is foolish" and I turned around again going to the short-cut. "Go the other way!" The voice spoke, I turned around and retraced my steps and after a few paces stopped. This is non-sense, it is late, and I am tired I want to get home, I turned around again, "Go back, do not go this way!" The urging seemed to scream at me. I chose to ignore the promptings and went my way.

Close to central station is a park. As I walked through the park, I was attacked, beaten, and robbed.

My point is simple. The protection of God is real, but it is not without conditions, conditions of being about His business and listening to him. Both are required to receive His protection.

Blood covenant is not a cast iron guarantee against all calamity or danger, but the promise of protection is real, and while I am listening to His Spirit and involved in His work – on the mission-field or the factory, the marketplace or the office I am assured of this truth.

> *After these things the word of the LORD came to Abram in a vision, saying, "Do not fear, Abram, I am a shield to you; Your reward shall be very great." Genesis 15:1*

End Of Chapter Questions

1. Discuss why are weapons exchanged in the Blood Covenant Ceremony?
2. What is the promise of Genesis 15:1?
3. Discuss the how God fulfills his promise to protect his people, give three old testament examples.
4. Explain the Armour of God in view of Blood covenant promises and principles.

Chapter 6:

The Exchange Of Names

Introduction

When a man and woman marry, there is an exchange of names. In almost every culture everywhere, this is a recognized principle. The principle was recognized in the days of Jesus, and was recognized in Blood Covenant times.

This exchange is not simply a matter of a woman accepting the man's name as hers, the significance of accepting the man's name is to show the world that these two people are now one unit. All they have is the possession of the other and the care and protection of the woman is now the responsibility of her husband, the protection and care of the husband is the responsibility of the wife.

In the Covenant ceremony both of the Covenant partners would accept a part of each other's name as theirs with equally powerful significance. Occasionally we see this principle in marriage today when Mr. Smith marries Miss Jones and they become Mr. and Mrs. Smith-Jones. Regardless of how this exchange is made, it is significant of a total commitment to each other as the couple pledge themselves, until "death us do part." The principle of this pledge applies not only to the marriage of a man and a woman but also to the Blood Covenant partners.

Old Testament

When God entered the Covenant with Abraham there was an exchange of names. The first indication of this is with Abram, as he was then known, and his wife Sarai. The references are found in Genesis 17.

> *"As for Me, behold, My covenant is with you, And you will be the father of a multitude of nations. "No longer shall your name be called Abram, But your name shall be Abraham; For I have made you the father of a multitude of nations. Genesis 17:4-5*
>
> *Then God said to Abraham, "As for Sarai your wife, you shall not call her name Sarai, but Sarah shall be her name. "I will bless her, and indeed I will give you a son by her. Then I will bless her, and she shall be a mother of nations; kings of peoples will come from her." Genesis 17:15-16*

It is important for us to notice the actual change that has taken place in the name. In many cultures, including those of the Middle and Far East, a persons name is significant. The meaning of the name was supposed to indicate the qualities or characteristics of the person the name is given to, or at least the parent's aspirations for their child.

When their names were changed they were given completely new meanings. Abram, which means "high father" was renamed Abraham the "father of many nations" and Sarai, which means "Dominative," became Sarah the "mother of princes." The change in their names brought about a change in the persons and in their destiny, for the meaning of the name influenced the life of the person.

The difference however is much more profound than this. There is a common change in the names of both Abram and Sarai it lies in the letter "H". In the Hebrew alphabet the equivalent change in their names is not just a letter; there is a special significance to the characters used for this change. The meaning of the characters used for the change in their names is that they denote Deity. God has not just changed their names but he has also added deity to the name of ABRAM and SARAI making them ABRAHAM and SARAH. They have become part of the family of God. They are married to him as shown by the giving of his name to them.

It is not sufficient to see that God has added his name to Abram's name making it Abraham. We should also note that God added Abraham to his name.

Throughout his word we find God referring to himself, as called "THE GOD OF ABRAHAM" no less than 17 times. Even though he also uses such names as "Jehovah", "the Lord your God," "Elohim", "I Am" and the "Lord", we cannot afford to overlook the fact that in the Covenant relationship God adds the name "Abraham" to his name.

> *"Go and gather the elders of Israel together and say to them, 'The LORD, the God of your fathers, the God of Abraham, Isaac and Jacob, has appeared to me, saying, "I am indeed concerned about you and what has been done to you in Egypt. Exodus 3:16*

See also Genesis 31:53, 1 Kings 18:36, Matthew 22:32, Mark 12:26, Luke 20:33 and Acts 3:13.

> *"The God of Abraham and the God of Nahor, the God of their father, judge between us." So Jacob swore by the fear of his father Isaac. Genesis 31:53*

As God reaffirms his Covenant with Moses, he refers to himself as the "God of Abraham," Exodus 3:1-22.

When Elijah faced the prophets of Baal he challenged them to serve the only true God and to decide who the true God was by calling on the only true God to answer by fire. He also called upon the God of Abraham.

> *The water flowed around the altar and he also filled the trench with water. At the time of the offering of the evening sacrifice, Elijah the prophet came near and said, "O LORD, the God of Abraham, Isaac and Israel, today let it be known that You are God in Israel and that I am Your servant and I have done all these things at Your word. "Answer me, O LORD, answer me, that this people may know that You, O LORD, are God, and that You have turned their heart back again." Then the fire of*

> *the LORD fell and consumed the burnt offering and the wood and the stones and the dust, and licked up the water that was in the trench. When all the people saw it, they fell on their faces; and they said, "The LORD, He is God; the LORD, He is God."*
> *1 Kings 18:35-39*

From the time that God identified himself as the God of Abraham, the Hebrews understood that they had a special relationship with God. The Hebrews were the only people who were the people of a particular God. Jehovah was the God of the Jews. The Jew's God is a personal God who cared for His people personally and individually. They were persecuted for having no gods of stone or wood, no statue, image or other evidence. The God of the Jews was unseen.

All other nations worshipped other gods. They worshiped the gods of the sun or the moon or the harvest or fish. They gave themselves over to the gods of love and the gods of war. They entertained family gods and gods of their industries. They embraced gods of mercy and fortune or revenge but they never had a God of the people. In this, the Jews were different; they were different because their God was different. Jehovah was as peculiar to the people of Israel as they were to him.

New Testament

The only other person with whom God exchanged a name was Jesus. In the first instance, God took upon himself the name of a man, Jesus. The name Jesus means Saviour; it was a significant name, but also a common name at that time. It was an appropriate name since God took upon himself the nature and form of man to become man's saviour. It is also the name that God reserved for this man.

Christ means the anointed one. It is as significant in its meaning as the name Jesus. It not only means the anointed one, it is also his title.

God took upon himself the nature, form, and name of a man. He then made the person, and the name of that man to be deity. There are many scriptures to show this truth

> *He predestined us to adoption as sons through Jesus Christ to Himself, according to the kind intention of His will, to the praise of the glory of His grace, which He freely bestowed on us in the Beloved. In Him we have redemption through His blood, the forgiveness of our trespasses, according to the riches of His grace which He lavished on us. In all wisdom and insight He made known to us the mystery of His will, according to His kind intention which He purposed in Him with a view to an administration suitable to the fullness of the times, that is, the summing up of all things in Christ, things in the heavens and things on the earth. In Him also we have obtained an inheritance, having been predestined according to His purpose who works all things after the counsel of His will, to the end that we who were the first to hope in Christ would be to the praise of His glory. Ephesians 1:5-12*
>
> *Have this attitude in yourselves which was also in Christ Jesus, who, although He existed in the form of God, did not regard equality with God a thing to be grasped, but emptied Himself, taking the form of a bond-servant, and being made in the likeness of men. Being found in appearance as a man, He humbled Himself by becoming obedient to the point of death, even death on a cross. For this reason also, God highly exalted Him, and bestowed on Him the name which is above every name, so that at the name of Jesus EVERY KNEE WILL BOW, of those who are in heaven and on earth and under the earth, and that every tongue will confess that Jesus Christ is Lord, to the glory of God the Father. Philippians 2:5-11*

Apart from the direct reference to his deity, there are many implied references. Only God could forgive sins as it is against God that sins are committed. Jesus forgave sins as He is the one through whom forgiveness is granted and received.

> *Peter said to them, "Repent, and each of you be baptized in the name of Jesus Christ for the forgiveness of your sins; and you will receive the gift of the Holy Spirit. Acts 2:38*

Further evidence of the deity of Jesus lies in the fact of healing being provided through and in the name of Jesus.

> *let it be known to all of you and to all the people of Israel, that by the name of Jesus Christ the Nazarene, whom you crucified, whom God raised from the dead--by this name this man stands here before you in good health. Acts 4:10*

One of the most emphatic scriptures on the divinity of Jesus is found in Romans as Jesus is declared to be the Son of God by the apostle Paul.

> *who was declared the Son of God with power by the resurrection from the dead, according to the Spirit of holiness, Jesus Christ our Lord, Romans 1:4*

The descendants of Abraham were also given a name as a means of identification. That name was the name of their faith - JEW. It was by this name that they were to be recognized as the people of God. Throughout the centuries since the children of Israel, Abraham's descendants have been known as Jews it is the name that God has given to them, it is their covenant name.

We Have A New Name

When a person accepts Jesus Christ as saviour, they become known as "CHRISTIAN." That person takes the name of Jesus as theirs in the same way that the children of Israel were known as the people of God by the term Jew. The Christian is identified as a child of God by the term Christian, one who belongs to Christ. It works in the same way and with the same principle of the marriage Covenant for we are a part of his bride.

We take upon ourselves the name of God as Christians, just as God took the name of a man in Jesus.

and when he had found him, he brought him to Antioch. And for an entire year they met with the church and taught considerable numbers; and the disciples were first called Christians in Antioch. Acts 11:26

Again, we find confirmation in the book of Galatians with regards to our oneness in Christ,

Galatians 3:27-29 As many of you as were baptised into Christ have clothed yourselves with Christ. There is no longer Jew or Greek, there is no longer slave or free, there is no longer male and female; for all of you are one in Christ Jesus. And if you belong to Christ, then you are Abraham's offspring, heirs according to the promise.

When we become Christians we are identified as the possession of God in just the same way that a husband and wife belong to each other. We belong to him and at the same time, God belongs to us. Just as He was the God of Abraham, he is now the God of every individual Christian. As individuals we enter this Covenant relationship.

We belong to him as a wife belongs to her husband, in the traditional sense, and as a husband belongs to his wife.

In a similar way that everything that a husband owns he gives to his bride on their wedding day, and she owns his possessions so too God has given all that He owns to us and we own it as our possession, as we own Him.

While we have a collective name, "Christian" we have also been given, individually, a new name. It is to the Church in Pergamum[25]

---

[25] **Pergamos:** now Bergamo, the ancient metropolis of Mysia, and the residence of the Attalian kings, is situated on the river Caicus, about sixty miles north of Smyrna, in long. 27 degrees e lat. 39 degrees 11 minutes n. It still retains some measure of its ancient importance; containing a population of 15,000 souls, and having nine or ten mosques, two churches, and one synagogue. Treasury of Scripture Knowledge.

that this truth is revealed and not only to the church of Pergamum but to all saints everywhere.

> *'He who has an ear, let him hear what the Spirit says to the churches. To him who overcomes, to him I will give some of the hidden manna, and I will give him a white stone, and a new name written on the stone which no one knows but he who receives it.' Revelation 2:17*

What is this "white stone" with new name written upon it? This token of favour in the stone a new name that only Jesus and ourselves could possibly know. The stone and the name is explained for us by Albert Barnes.

1. A white stone was regarded as a token of favor, prosperity, or success everywhere - whether considered as a vote, or as given to a victor, etc. As such, it would denote that the Christian to whom it is said to be given would meet with the favor of the Redeemer, and would have a token of his approval.

2. The name written on this stone would be designed also as a token or pledge of his favor - as a name engraved on a signet or seal would be a pledge to him who received it of friendship. It would be not merely a white stone - emblematic of favor and approval - but it would be so marked as to indicate its origin, with the name of the giver on it. This would appropriately denote, when explained, that the victor Christian would receive a token of the Redeemer's favor, as if his name were engraved on a stone, and given to him as a pledge of his friendship; that is, that he would be as certain of his favor as if he had such a stone. In other words, the victor would be assured from the Redeemer, who distributes rewards, that his welfare would be secure.

3. This would be to him as if he should receive a stone so marked that its letters were invisible to all others, but apparent to him who received it. It is not needful to suppose that in the Olympic games, or in the prizes distributed by Roman emperors, or in

any other custom, such a case had actually occurred, but it is conceivable that a name might be so engraved - with characters so small, or in letters so unknown to all others or with marks so unintelligible to others - that no other one into whose hands it might fall would understand it. The meaning then probably is, that to the true Christian - the victor over sin - there is given some pledge of the divine favor which has to him all the effect of assurance, and which others do not perceive or understand. This consists of favors shown directly to the soul - the evidence of pardoned sin; joy in the Holy Spirit; peace with God; clear views of the Saviour; the possession of a spirit which is properly that of Christ, and which is the gift of God to the soul. The true Christian understands this; the world perceives it not. The Christian receives it as a pledge of the divine favor, and as an evidence that he will be saved; to the world, that on which he relies seems to be enthusiasm, fanaticism, or delusion. The Christian bears it about with him as he would a precious stone given to him by his Redeemer, and on which the name of his Redeemer is engraved, as a pledge that he is accepted of God, and that the rewards of heaven shall be his; the world does not understand it, or attaches no value to it.

And in the stone a new name written - A name indicating a new relation, new hopes and triumphs. Probably the name here referred to is the name of the Redeemer, or the name Christian, or some such appellation. It would be some name which he would understand and appreciate, and which would be a pledge of acceptance[26]

Marriage Is A Blood Covenant

Today the truth that marriage is a blood covenant, like most Blood Covenant truths, has been forgotten.

---

[26] Albert Barnes' Notes on the Bible Albert Barnes (1798-1870)

Until our very recent past, in almost every culture, almost every man wants his bride to be a virgin and in almost every culture, almost every woman wants to be a virgin on her wedding night.

In the past, shame was brought to a family if a man is caught with a woman before marriage, and if a woman was to loose her virginity before marriage the shame was such in some cultures, even today, that she may loose her life. Among many Islamic cultures she will be stoned to death as will the man if found guilty. In some Hindu cultures, even today, a woman is burned to death for losing her virginity before marriage.

The tearing of the hymen in the first act of sexual intercourse is a Blood Covenant act. The force of this truth is found in the scripture itself as we are urged to remain chaste until our wedding day.

The bond that comes from this act is, and should be still, a sacred bond that is unbreakable and the consequences of breaking the marriage covenant includes the damage to families and children, the ruin of society itself, as these values are diminished. Although largely unrecognized the consequences are horrific.

In the 20th and 21st Century, the "modern western culture" is reaping the result of the devaluing of this wonderful covenant. We may, in our so-called modern thinking, put aside the "old way of thinking" for a more liberal view and morality. Yet we must remember that the force and power of a blood covenant is not minimised because we choose to think and act differently.

Blood Covenant is so powerful, so sacred, so filled with ritual, meaning and relationship that God sees His relationship with Israel and then with the church as a Marriage.

God has often seen his Covenant partner in the light of a marriage. This is demonstrated first for us with the Jews, through Jeremiah God makes it clear that He saw Israel as wife.

> *"Behold, days are coming," declares the LORD, "when I will make a new covenant with the house of Israel and with the*

house of Judah, not like the covenant which I made with their fathers in the day I took them by the hand to bring them out of the land of Egypt, My covenant which they broke, although I was a husband to them," declares the LORD. Jeremiah 31:31-32

Jesus also refers to his church as his bride.

Husbands, love your wives, just as Christ also loved the church and gave Himself up for her, so that He might sanctify her, having cleansed her by the washing of water with the word, that He might present to Himself the church in all her glory, having no spot or wrinkle or any such thing; but that she would be holy and blameless. So husbands ought also to love their own wives as their own bodies. He who loves his own wife loves himself; for no one ever hated his own flesh, but nourishes and cherishes it, just as Christ also does the church, because we are members of His body. FOR THIS REASON A MAN SHALL LEAVE HIS FATHER AND MOTHER AND SHALL BE JOINED TO HIS WIFE, AND THE TWO SHALL BECOME ONE FLESH. This mystery is great; but I am speaking with reference to Christ and the church. Ephesians 5:25-32

An Application

Although I have referred to the Covenant of marriage and to the exchange of names, we should remember that the Blood Covenant is far more binding than a human marriage. The marriage is only for the lifetime of the couple married. The Blood Covenant of God however is an *Eternally Binding Covenant*, for we are given eternal life through him.

As individuals and collectively we all become a part of the bride of Christ, all of the people of God are the Bride. As such we are covenanted together as his people, as a part of him, and he is part of us. We are the family of God. We are his children because we are the children of Abraham. We are the children of Abraham because of the sacrificial work of Jesus Christ and our faith in all that Jesus has done for us at Calvary. The whole of Ephesians ch. 4 makes this point very clear to us.

Names are exchanged at a marriage. This ancient rite is performed in one form or another in almost every society, in almost every country or province or state throughout the world, and has been so through all time. It provides emotional and material security for both partners. It is a security granted out of the love of the husband and the wife to each other. For the rest of their lives they are pledged to look after each other. They indicate this to the entire world by exchanging their names. So it is for us when we become Christians. We receive the security of the name of Christ, God himself. It is unmerited, un-earned security.

Security for all is born out of his love for us as his supreme creation and his desire to enjoy a relationship with us, a relationship that can best be considered in the terms of a good marriage. His love for us will allow nothing to stand between himself as his people, his bride.

> *Who will separate us from the love of Christ? Will tribulation, or distress, or persecution, or famine, or nakedness, or peril, or sword? Just as it is written, "FOR YOUR SAKE WE ARE BEING PUT TO DEATH ALL DAY LONG; WE WERE CONSIDERED AS SHEEP TO BE SLAUGHTERED." But in all these things we overwhelmingly conquer through Him who loved us. For I am convinced that neither death, nor life, nor angels, nor principalities, nor things present, nor things to come, nor powers, nor height, nor depth, nor any other created thing, will be able to separate us from the love of God, which is in Christ Jesus our Lord. Romans 8:35-39*

End Of Chapter Questions

1. How does and exchange of names relate to Blood Covenant?
2. How does God show that he has added His name to Abram and Sarai?
3. Discuss the manner is which God has given us a name.

End Of Chapter Questions

Chapter 7:

Exchange Of Memorial Gifts

Historical

During the ceremony there was an exchange of the Covenant Gift[27]. Often two gifts were given, a personal[28] gift and a public gift. Usually the gifts came from the Great King to the Vassal King but sometimes the Vassal would also give a gift.

While both gifts were given as a memorial of the Covenant, the personal gift was exactly that, a personal gift between the kings themselves. They may or may not reveal this personal gift to others.

The public gift was for the public, to remind the kings, and all parties concerned, of the existence of the Covenant and their responsibility to it. For this gift could include mountains, hills, huge stones or rivers, or other natural objects that should remain indefinitely. Sometimes a flock of animals or a grove of trees was given as a memorial gift.

If the gift was some form of natural prominent feature such as a mountain or river, or if it was a man made monument, (it had to be very substantial), the meaning behind the gifts was that as long as the gift remained the covenant was in place. If gift was the trees or a flock or herd of animals then the meaning was that as long as the flock or heard flourished so should the benefits of the Covenant

---

[27] See also The Blood Covenant, E. W. Kenyon pp14

[28] The terms "personal" and "public" are mine and are offered simply for the purpose of distinction between the gifts themselves.

continue and grow. These are not different meanings, simply shades of the same, relevant to the gift.

Old Testament

The principle of covenant gifts is first shown through Abraham as God begins to deal with him. Although Abraham is not yet a family much less a nation, he is given a public covenant gift. It is the land of Canaan, the Promised Land. At the time he may not have realised what was happening, none-the-less to Abraham, his sons and the nation that was to come God gave the Promised Land. It was public the covenant Gift of God to the nation is Israel.

> *Now the LORD said to Abram, "Go forth from your country, And from your relatives And from your father's house, To the land which I will show you; And I will make you a great nation, And I will bless you, And make your name great; And so you shall be a blessing; And I will bless those who bless you, And the one who curses you I will curse. And in you all the families of the earth will be blessed." So Abram went forth as the LORD had spoken to him; and Lot went with him. Now Abram was seventy-five years old when he departed from Haran. Abram took Sarai his wife and Lot his nephew, and all their possessions which they had accumulated, and the persons which they had acquired in Haran, and they set out for the land of Canaan; thus they came to the land of Canaan. Abram passed through the land as far as the site of Shechem, to the oak of Moreh. Now the Canaanite was then in the land. The LORD appeared to Abram and said, "To your descendants I will give this land." So he built an altar there to the LORD who had appeared to him. Then he proceeded from there to the mountain on the east of Bethel, and pitched his tent, with Bethel on the west and Ai on the east; and there he built an altar to the LORD and called upon the name of the LORD. Genesis 12:1-8*

A private gift was to follow. When God established his Covenant with Abraham, Abraham wanted a specific memorial gift. It is unusual to actually request a specific gift. However, he wanted something special to remind him personally of the earnestness of God in the promises of his Covenant. He wanted a son. His culture prevented him from actually asking specifically, such a direct request would be seen as offensive, even so, he made it clear what he wanted. Consequently, the memorial gift to Abraham was Isaac.

> *After these things the word of the LORD came to Abram in a vision, saying, "Do not fear, Abram, I am a shield to you; Your reward shall be very great." Abram said, "O Lord GOD, what will You give me, since I am childless, and the heir of my house is Eliezer of Damascus?" And Abram said, "Since You have given no offspring to me, one born in my house is my heir." Then behold, the word of the LORD came to him, saying, "This man will not be your heir; but one who will come forth from your own body, he shall be your heir." And He took him outside and said, "Now look toward the heavens, and count the stars, if you are able to count them." And He said to him, "So shall your descendants be." Genesis 15:1-5*

At that time, Abraham was 75 years of age. It was to be a further 25 years before Isaac was to be born. Sarah was ninety years of age before she gave birth to Isaac. This also established the fact that only God could have performed such a miracle. It was to be through the birth of Isaac that the promises of God to Abraham were to be fulfilled, and Isaac was Abraham's personal covenant gift.

Just as Abraham required a memorial gift from God, so God required a memorial gift from Abraham and the Jews. The memorial gift to God was to be the circumcision of Abraham and all of his people. As the "Great King," it was right and proper for God to demand of Abraham his Covenant gift.

Although it is not customary for Abraham, the Vassal to dictate the gift it was quite proper for the Great King, in this case God, to make such a demand. The cultural niceties of the Vassal King did not limit the Great King as he has conquered the Vassal and the Vassal is subservient to him. God required a very personal gift that would always serve to remind them of their relationships.

> *God said further to Abraham, "Now as for you, you shall keep My covenant, you and your descendants after you throughout their generations. "This is My covenant, which you shall keep, between Me and you and your descendants after you: every male among you shall be circumcised. "And you shall be circumcised in the flesh of your foreskin, and it shall be the sign of the covenant between Me and you. "And every male among you who is eight days old shall be circumcised throughout your generations, a servant who is born in the house or who is bought with money from any foreigner, who is not of your descendants. "A servant who is born in your house or who is bought with your money shall surely be circumcised; thus shall My covenant be in your flesh for an everlasting covenant. "But an uncircumcised male who is not circumcised in the flesh of his foreskin, that person shall be cut off from his people; he has broken My covenant." Genesis 17:9-14*

God required circumcision as a personal and national covenant gift. It was, and still is required of every male in the nation, those born as a Jew, those who have migrated, and those who are slaves or those "bought with money," along with the willing slave were to be circumcised. No male in Israel is to escape this requirement.

Abraham and Abimelech[29] enter into a covenant. Abimelech's men continuously persecute Abraham and his people without Abimelech's knowledge or consent. Abraham speaks with Abimelech and they enter into a blood covenant. Abraham gave Abimelech seven[30] ewe lambs. The lambs were the witness of the Covenant. As the flock grew and thrived, they would remind Abimelech and his people, the Philistines, of the Covenant that he had entered with Abraham and his people.

Abraham took sheep and oxen and gave them to Abimelech, and the two of them made a covenant. Then Abraham set seven ewe lambs of the flock by themselves. Abimelech said to

---

[29] **Abimelech** my father a king, or father of a king, a common name of the Philistine kings, as "Pharaoh" was of the Egyptian kings. (1.) The Philistine king of Gerar in the time of Abraham (Gen 20:1-18). By an interposition of Providence, Sarah was delivered from his harem, and was restored to her husband Abraham. As a mark of respect he gave to Abraham valuable gifts, and offered him a settlement in any part of his country; while at the same time he delicately and yet severely rebuked him for having practised a deception upon him in pretending that Sarah was only his sister. Among the gifts presented by the king were a thousand pieces of silver as a "covering of the eyes" for Sarah; i.e., either as an atoning gift and a testimony of her innocence in the sight of all, or rather for the purpose of procuring a veil for Sarah to conceal her beauty, and thus as a reproof to her for not having worn a veil which, as a married woman, she ought to have done. A few years after this Abimelech visited Abraham, who had removed southward beyond his territory, and there entered into a league of peace and friendship with him. This league was the first of which we have any record. It was confirmed by a mutual oath at Beer-sheba (Gen 21:22-34). M.G. Easton M.A., D.D., Illustrated Bible Dictionary, Third Edition, published by Thomas Nelson, 1897.

[30] In the Hebrew alphabet there are no numbers only characters, some of which serve a dual purpose. The characters for seven (7) are also the word for Promise or Covenant and is also the number of Perfection and is symbolic for God. It is important to note the typology of God, Promise, Covenant. It is also important not to build a doctrinal position on these interesting types. The last well that Abraham dug well is called Beer-Sheba, (the anglicized name for Beer-Sheva) the well of Sevens or the Well of Covenant. It is still in existence today and is so revered that in both world wars and in all of the Middle Eastern conflicts since that time it is a place that is protected by all parties.

> *Abraham, "What do these seven ewe lambs mean, which you have set by themselves?" He said, "You shall take these seven ewe lambs from my hand so that it may be a witness to me, that I dug this well." Therefore he called that place Beersheba, because there the two of them took an oath. So they made a covenant at Beersheba; and Abimelech and Phicol, the commander of his army, arose and returned to the land of the Philistines. Abraham planted a tamarisk tree at Beersheba, and there he called on the name of the LORD, the Everlasting God. And Abraham sojourned in the land of the Philistines for many days. Genesis 21:27-34*

Abraham also planted a grove of trees in Beersheba as a memorial to his own people so that they too will remember the covenant they have entered into. In this case Abraham has offered both of the memorial Gifts. In so doing he is signifying that he is the greater of the two Covenant Heads. This is remarkable seeing as Abraham is the visitor in the land. His integrity is recognized in spite of his earlier indiscretion, and this worldly king, a man whose integrity even God recognized, could see the fact of God's blessing in the life of Abraham.

Abimelech was also the King of the Philistines. Here is the solution to a mystery and an example of a value of Blood Covenant. It is clear in the Old Testament that God fought fiercely against the Philistines for the children of Israel. Why was this so?

The answer lies the fact that Abraham and Abimelech entered into a Blood Covenant for themselves and their people for all time. Abraham is the Great King, this is evidenced by the fact that it is Abraham that is giving the covenant gifts. Later when Abraham rescues his and Abimelech's people from captivity, he refused payment or reward of any kind. The Philistine people are to honour Abraham's God, respect, and protect Abraham's people.

This is covenant law. When the philistines preferred to remain in idolatry and fight against the Israelites God, Abraham's Great King was duty bound to come to Abraham's rescue. This is the cause of much of the anguish between the Israelites and the Philistines and the cause of their defeat.

This principle and promise has never changed and should serve as a lesson to us.

In Genesis 29:1 to 31:55 we have another example. Jacob had promised to work for Laban for seven years to marry his daughter Rachel. He was tricked into, marrying her older sister, Leah, and then had to work for another seven years before he could marry Rachel. Jacob is tricked and cheated yet remains with Laban for twenty years and prospers greatly in all he does. When Jacob finally leaves to establish his own family in his own country he is pursued by Laban and falsely accused of stealing (unbeknown to Jacob Rachel had stolen from her father's house).

On being proven innocent Jacob and Laban entered a Covenant of peace. The memorial for this was a pillar of stones, a memorial pillar. This pillar was to remind them of the Covenant between them. It was called on as a reminder that God was to watch over Jacob, and see that he should not hurt Laban's daughters. It was also to provide a reminder that neither of them would cross over that border to hurt the other.

An example with Moses. God enters into a Blood Covenant with Moses. He speaks to Moses through the burning bush where God gave his name to the children of Israel as a memorial gift, later he is to give them the land of promise, Israel, and the mountain to Moses.

> *And He said, "Certainly I will be with you, and this shall be the sign to you that it is I who have sent you: when you have brought the people out of Egypt, you shall worship God at this mountain." Then Moses said to God, "Behold, I am going to the sons of Israel, and I will say to them, 'The God of your fathers has sent me to you.' Now they may say to me, 'What is His name?' What shall I say to them?" God said to Moses, "I AM WHO I AM"; and He said, "Thus you shall say to the sons*

> *of Israel, 'I AM has sent me to you.'" God, furthermore, said to Moses, "Thus you shall say to the sons of Israel, 'The LORD, the God of your fathers, the God of Abraham, the God of Isaac, and the God of Jacob, has sent me to you.' This is My name forever, and this is My memorial-name to all generations. Exodus 3:12-15*

The Tribe of Levi were a gift of God to the nation of Israel as Levitical Priesthood. They were the "ministering priests" who stood before the people on behalf of God and before God on behalf of the people. The garments of the High Priest were also memorials of the people of Israel. As the High Priest completed his duties he came into the presence of God in his Priestly robes, he holds the nation of Israel before God constantly. It is done to remind God of his Covenant with his people, Exodus 28:1-43.

At the end of his life, Joshua reminds the children of Israel of the Covenant to which they are committed. They are reminded of their promise to God and of his benefits to them. As he does so he sets up a huge stone as a memorial. As often as the people see the stone they were to remember all that they promised to do. It is a Covenant memorial stone, Joshua 24:1-31, note vs. 24-28.

> *The people said to Joshua, "We will serve the LORD our God and we will obey His voice." So Joshua made a covenant with the people that day, and made for them a statute and an ordinance in Shechem. And Joshua wrote these words in the book of the law of God; and he took a large stone and set it up there under the oak that was by the sanctuary of the LORD. Joshua said to all the people, "Behold, this stone shall be for a witness against us, for it has heard all the words of the LORD which He spoke to us; thus it shall be for a witness against you, so that you do not deny your God." Then Joshua dismissed the people, each to his inheritance. Joshua 24:24-28*

There are many more examples of Covenant memorial gifts in the Old Testament that help us to see the truth of this principle.

New Testament

For the Christian there are also memorial gifts. Gifts that God gives to us that help to remind us of our relationship with Him, our standing, and responsibility to Him and they help us to understand how our Covenant God sees us.

Jesus sees us as worthy of eternal life even though we are worthy of death. Even in his pronunciation of our sinful state he is offering us eternal life.

> *For the wages of sin is death, but the free gift of God is eternal life in Christ Jesus our Lord. Romans 6:23*
>
> *And the testimony is this, that God has given us eternal life, and this life is in His Son. 1 John 5:11*
>
> *For we also once were foolish ourselves, disobedient, deceived, enslaved to various lusts and pleasures, spending our life in malice and envy, hateful, hating one another. But when the kindness of God our Savior and His love for mankind appeared, He saved us, not on the basis of deeds which we have done in righteousness, but according to His mercy, by the washing of regeneration and renewing by the Holy Spirit, whom He poured out upon us richly through Jesus Christ our Savior, so that being justified by His grace we would be made heirs according to the hope of eternal life. This is a trustworthy statement; and concerning these things I want you to speak confidently, so that those who have believed God will be careful to engage in good deeds. These things are good and profitable for men. Titus 3:3-8*

Salvation and inheritance do not depend in any way upon anything we can do. It is not our good works, but by his grace that we have been given salvation, position, authority, rank of member in the Royal Family of God. We have been made Kings and Priests of his household.

No matter how dead you may have been in sin, in Christ God has made you alive! Our part is to accept this new identity, and to begin to live it out.

The very first gift that God gives to us is eternal life. He gives it to us when we enter a relationship with him. It is not something we can earn, nor can we gain this gift by merit. We cannot buy this; it is a gift from God to us.

> *For by grace you have been saved through faith; and that not of yourselves, it is the gift of God; Ephesians 2:8*

The personal gift of Eternal life and other gifts that God gives us at the time of salvation are his Memorial Gifts to us. We receive other gifts. Things we desire personally or need. These gifts often include a remarkable healing, deliverance from evil spirits, the restoration of a broken family or even the financial recovery of an individual, family, or business.

Additionally we can call upon him for anything that we need, especially for life and godliness. Our Great King spares us nothing in this regard. For life and godliness he will give us as a gift, giving us all that we require.

> *Grace and peace be multiplied to you in the knowledge of God and of Jesus our Lord; seeing that His divine power has granted to us everything pertaining to life and godliness, through the true knowledge of Him who called us by His own glory and excellence. For by these He has granted to us His precious and magnificent promises, so that by them you may become partakers of the divine nature, having escaped the corruption that is in the world by lust. Now for this very reason also, applying all diligence, in your faith supply moral excellence, and in your moral excellence, knowledge, and in your knowledge, self-control, and in your self-control, perseverance, and in your perseverance, godliness, and in your godliness, brotherly kindness, and in your brotherly kindness, love. 2 Peter 1:2-7*

James kindly reminds us that it is the attempted abuse of these gifts or misunderstanding of our relationship with God and each other that nullify the expected gift, not the promise itself.

> *What is the source of quarrels and conflicts among you? Is not the source your pleasures that wage war in your members? You lust and do not have; so you commit murder. You are envious and cannot obtain; so you fight and quarrel. You do not have because you do not ask. You ask and do not receive, because you ask with wrong motives, so that you may spend it on your pleasures. You adulteresses, do you not know that friendship with the world is hostility toward God? Therefore whoever wishes to be a friend of the world makes himself an enemy of God. Or do you think that the Scripture speaks to no purpose: "He jealously desires the Spirit which He has made to dwell in us"? But He gives a greater grace. Therefore it says, "GOD IS OPPOSED TO THE PROUD, BUT GIVES GRACE TO THE HUMBLE." James 4:1-6*

These gifts are for us memorial gifts to us in just the same way that God granted a son to Abraham.

We are offered a great deal more than just eternal life both now and in eternity as we can see from the disciple's questions in the Gospels

> *Peter began to say to Him, "Behold, we have left everything and followed You." Jesus said, "Truly I say to you, there is no one who has left house or brothers or sisters or mother or father or children or farms, for My sake and for the gospel's sake, but that he will receive a hundred times as much now in the present age, houses and brothers and sisters and mothers and children and farms, along with persecutions; and in the age to come, eternal life. Mark 10:28-30*

God gives us these gifts to help establish our relationship with him at the beginning of that relationship. They are given to us to help increase our faith. Jesus brings the point home to us as he speaks to his disciples.

> *"Believe Me that I am in the Father and the Father is in Me; otherwise believe because of the works themselves. John 14:11*

These are not the only gifts that are given to us.

The abilities and talents of individuals that were established in eternity past, before our birth, become ministry gifts to his body the church. These ministry gifts enable us to fulfil our role in the body of Christ and show the nature of Jesus to the world. They are also reminders to us of the love grace and ministry of Christ. These Gifts are memorial Gifts to remind us of His Covenant with us. We find our place in the body of Christ as apostles, pastors, teachers prophets or evangelists, or indeed in any role that Jesus may place us in (Ephesians 4:7-8 and 11-13). These gifts are Covenant gifts to the church, without the Covenant with Jesus, none of these gifts would have been given.

> *But to each one of us grace was given according to the measure of Christ's gift. Therefore it says, "WHEN HE ASCENDED ON HIGH, HE LED CAPTIVE A HOST OF CAPTIVES, AND HE GAVE GIFTS TO MEN." (Now this expression, "He ascended," what does it mean except that He also had descended into the lower parts of the earth? He who descended is Himself also He who ascended far above all the heavens, so that He might fill all things.) And He gave some as apostles, and some as prophets, and some as evangelists, and some as pastors and teachers, for the equipping of the saints for the work of service, to the building up of the body of Christ; Ephesians 4:7-12*

God requires a memorial gift from us as we enter into this relationship. Just as God called on Abraham to be circumcised there is a call to us also.

A call, indeed a command to circumcision[31], but not a physical circumcision, indeed not, this circumcision is a circumcision of the heart. This circumcision will require no blade, will leave no scar but will rather heal, is for men and women, not just the males, and while invisible to man is so clearly visible to God.

> *But he is a Jew who is one inwardly; and circumcision is that which is of the heart, by the Spirit, not by the letter; and his praise is not from men, but from God. Romans 2:29*
>
> *and in Him you were also circumcised with a circumcision made without hands, in the removal of the body of the flesh by the circumcision of Christ; having been buried with Him in baptism, in which you were also raised up with Him through faith in the working of God, who raised Him from the dead. When you were dead in your transgressions and the uncircumcision of your flesh, He made you alive together with Him, having forgiven us all our transgressions, having canceled out the certificate of debt consisting of decrees against us, which was hostile to us; and He has taken it out of the way, having nailed it to the cross. Colossians 2:11-14*

To put this as plainly as possible it means that each individual human being must commit their lives to God and allow God to live through their life.

> *There will be tribulation and distress for every soul of man who does evil, of the Jew first and also of the Greek, Romans 2:9*

It is not possible for man to enter a Covenant with him without fully committing our lives to him. That is the first requirement of a Blood Covenant relationship.

Once we have committed our life to Jesus, it is impossible to maintain this relationship without fulfilling the memorial gift that is required of

---

[31] I shall deal with this in greater detail in the chapter the "Seal of the Covenant".

us. We cannot have part of the Covenant. Only the total acceptance of the whole of the Covenant is acceptable to God for He has given to us all that he is for all that we were that he might make us to be all he wants us to be. We become a gift

An Application

There are times in our walk with God that doubt, fear, anxiety, forgetfulness or even the familiarity that we can have with God causes us to loose sight of who and what He really is.

We can forget the blessings promised for the trial in front of us. It is at such times that we need to take stock of what God has done. Not for the sentimentality of "counting your blessings" but for the certain security that what God has given us is a sure guarantee of what is to come.

Our faith will rise, our relation shall be invigorated and our confidence in these times of stress will be renewed as we remember we are not just "Christians, simple attendees of a local church, ordinary believers in Jesus."

Indeed not, we will recall that we are Blood Covenant partners with almighty God in a relationship that cannot be broken, that is built on the security and surety that God has pledged himself for our good benefit, and He will not be moved.

> *For those whom He foreknew, He also predestined to become conformed to the image of His Son, so that He would be the firstborn among many brethren; and these whom He predestined, He also called; and these whom He called, He also justified; and these whom He justified, He also glorified. What then shall we say to these things? If God is for us, who is against us? He who did not spare His own Son, but delivered Him over for us all, how will He not also with Him freely give us all things? Who will bring a charge against God's elect? God is the one who justifies; who is the one who condemns? Christ Jesus is He who died, yes, rather who was raised, who is*

at the right hand of God, who also intercedes for us. Who will separate us from the love of Christ? Will tribulation, or distress, or persecution, or famine, or nakedness, or peril, or sword? Just as it is written, "FOR YOUR SAKE WE ARE BEING PUT TO DEATH ALL DAY LONG; WE WERE CONSIDERED AS SHEEP TO BE SLAUGHTERED." But in all these things we overwhelmingly conquer through Him who loved us. For I am convinced that neither death, nor life, nor angels, nor principalities, nor things present, nor things to come, nor powers, nor height, nor depth, nor any other created thing, will be able to separate us from the love of God, which is in Christ Jesus our Lord. Romans 8:29-39

End Of Chapter Questions

1. Why were there the kinds of Covenant Gift?
2. What was God's covenant Gift to Abraham?
3. Compare the Jews "Covenant Gift" to God and the New Testament equivalent?
4. What are our "Covenant Gifts"?

Chapter 8:

Cutting The Covenant

Historical Perspective

To "Cut the Covenant" is the proper term given when the sacrificial animal is prepared and killed for the Covenant partners as the substitute sacrifice on behalf of each other. Without the Cutting of the Covenant, there is no Blood Covenant. There can be agreements, leagues and promises, yet not a Blood Covenant.

The provision of the sacrificial animal is the responsibility of the Vassal King as it is his life that has been spared. It is the Great King who decides what kind of animal is to be used in the sacrifice. The sacrifice must be perfect, without any kind of fault or deformity. It must be the very best that was available to the Vassal, and it must be owned or purchased by the Vassal himself. He must not use a gift to himself for the sacrifice as this would have been provided at no cost to himself and therefore could be a true substitute of himself.

The actual killing of the sacrifice was usually done by the Priest of the Great King. The beast, usually a domesticated animal such as a calf or a bullock, a lamb or a goat, is to be taken to a place determined by the Great King or his high priest. At this site the sacrifice must be made.

The beast was cut into two equal parts down the spinal cord. The animal was laid open in two halves; hide down, with the backs facing each other, exposing the internal organs of the beast to the air. In some cultures the animal was killed before it was cut in half for the sacrifice. In some cultures it died as a result of being prepared, that is to say that it dies whilst being cut in half, for the sacrifice, thereby providing a living sacrifice.

Now came one of the most sacred parts of the whole procedure. The two kings stand between the halves of the sacrifice and face each other. From this position they begin to walk around each half of the animal in the opposite direction from each other, in a figure eight (8) pattern. As they did so they would pronounce great blessings upon each other. Quite often this became almost a competition of trying to outdo each other as to who could pronounce the greatest blessing on the other while still being serious and sincere in the intent of the blessing.

As they meet for the first time between the parts of the sacrifice they change from blessing each other to a declaration that all their possessions are the possession of the other. They began to list their possessions, rather like giving an inventory of what they own to each other. This inventory includes personal possessions, lands, people, towns and villages, flocks and herds.

As they began to walk around the other half of the sacrifice they pronounce curses upon each other if they should break the Covenant. This would also become a matter or trying to outdo one another in the strength of the curse. The whole affair was taken very seriously. No matter how horrific the curse, it would always end in the death of the Covenant breaker and his family. This part of the ceremony would end with a comment similar to "So shall it be done to you, (or unto me) as it was to this animal if this Covenant should be broken."[32]

As they finished this part of the ceremony they would call upon their gods to ratify the Covenant. Their gods must be a witness that the Covenant Ceremony has been completed and that nothing has been left undone. In every case, the gods of the Great King must now take pre-eminence over the gods of the Vassal King.

It is important to realise that the sacrificial beast has been killed. The vows have already been exchanged by the Covenant Heads and from this time on. There is no turning back from the Covenant into which they have entered.

It is following this part of the ceremony that the Covenant Heads cut their flesh and become Blood Brothers[33]. This was possibly the most sacred part of the entire proceedings of the Covenant.

The cut is usually on the right wrist or arm. Blood from each wound is caught in a cup and usually mingled with some form of wine and both of the covenant heads drink it. They press their open wounds together, and allow their blood to mingle as it runs from their wounds. As they do so they believe that the blood of the Great King has entered into the body of the Vassal King and the Blood of the Vassal King has entered into the body of the Great King, therefore the life of each other has become their own life. From this point there can be no turning back from the Covenant agreement. They have chosen to become blood brothers with each other, to defend each other to the death if necessary, to live for each other's benefit. Each sees the exchange of blood as an

---

[32] Note God's comment to the nation of Israel in Jeremiah 34:18-19

[33] As Stanley went into Africa he is reported to have cut over 50 covenants with various chief. An unusual way that the cutting was done by one tribe was for the chief to bring one of his princes and Stanley brought one of his English assistants and the cut was made in their flesh as substitutes instead of on the flesh of Stanley and the chief. (The Blood Covenant, E.W, Kenyon)

exchange of life and identity, although for the Vassal King it is the life of the Great King's that is to be dominant for both of them.

Blood is believed by almost all societies to be sacred. It is this shedding of blood that makes a Blood Covenant irrevocable and sacred. It was believed that the life of a man or the woman or any other animal was in the blood itself.

Biblical Blood References

The word of God declares the "life is in the blood." Leviticus 17:11. It is because of this that we are expected to hold blood sacred. This is the reason that God holds us accountable for the spilling of blood (murder) and eating raw meat (eating meat with the blood in it or the drinking of blood) and His command not to eat the blood.

> *"Only you shall not eat flesh with its life, that is, its blood. Genesis 9:4*
>
> *'For the life of the flesh is in the blood, and I have given it to you on the altar to make atonement for your souls; for it is the blood by reason of the life that makes atonement.' "Therefore I said to the sons of Israel, 'No person among you may eat blood, nor may any alien who sojourns among you eat blood.' "So when any man from the sons of Israel, or from the aliens who sojourn among them, in hunting catches a beast or a bird which may be eaten, he shall pour out its blood and cover it with earth. "For as for the life of all flesh, its blood is identified with its life. Therefore I said to the sons of Israel, 'You are not to eat the blood of any flesh, for the life of all flesh is its blood; whoever eats it shall be cut off.' Leviticus 17:11-14*
>
> *"Only be sure not to eat the blood, for the blood is the life, and you shall not eat the life with the flesh. "You shall not eat it; you shall pour it out on the ground like water. "You shall not eat it, so that it may be well with you and your sons after you,*

for you will be doing what is right in the sight of the LORD. Deuteronomy 12:23-25

It is interesting to note that very few things are carried over from the Old Covenant to the New Covenant. These carry-overs included the abstinence from eating blood. These things are outlined for us at the first general council of Christians as the apostles sought to understand the new Covenant, its responsibilities, regulations and its application to our lives

"For it seemed good to the Holy Spirit and to us to lay upon you no greater burden than these essentials: that you abstain from things sacrificed to idols and from blood and from things strangled and from fornication; if you keep yourselves free from such things, you will do well. Farewell." Acts 15:28-29

Clearly for the Christian blood is to be held sacred.

Old Testament

It should not come to us as a surprise to see that God himself has "Cut a Covenant." The occasion of this cutting of the Covenant was with Abraham, Genesis 15:1-18 note vs. 9-17.

So He said to him, "Bring Me a three year old heifer, and a three year old female goat, and a three year old ram, and a turtledove, and a young pigeon." Then he brought all these to Him and cut them in two, and laid each half opposite the other; but he did not cut the birds. The birds of prey came down upon the carcasses, and Abram drove them away. Now when the sun was going down, a deep sleep fell upon Abram; and behold, terror and great darkness fell upon him. God said to Abram, "Know for certain that your descendants will be strangers in a land that is not theirs, where they will be enslaved and oppressed four hundred years. "But I will also judge the nation whom they will serve, and afterward they will come out with many possessions. "As for you, you shall go to your fathers in peace; you will be buried at a good old age. "Then in the fourth generation they will return here, for the iniquity of the Amorite is not yet complete." It came about when the sun had set, that it was very dark, and behold, there appeared a smoking oven and a flaming torch which passed between these pieces. Genesis 15:9-17

Abraham is called upon to provide the sacrificial animal. He is the Vassal. Abraham[34] is a great man in his own right. He is a great chief or leader and possibly even seen as a king. This can be seen in the response of Abimelech to Abraham, and by his conquest over the giants he fights to rescue Lot, the men and woman of Abimelech at Ched-or-la'o-mer, Genesis 14:1-17, and the response of the King of Sodom to Abraham.

This is the same Abraham that God has called out of Ur of the Chaldees. The same Abraham was called on by Melchizedek, the King of Salem and high priest of God. He is recognized as a powerful man by his peers and by God.

Nevertheless, it is his standing with God, because of his faithfulness, that caused him to be seen as a friend of God. It is the basis of his faithfulness not his "kingship" or conquests that God is calling upon for the purpose of establishing his Covenant with him.

As God begins to outline the required sacrifice he demands more than just a calf. God demands a three-year-old heifer, a female goat, a ram of three years and a turtledove and a young pigeon.

There is no Biblical explanation for God's demand for such a variety of sacrificial offerings, however, there are certain observations that can be made.

God demands these same sacrifices in the book of Leviticus for peace offerings (Leviticus ch. 3), and offerings for the sins of

---

[34] The greatness of Abraham is indicated by the response of Abimelech to him when they cut covenant, It is further reflected in his rescue of the King of Sodom's family and also in the fact that He is mentioned in the Mari tablets, see Appendix II.

ignorance (Leviticus 4:22-35). The same offerings were required for offences against another person, against God or Holy things, (Leviticus ch 5:1 to 6:7). It is possible that the purpose of these sacrifices, and their future use, was to remind offenders of their Covenant relationship, and that sacrifice is required to restore Covenant relationship.

Perhaps in choosing these particular animals and birds God has embraced all of the acceptable sacrificial animals that have been used in human Covenants throughout the world. Typologically he has embraced all people by recognizing their own particular sacrificial animals.

He requires Abraham to take these animals, divide them in half and lay them upon the ground. He must do this in exactly the same way that other Covenant sacrifices are laid out.

> *He said, "O Lord GOD, how may I know that I will possess it?" So He said to him, "Bring Me a three year old heifer, and a three year old female goat, and a three year old ram, and a turtledove, and a young pigeon." Then he brought all these to Him and cut them in two, and laid each half opposite the other; but he did not cut the birds. Genesis 15:8-10*

After killing and preparing the animals for the Blood Covenant Abraham is told to watch over the offerings. He must not allow them to become spoilt by birds or animals. This must have been a severe test of Abraham's loyalty and his commitment to God. It would have been a test of his faithfulness, sitting in the wilderness watching and waiting for God to respond to him, for it is not until the evening that something begins to happen.

God causes a deep sleep to fall on Abraham. As he enters into this sleep a sense of being totally alone comes upon him. Abraham is only aware of the presence of God. Whilst he is in this state God speaks to him and outlines some of the blessings of the Covenant and the fact of it.

> *Genesis 15:12-15 As the sun was going down, a deep sleep fell upon Abram, and a deep and terrifying darkness descended upon him. Then the LORD said to Abram, "Know this for certain, that your offspring shall be aliens in a land that is not theirs, and shall be slaves there, and they shall be oppressed for four hundred years; but I will bring judgement on the nation that they serve, and afterward they shall come out with great possessions. As for yourself, you shall go to your ancestors in peace; you shall be buried in a good old age.*

The next thing that was seen is a "smoking furnace and a burning lamp" that passes through the halves.

> *Now when the sun was going down, a deep sleep fell upon Abram; and behold, terror and great darkness fell upon him. God said to Abram, "Know for certain that your descendants will be strangers in a land that is not theirs, where they will be enslaved and oppressed four hundred years. "But I will also judge the nation whom they will serve, and afterward they will come out with many possessions. "As for you, you shall go to your fathers in peace; you will be buried at a good old age. Genesis 15:12-15*

Two things should be understood at this point.

1. A flaming torch or a burning lamp was understood to be an emblem of Divine Presence in most Eastern and Middle Eastern cultures.

2. In the east it was often a custom to light a torch when making a Covenant or in celebration of a marriage. This symbolised the fire of warmth and light as the Covenant is continued or the fires of destruction if the agreement should be broken.

God himself has passed through the halves of the calf. By putting Abraham to sleep he ensured that he could not make any claim to the Covenant by his own virtue. Nor could he claim that it is established by any quality or ability of his own. This is God's

Covenant. It is given by God, established by God, ratified by God, drawn up by God, and written by God.

It is to be another thirteen years before this Covenant is fulfilled as we read in Genesis 17:1-10.

> *Now when Abram was ninety-nine years old, the LORD appeared to Abram and said to him, "I am God Almighty; Walk before Me, and be blameless. "I will establish My covenant between Me and you, And I will multiply you exceedingly." Abram fell on his face, and God talked with him, saying, "As for Me, behold, My covenant is with you, And you will be the father of a multitude of nations. "No longer shall your name be called Abram, But your name shall be Abraham; For I have made you the father of a multitude of nations. "I will make you exceedingly fruitful, and I will make nations of you, and kings will come forth from you. "I will establish My covenant between Me and you and your descendants after you throughout their generations for an everlasting covenant, to be God to you and to your descendants after you. "I will give to you and to your descendants after you, the land of your sojournings, all the land of Canaan, for an everlasting possession; and I will be their God." God said further to Abraham, "Now as for you, you shall keep My covenant, you and your descendants after you throughout their generations. "This is My covenant, which you shall keep, between Me and you and your descendants after you: every male among you shall be circumcised. Genesis 17:1-10*

The next time that God cuts a Covenant is on Mount Sinai with Moses and the elders of Israel, Exodus 24. This is the event that God refers to when he speaks of walking between the "parts of the calf" or the cutting of the Covenant in Jeremiah.

> *'I will give the men who have transgressed My covenant, who have not fulfilled the words of the covenant which they made before Me, when they cut the calf in two and passed between its parts-- the officials of Judah and the officials of Jerusalem, the*

> *court officers and the priests and all the people of the land who passed between the parts of the calf-- Jeremiah 34:18-19*

We should remember the curses that were pronounced on those who broke the Covenant. A terrible death, awful sickness and disease, poverty and every horror that can be imagined are a part of the penalty of breaking the Covenant.

When the Old Covenant was done away with, even though it was to introduce another better Covenant, the New Covenant had to pay the penalty of and incorporate the blessings of the old Covenant. The issues of righteousness, holiness, and justice must still be handled and fulfilled before the Old Covenant can be done away with for it is an Everlasting Covenant.

New Testament

When God was preparing to cut the new Blood Covenant with Jesus for us it became necessary for the penalty of sin to be paid. Jesus, as the sacrifice must pay the old penalty as well as provide a new penalty. Sickness and disease, the consequence of sin, were to be handled in the scourging of Jesus.

It was required that Jesus should bear the full force and brunt of sickness in every form; as a result he was disfigured more than any other man. His appearance was so totally changed that he became unrecognisable as his flesh was torn apart and ripped from his body by the scourge.

> *1 Peter 2:24 (KJV) Who his own self bare our sins in his own body on the tree, that we, being dead to sins, should live unto righteousness: by whose stripes ye were healed.*

Sin itself was to be dealt with through the false trial, the mockery and finally the cruel death of Jesus. The scourging of Jesus and his crucifixion at Calvary paid the penalty of sin. It was formally dealt with in the body of Jesus as he offered himself as the living sacrifice for the sins of the world.

> *As many were astonied at thee; his visage was so marred more than any man, and his form more than the sons of men... Isaiah 52:14 (KJV)*
>
> *Just as many were astonished at you, My people, So His appearance was marred more than any man And His form more than the sons of men. Isaiah 52:14*

The point is reinforced for us in the Gospel of John. The sacrifice of Jesus was a willing sacrifice, a matter of choice, to pay the full penalties, and not the execution of a punishment over which he had no control. He Gave Up the ghost.

> *Therefore when Jesus had received the sour wine, He said, "It is finished!" And He bowed His head and gave up His spirit. John 19:30*

Unwittingly the Roman[35] soldier that pierced Jesus side with his spear plays a critical part in the history of man as he became the instrument for the actual cutting of the Covenant. As the spear pierced the body of both God and man and the blood of Jesus was shed for God and man providing the price of the remission of sin. The blood of God and man is already mingled within Jesus. The wound leaves a permanent scar, as do the nail prints in his hands and feet.

The shedding of his blood has become all-important. It is the Blood that has dealt with sin as the cleansing agent; it is the blood of Jesus and the life of Jesus in that blood that imparted eternal life to us. Jesus gave his blood, and then presented it to his father in heaven as the required penalty for the remission sin; it was accepted by God the Father.

We can take on His life with all its quality and benefit and glorious position because Jesus has already received our life with all its sin,

---

[35] A Roman soldier, a representative of the Gentile authority of the day, has cut covenant for God and all Gentile nations for the covenant between God and all Gentile nations.

shame and failure, and he dealt with it. Justice has been done. The penalty of sin was paid in the sacrifice of Jesus; forgiveness was imparted to us with the life of Jesus as we accept his sacrifice for us and choose to live for him.

> *If we confess our sins, He is faithful and righteous to forgive us our sins and to cleanse us from all unrighteousness. 1 John 1:9*

It was unnecessary for Jesus to be "cut in half." This was normally done with the sacrificial beast so that each half of the beast could represent one of the two Covenant Heads. Jesus was in himself both God and man, and in being so was able to fully represent both God and man, and bearing the full force and price of the sacrifice in his body. As He died on Calvary, Jesus was not just representing man but he was also representing God. In doing so, he paid the price of the Covenant in the same way that a goat, bullock, or sacrificial animal had done for Abraham, Moses or the other Old Testament saints of God.

Jesus, by his death and resurrection provided a bridge between both God and man, a bridge that both God and man can use. He is our reconciliation and has done away with the enmity between God and man.

Now we are able to live in peace with God and know that God is at peace with us. The book of Hebrews makes the issue clear for us; Jesus becomes the mediator of a better Covenant. He fulfilled the demands of the Old Covenant. Jesus paid its penalty and absorbed in himself the full consequences of sin. At the same time he provided better promises and a better life, not just for when we die, from the time we receive Jesus as our saviour, our substitute, our Covenant Head, Hebrews Ch. 8.

> *Now the main point in what has been said is this: we have such a high priest, who has taken His seat at the right hand of the throne of the Majesty in the heavens, a minister in the sanctuary and in the true tabernacle, which the Lord pitched, not man. For every high priest is appointed to offer both gifts*

and sacrifices; so it is necessary that this high priest also have something to offer. Now if He were on earth, He would not be a priest at all, since there are those who offer the gifts according to the Law; who serve a copy and shadow of the heavenly things, just as Moses was warned by God when he was about to erect the tabernacle; for, "SEE," He says, "THAT YOU MAKE all things ACCORDING TO THE PATTERN WHICH WAS SHOWN YOU ON THE MOUNTAIN." But now He has obtained a more excellent ministry, by as much as He is also the mediator of a better covenant, which has been enacted on better promises. For if that first covenant had been faultless, there would have been no occasion sought for a second. For finding fault with them, He says, "BEHOLD, DAYS ARE COMING, SAYS THE LORD, WHEN I WILL EFFECT A NEW COVENANT WITH THE HOUSE OF ISRAEL AND WITH THE HOUSE OF JUDAH; NOT LIKE THE COVENANT WHICH I MADE WITH THEIR FATHERS ON THE DAY WHEN I TOOK THEM BY THE HAND TO LEAD THEM OUT OF THE LAND OF EGYPT; FOR THEY DID NOT CONTINUE IN MY COVENANT, AND I DID NOT CARE FOR THEM, SAYS THE LORD. "FOR THIS IS THE COVENANT THAT I WILL MAKE WITH THE HOUSE OF ISRAEL AFTER THOSE DAYS, SAYS THE LORD: I WILL PUT MY LAWS INTO THEIR MINDS, AND I WILL WRITE THEM ON THEIR HEARTS. AND I WILL BE THEIR GOD, AND THEY SHALL BE MY PEOPLE. "AND THEY SHALL NOT TEACH EVERYONE HIS FELLOW CITIZEN, AND EVERYONE HIS BROTHER, SAYING, 'KNOW THE LORD,' FOR ALL WILL KNOW ME, FROM THE LEAST TO THE GREATEST OF THEM. "FOR I WILL BE MERCIFUL TO THEIR INIQUITIES, AND I WILL REMEMBER THEIR SINS NO MORE." When He said, "A new covenant," He has made the first obsolete. But whatever is becoming obsolete and growing old is ready to disappear. Hebrews 8:1-13

An Application

The Old Covenant is now gone. It is done away with and in its place a new and better Covenant has been provided. It has been ratified by the cutting of the sacrifice of Jesus, no less than God himself.

No longer do we struggle with laws and ritual. No more sacrifices. No need for fear. Gone are the class distinctions between priesthood and laity. Now we walk in relationship. We have been made joint heirs with Christ not of a natural order but of a supernatural one.

> [36]There are those who are kings because they are born with a crown upon their heads; there are those who are kings because they have been adopted **into a royal family; and there are those who have seized a throne by force**. But in all history, only God's chosen people hold the throne by this triple right! Their claim could hardly be more secure. No coup against them can hope to succeed. No insurrection can disturb their dominion. Their sovereignty is invincible!

Your right to the throne is established

- **By the new birth**, which has made you the Father's child.
- **by adoption in Christ**, which has doubly strengthened your legal claim.
- **by conquest**, through your access by faith to the triumph of Christ's resurrection and ascension.

And all of this is confirmed by a set of immutable parchments, your personal "*letters patent*" - the Holy Scriptures. One passage in particular is outstanding -

---

[36] Quoted from "Throne Rights", Ch. 1 page 7. Rev. Dr, K. Chant, Vision Christian College.

> *"Our God is rich in mercy; so out of the great love he had for us, even when we were 'dead' because of our sins, he made us alive together with Christ (you are saved by grace). But then, through our union with Christ, <u>God has also raised us up with him and enthroned us with him in 'the heavenly places'</u>. His purpose in showing this kindness toward us in Christ Jesus, is that in the coming ages he might reveal the immeasurable riches of his grace" (Ep. 2:4-9, free translation).*

Our position in Christ could not be more secure, our relationship with Him is bound up with His own word that he will be our shield and defender our protector and provider and He has committed his very existence to that promise for *He is God and He cannot lie*[37].

We do not need to prove ourselves, we cannot earn our ranking, and we do not need to adopt or strive towards a pious position. It is timely for us to realize that everything that needs to be done has been done and He is pleased to welcome you as His child, a member of his royal household, a king and a priest. It is His declaration

> *But you are A CHOSEN RACE, A royal PRIESTHOOD, A HOLY NATION, A PEOPLE FOR God's OWN POSSESSION, so that you may proclaim the excellencies of Him who has called you out of darkness into His marvelous light; 1 Peter 2:9*
>
> *and from Jesus Christ, the faithful witness, the firstborn of the dead, and the ruler of the kings of the earth. To Him who loves us and released us from our sins by His blood-- and He has made us to be a kingdom, priests to His God and Father--to Him be the glory and the dominion forever and ever. Amen. Revelation 1:5-6*

---

[37] Titus 1:2

End Of Chapter Questions

1. Explain what is meant by the expression "Cutting the Covenant"

2. What is the universal significance of the Blood that makes it the vital element of blood covenant?

3. Give references from the Old and the New Testament that testify to the value of Blood.

Chapter 9:

The Covenant Feast

Historical Perspective

When the "Covenant Cutting" ceremony is finished everyone is invited to a feast. This is the "Covenant Feast." A particular part of the Covenant Feast is called the "Memorial Meal." The Covenant Heads are the guests of honour for this meal, which is hosted at the Great King's palace. Guests would include all the families of the Covenant Heads. To be absent would be seen as a personal insult, and at that time, could result in the renewal of animosities, or at the very least, the death penalty for the absentee.

Other invited guests would be heads of other families, tribes, or states known to either or both kings and would always include those who are in Covenant relationship with the Great King, as this is the time to introduce the new "Vassal King" to his "Brother Vassal Kings[38]". This introduction to his new family will prevent future misunderstandings or hostilities between them, as; despite previous animosities, they will now consider themselves to be friends and allies.

Often the elders of both tribes, men of wisdom, priests and, often, all the people living in the towns or villages of the Vassal King will attend the feast. A national feast day will be called and every town and village was commanded to celebrate if they could not attend the feast themselves because of distance.

---

[38] Some Great Kings had many Vassal Kings and the continued peace of the covenant demanded that all Vassals new who their brother Vassals were. In his quest for Livingstone, Stanley cut over 50 covenants, Pharaoh Akhenaton cut at least 13 covenants during his rule of Egypt. Wycliffe Bible Encyclopaedia; Blood Covenant E.W. Kenyon

This feast could go on for many days, or even weeks depending on the cultures of the people involved. It is a great time of festivity and celebration. Old enemies let bygones be bygones. The proverbial hatchet is buried and, by Royal Decree, all animosity is forgiven and forgotten. More often than not, the people involved in the feasting had no personal animosity. Their feuds were more traditional than personal and often they had forgotten why they were fighting at all. They usually found that they had more in common with each other, than differences.

In Eastern and Middle Eastern Covenant agreements the Great King would have a clause inserted into the Covenant agreement that demanded at least an annual renewal and commemorative feast. This was a part of the continuation of the Covenant. Examples of this are found in the Aramaean and Hittites Treaties.

The Memorial Meal

One of the most remarkable aspects of the Covenant Feast, and one of the last rites of the entire proceedings, is the "Memorial Meal", better known to us as a "Breaking of Bread Ceremony", or communion. In almost all the Blood Covenants around the world this rite, in some form or another, is included.

The "Memorial Meal" would be repeated as often as the Covenant Heads came together. Not only the Covenant Heads but also the other Vassal Kings would share in a memorial meal when they met to remind each other of the common bond between them.

As discussed, an animal has been killed and its blood spilt on behalf of the two men who are entering the Covenant. At sometime during the Covenant meal the two Covenant Heads will stand to partake of the "Memorial Meal." A loaf of bread is produced and they will declare that the bread represents the body of the animal that has been sacrificed for them. Each of them will take a piece of bread from the loaf. They will declare that they are "eating the body of the sacrifice." In some countries, an actual piece of the slain animal is eaten, sometimes instead of, or with the bread.

The meaning behind the declaration is that as surely as the animal has died for all of their offences against each other, by eating the "flesh of the animal in the bread, so too have all the hatred and animosity they held against the other. By eating this bread, declared to be the body of the sacrificed animal they are eating the benefits of sacrifice, the penalty for all their offences has been paid and now they enjoy peace and prosperity with each other; they are now alive in its place.

As the animal is representing them, they are declaring once again that they see themselves in the slain beast. As they look to each other, they are able to declare that, as they have died to themselves, they are now alive to and living for each other.

Of course the benefit is greatest to the Vassal King who, having been conquered has nothing to offer the Great King, other than loyalty. The Vassal King is then able to enjoy the benefits of the Great King life as though he were the Great King himself. The Great King now absorbs and deals with, in forgiveness, all the offences of the Vassal King.

Justice has been totally satisfied in the sacrificial animal. As the bread is eaten, the relationship is cemented together. Their personal acknowledgement of the Covenant agreement is almost completed.

They must then drink the blood of the animal. Their culture may actually determine exactly what was drunk. In some cultures they actually drank the blood of the animal. In other cultures the blood would be mixed with wine or herbs and drank. In some cultures the blood was substituted with wine. In China a few drops of blood was mingled with tea and this mixture was then drunk.

Regardless of what was drunk, it was declared to be the blood of the sacrifice. They saw themselves drinking the blood of the sacrifice and therefore the blood of their Covenant partner. It was held that as they drank the blood it entered into their own blood stream, therefore as they drink this "blood" their Covenant partner's blood is now flowing through their veins. Their respective lives are flowing through each other; they are now one with each other, living for each other's benefit.

They consider themselves to be closer than natural brothers, for their brotherhood is a brotherhood of choice. As they believe that their blood is flowing through the veins of each other they believe that their personality and qualities have been exchanged and mingled with each other with the life of the Great King dominant in each of them. His blood, and therefore his life, will dominate the life of the Vassal King.

To take this memorial meal and then to walk away from it without accepting the obligations associated with it, or to treat it with less respect than it deserved was to reinstate an act of war with the Covenant Head. It would be tantamount to declaring a death penalty on yourself, your family, and your people.

It was the greatest possible insult to despise, or even take lightly the "Memorial Meal". To do so would be to despise the Covenant itself. It is doubtless with this in mind that Paul urges us to be careful about taking communion, that we should take it with the right mind and heart.

Old Testament

Throughout the word of God we find many examples of Covenant Feasts, identical with the Covenant Feasts of the Middle Eastern covenants. It is certain that these covenant principles were familiar to the Israelites. God used this familiarity in the institution of his Covenant with man, with both the establishment and re-establishment of the Covenant, both with God and men and between men and men.

Some of these examples of Covenant Feasts between men are found with Isaac and Abimelech in Genesis 26:26-33. As Abimelech[39] sees that God is with Isaac, Abimelech becomes afraid of Isaac's wealth and power. To protect himself he enters into a Covenant with Isaac and it ends with a feast.

> *Then he went up from there to Beersheba. The LORD appeared to him the same night and said, "I am the God of your father Abraham; Do not fear, for I am with you. I will bless you, and multiply your descendants, For the sake of My servant Abraham." So he built an altar there and called upon the name of the LORD, and pitched his tent there; and there Isaac's servants dug a well. Then Abimelech came to him from Gerar with his adviser Ahuzzath and Phicol the commander of his army. Isaac said to them, "Why have you come to me, since you hate me and have sent me away from you?" They said, "We see plainly that the LORD has been with you; so we said, 'Let there now be an oath between us, even between you and us, and let us make a covenant with you, that you will do us no harm, just as we have not touched you and have done to you nothing but good and have sent you away in peace. You are now the blessed of the LORD.'" Then he made them a feast, and they ate and drank. In the morning they arose early and exchanged oaths; then Isaac sent them away and they departed from him in peace. Now it came about on the same day, that Isaac's servants came in and told him about the well which they had dug, and said to him, "We have found water." So he*

---

[39] A King of Gerar in the time of Isaac, probably the son of the preceding one, (Gen_26:1-22). Isaac sought refuge in his territory during a famine, and there he acted a part with reference to his wife Rebekah similar to that of his father Abraham with reference to Sarah. Abimelech rebuked him for the deception, which he accidentally discovered. Isaac settled for a while here, and prospered. Abimelech desired him, however, to leave his territory, which Isaac did. Abimelech afterwards visited him when he was encamped at Beer-sheba, and expressed a desire to renew the covenant which had been entered into between their fathers (Gen_26:26-31). M.G. Easton M.A., D.D., Illustrated Bible Dictionary, Third Edition, published by Thomas Nelson, 1897.

called it Shibah; therefore the name of the city is Beersheba to this day. Genesis 26:23-33

Jacob and Laban end their Covenant of peace with a meal (Genesis 31:36-55).

Both before and after the Exodus, the Passover feast is given as a memorial of the Covenant of God to the people of God, Exodus 12:1-51. Every year the Jews were to hold the Passover feast as a memorial of how God brought the children of Israel out of Egypt, thus renewing his Covenant with them.

Not all the covenant agreements recorded in the Bible provide all the details of the covenant ceremony, but enough is known of the people, their philosophy, and their culture, to know that the ceremony would be completed with a meal in each case.

Examples of Covenant Feasts between God and man are found as the Covenant is instituted on Mount Sinai. God and the Elders of Israel eat together (Exodus 24).

Then He said to Moses, "Come up to the LORD, you and Aaron, Nadab and Abihu and seventy of the elders of Israel, and you shall worship at a distance. "Moses alone, however, shall come near to the LORD, but they shall not come near, nor shall the people come up with him." Then Moses came and recounted to the people all the words of the LORD and all the ordinances; and all the people answered with one voice and said, "All the words which the LORD has spoken we will do!" Moses wrote down all the words of the LORD. Then he arose early in the morning, and built an altar at the foot of the mountain with twelve pillars for the twelve tribes of Israel. He sent young men of the sons of Israel, and they offered burnt offerings and sacrificed young bulls as peace offerings to the LORD. Moses took half of the blood and put it in basins, and the other half of the blood he sprinkled on the altar. Then he took the book of the covenant and read it in the hearing of the people; and they said, "All that the LORD has spoken we will do, and we will be obedient!" So Moses took the blood and sprinkled it on the people, and said, "Behold the blood of the covenant, which the LORD has made with you in accordance with all these words." Then Moses went up with Aaron, Nadab and Abihu, and seventy of the elders of Israel, and they saw the God of Israel; and under His feet there appeared to be a pavement of sapphire, as clear as the sky itself. Yet He did not stretch out His hand against the nobles of the sons of Israel; and they saw God, and they ate and drank. Exodus 24:1-11

The weekly Sabbath, which means a day of rest and feasting, was given as a sign between God and the children of Israel, of their perpetual Covenant (Exodus 31:12-17). The feast was to remind the children of Israel of their relationship with God.

In 2 Kings 22:1 to 2 Kings 23:25, we read of the greatest feast and celebration in the history of the Kings of Israel since Samuel, as King Josiah re-establishes the Covenant of God with his people. This event is also found in 2 Chronicles 34:1 to 2 Chronicles 35:19.

Although all the feasts of the Jews, as instituted by God, had a direct relationship with the Covenant, the feasts most properly identified with the Covenant is the "Feast of Unleavened Bread" and the "Passover."

Almost, if not every revival, or re-establishment of the Covenant relationship with God, came with the Passover feast, beginning with the original Passover itself as found in Exodus 12:1-11. It came at the beginning of the year and was the first feast. In each case, God gave them a new start.

New Testament

Therefore it should be no surprise to us, to see that God chooses the Passover, a feast that spoke of the sacrifice of Jesus and the redemption of the people of God, as the very event that Jesus chooses to establish the New Covenant with his people.

And He said to them, "When you have entered the city, a man will meet you carrying a pitcher of water; follow him into the house that he enters. "And you shall say to the owner of the house, 'The Teacher says to you, "Where is the guest room in which I may eat the Passover with My disciples?"' "And he will show you a large, furnished upper room; prepare it there." And they left and found everything just as He had told them; and they prepared the Passover. When the hour had come, He reclined at the table, and the apostles with Him. And He said to them, "I have earnestly desired to eat this Passover with you before I suffer; for I say to you, I shall never again eat it until it is fulfilled in the kingdom of God." And when He had taken a cup and given thanks, He said, "Take this and share it among yourselves; for I say to you, I will not drink of the fruit of the vine from now on until the kingdom of God comes." And when He had taken some bread and given thanks, He broke it and gave it to them, saying, "This is My body which is given for you; do this in remembrance of Me." And in the same way He took the cup after they had eaten, saying, "This cup which is poured out for you is the new covenant in My blood. "But behold, the hand of the one betraying Me is with Mine on the table. "For indeed, the Son of Man is going as it has been determined; but woe to that man by whom He is betrayed!" And they began to discuss among themselves which one of them it might be who was going to do this thing. And there arose also a dispute among them as to which one of them was regarded to be greatest. And He said to them, "The kings of the Gentiles lord it over them; and those who have authority over them are called 'Benefactors.' "But it is not this way with you, but the one who is the greatest among you must become like the youngest, and the leader like the servant. "For who is greater, the one who reclines at the table or the one who serves? Is it not the one who reclines at the table? But I am among you as the one who serves. "You are those who have stood by Me in My trials; and just as My Father has granted Me a kingdom, I grant you that you may eat and drink at My table in My kingdom, and you will sit on thrones judging the twelve tribes of Israel. Luke 22:10-20[40]

Jesus fully recognized what he was doing. He declared that his body is broken for us and his blood is the blood of the New Covenant. He literally died in our place and we are alive in his place.

The disciples understood what he was saying so they did not question Jesus at this time. Even though he referred to himself as the sacrifice, the Lamb of God. If they had questioned him, as we would likely have, we would be alerted also to their concern and doubts, but instead they simply accepted all that he had to say.

If they had questioned him at this point, it would have been due to their lack of faith in Him, they would have no choice but to accuse him of blasphemy. Indeed to declare himself as the Passover lamb, the final sacrifice, and call himself the Lamb of God would have been blasphemous if indeed he were not who He declared Himself to be (Luke 22:14-20).

The fact that Jesus made this statement and the disciples maintained their love for Him, continuing to follow him, indicated that they understood what he was saying and they believed him. If they did not, then no matter how much they loved him and in spite of his miracles, they would have to denounce him as a blasphemer. Their cultural background demanded this of them.

Instead they partook of this Passover with him. As they partook of this supper Jesus declared to them that he is their Passover.

> *While they were eating, Jesus took some bread, and after a blessing, He broke it and gave it to the disciples, and said, "Take, eat; this is My body." And when He had taken a cup*

---

[40] There are four accounts of the institution of the Lord's Supper, three in the Gospels Mat. 26:26-30; Mar. 14:22-2; Luke 22:14-20; and one in Paul's letter to the Corinthians, 1 Cor. 11:23-25.

> *and given thanks, He gave it to them, saying, "Drink from it, all of you; for this is My blood of the covenant, which is poured out for many for forgiveness of sins. "But I say to you, I will not drink of this fruit of the vine from now on until that day when I drink it new with you in My Father's kingdom." After singing a hymn, they went out to the Mount of Olives. Matthew 26:26-30*

No longer do they need a Passover lamb, the feast of unleavened bread, or any of the other feast days to commemorate the New Covenant. From now on all they need do is share the bread and wine, the "Memorial Meal," as often as they wished (1 Corinthians 11:23-26). They will do this in just the same manner as the Covenant Heads in the past, in remembrance of him.

This bread had always been eaten with, and represented the Passover lamb, until that time. From that time on it will represent Jesus and his body that is given for all mankind.

Jesus has accomplished much more than we realise, doubtless that will always be true. Our capacity to understand what God has done is finite and yet His work in infinite.

Not only has he paid for our sins, he has taken the consequences of those sins as well. In doing so he has provided much more than simply providing healing for sickness and disease and forgiveness of sin. He has restored relationship between ourselves and God and he has enthroned us with him in heavenly places

> *But God, being rich in mercy, because of His great love with which He loved us, even when we were dead in our transgressions, made us alive together with Christ (by grace you have been saved), and raised us up with Him, and seated us with Him in the heavenly places in Christ Jesus, so that in the ages to come He might show the surpassing riches of His grace in kindness toward us in Christ Jesus. For by grace you have been saved through faith; and that not of yourselves, it is the gift of God; Ephesians 2:4-8*

He has provided the only real solution to the issues of poverty, drug addiction, the abuse of children, wives and husbands, personal degradation and failure and all of the common areas of human suffering, for all these things are but a part of the penalty of sin. When Jesus died he paid the penalty entirely. He has totally satisfied the issue of justice between God and man.

In doing so he has made it possible for us to access all the benefits of God the Great King as if we were the Great King ourselves. Just as the Vassal King accessed all the wealth, life, power, authority, peace and prosperity of the Great King, so do we, in exactly the same manner, for exactly the same reason - Blood Covenant.

The major difference between a human covenant and a covenant between God and Man is that the benefits and wealth of the Great King on earth are limited by his personal wealth. But our Great King, our heavenly Father, is unlimited wealth personified. He is totally unlimited in providing for the needs of his people. The context of those needs include all we require for life and godliness.

When we accept his sacrifice for us, we accept his life in our place. In him there was and is no sickness. If we lived our life as he did, in complete harmony with his Father, we would enjoy his health and fitness.

Not only did he die, He was also resurrected. He rose from the dead and passes on to us all the benefits of His resurrected life. It is in this sense that Paul declares to us that we are dead to self, but alive unto God.

> *Even so consider yourselves to be dead to sin, but alive to God in Christ Jesus. Romans 6:11*

We are not just alive because of him, we are alive in him, and he is alive in us.

Each time we partake of this communion meal, we are reaffirming our desire to be a part of this New Covenant. In the same way, taking part in the Passover was to reaffirm a desire to be a part of the Old Covenant.

Jesus speaks of the cup of the meal as the "New Testament" in his blood. New Testament is properly understood as New Covenant for the word "Testament" and "Covenant" are synonymous. This signified the acceptance of a new Covenant by all who were to partake of it. When the Jews ate the bread of the Passover and the Passover lamb, they were symbolically eating the flesh of the Passover sacrifice. When they took the Passover wine, it was to represent of the blood of the Passover or sacrificial animal.

Both Jesus and Paul remind us that this meal should be taken in remembrance of Jesus. It is the fulfilment of the typology of the Passover, and this remembrance is the only "act of remembrance" that is required of Christians. It is the only memorial that Jesus has asked of us and that we are expected to give him.

Jesus points to the bread and tells the disciple that it is his body, and refers to the wine as his blood. He identifies himself as the Passover sacrifice, and therefore the sacrifice of the New Covenant. The disciples understood this. Blood Covenant was something they understood. They had been saturated in these ideas since early childhood. When Jesus said these things to them, they instantly recognized what Jesus was saying: "I am the sacrifice for sin, you do not need to sacrifice lambs or goats or any other thing ever again."

This is the reason Paul reminds us be careful when we take communion (1 Corinthians 11:23-30).

When we eat the bread of communion, we declare that we are dead to the world and to sin. Our own selfish nature is as the dead beast of the covenant sacrifice. We are empowered in this by fact of the resurrection life of the resurrected Jesus (Romans 6:1-8).

Jesus died for us as individuals. As we accept his death as ours, we must also accept his resurrection. He died totally for us and he was totally resurrected. Now we must live totally for him. When we enter Covenant relationship we are agreeing to put on the nature of our Covenant partner. Paul reminds us of the need to put on the new man, and reminds us of how we should live (Colossians 3:1-17; Ephesians 4:23-32).

We should take note of Romans 13:11-12, Galatians 3:26-29, and Galatians 5:22-23. These scriptures also show us what our new nature is like and what is expected of us as we begin our relationship with Jesus.

> *Do this, knowing the time, that it is already the hour for you to awaken from sleep; for now salvation is nearer to us than when we believed. The night is almost gone, and the day is near. Therefore let us lay aside the deeds of darkness and put on the armor of light. Romans 13:11-12*

> *For you are all sons of God through faith in Christ Jesus. For all of you who were baptized into Christ have clothed yourselves with Christ. There is neither Jew nor Greek, there is neither slave nor free man, there is neither male nor female; for you are all one in Christ Jesus. And if you belong to Christ, then you are Abraham's descendants, heirs according to promise. Galatians 3:26-29*

> *But the fruit of the Spirit is love, joy, peace, patience, kindness, goodness, faithfulness, gentleness, self-control; against such things there is no law. Galatians 5:22-23*

When the Vassal King took part in this final act of the Covenant Ceremony he became a new man. As he entered this Covenant relationship, and confirmed it at this feast time, all the penalties for all his crimes were paid for. So it is for us. As we enter this relationship and partake of this feast we accept a new life.

The penalty for our sins has been paid in the same way that the penalty of the Vassal Kings crimes had been paid, through a substitute sacrifice.

> *Therefore if anyone is in Christ, he is a new creature; the old things passed away; behold, new things have come. Now all*

> *these things are from God, who reconciled us to Himself through Christ and gave us the ministry of reconciliation, 2 Corinthians 5:17-18*

We can also compare some of Paul's comments in Ephesians, and Colossians

> *by abolishing in His flesh the enmity, which is the Law of commandments contained in ordinances, so that in Himself He might make the two into one new man, thus establishing peace, Ephesians 2:15*

> *and have put on the new self who is being renewed to a true knowledge according to the image of the One who created him- - Colossians 3:10*

It is not simply a matter that our slate is wiped clean and we are given a new start with an old slate. Instead God has thrown the slate away. He no longer considers our past sins as they have been dealt with, as we can see in 2 Corinthians 5:19. Our life is hid in God and his life is to be lived out in ours.

> *namely, that God was in Christ reconciling the world to Himself, not counting their trespasses against them, and He has committed to us the word of reconciliation. 2 Corinthians 5:19*

Just as the cleansing properties of blood surge through our body and cleanse our system from impurities, the blood of Jesus surges through our spiritual being. It cleanses us, from the spirit out, effecting and purifying even our soul and body.

An Application

We take communion as a declaration that we accept this blood covenant relationship with Jesus. That is the purpose, we agree with the offer made and we accept it and our responsibility.

From this time on we should expect a change in our lives as the cleansing blood of Jesus begins to take effect and we begin to take on more of his personality and characteristics.

It is not given to us on a yearly or monthly period. We are not called upon to set aside a special time, although many churches do for the sake of convenience and to make possible this great feast time. Instead Jesus simply asks us to partake of these emblems, as often as we can and as often as we desire to take them.

> *For I received from the Lord that which I also delivered to you, that the Lord Jesus in the night in which He was betrayed took bread; and when He had given thanks, He broke it and said, "This is My body, which is for you; do this in remembrance of Me." In the same way He took the cup also after supper, saying, "This cup is the new covenant in My blood; do this, as often as you drink it, in remembrance of Me." For as often as you eat this bread and drink the cup, you proclaim the Lord's death until He comes. Therefore whoever eats the bread or drinks the cup of the Lord in an unworthy manner, shall be guilty of the body and the blood of the Lord. But a man must examine himself, and in so doing he is to eat of the bread and drink of the cup. For he who eats and drinks, eats and drinks judgment to himself if he does not judge the body rightly. For this reason many among you are weak and sick, and a number sleep. 1 Corinthians 11:23-30*

When we take the communion meal we are told to examine ourselves. The purpose of this examination is to see ourselves in the light of the Covenant, accepted blessed, and desired of God, loved and considered worthy, a part of God's family.

We should look to ourselves and see if there is some part of our life that is not maintaining the standards of the Covenant relationship that Jesus expects of us.

As we partake of the communion we should take time to reaffirm our desire to take part in the Covenant relationship.

Effectively we are declaring publicly that we accept the concepts, principles, ideals, laws, regulations, and responsibilities of the Covenant and that we wish to accept them fully, including its penalties for failing to maintain our part of the Covenant. It is no wonder that Paul declares that many are sick and weak from taking the cup of the communion in vain. The penalties of taking the Covenant lightly are very serious. God will not be mocked, especially where his Covenant is concerned (1 Cor. 11:27-30).

> *For as often as you eat this bread and drink the cup, you proclaim the Lord's death until He comes. Therefore whoever eats the bread or drinks the cup of the Lord in an unworthy manner, shall be guilty of the body and the blood of the Lord. But a man must examine himself, and in so doing he is to eat of the bread and drink of the cup. For he who eats and drinks, eats and drinks judgment to himself if he does not judge the body rightly. For this reason many among you are weak and sick, and a number sleep. But if we judged ourselves rightly, we would not be judged. 1 Corinthians 11:26-31*

The memorial Gift that God has given to us is the living gift of Jesus both as a sacrificial lamb, and as the living High Priest of the better Covenant. Hebrews 7:1 to Hebrews 10:31.

For so many people there are wonderful benefits to be found in taking communion. Often healing, deliverance, miracles, restoration of family, release into ministry are found, and however often these are mistakenly attributed to the communion elements. These blessings are not a part of the communion elements, the wine and the bread themselves.

These blessings are accessed because we recognize our place in Christ and we identify with him through taking the communion. It is relationship that releases God's rich blessings into us, not ceremony, not formula, not an act of obedience for such would make these blessings the result of our works.

God's blessing does not come to us based upon merit of our own doing. It comes from the grace of His heart and our willing acceptance of his provision.

After these things the word of the LORD came unto Abram in a vision, saying, Fear not, Abram: I am thy shield, and thy exceeding great reward. Genesis 15:1

End Of Chapter Questions

1. What was the purpose of the memorial meal?
2. Explain the significance of Exodus 24:1-11 in light of Blood Covenant.
3. What is the significance of our Communion Service in light of Blood Covenant?

Chapter 10:

The Reading Of The Word

A Historical Perspective

During the Covenant Feast, time must be set aside for the reading of the Covenant Law. The Vassal King had already agreed to the laws of the Great King however during the feast he was to be publicly reminded of them. Not only the Vassal but also his high priest and headmen, elders, or government members must also be made aware of these laws. If it was a tribal situation the whole tribe is to be made aware as the laws of the Great King are now to be the laws of the Vassal King.

The purpose of this reading was to ensure that the Vassal King and his people understood their new laws. From this time on there would be no excuses for failing to comply with the laws of the Great King.

Once a year, at a time and place to be determined by the Great King the re-reading of the Covenant Laws must also take place. This was usually during a renewal of the covenant feast, which would be held annually. This renewal may be in the Vassal's own land or at the capital city of the Great King. The location and frequency of this reading was determined by the Great King with some consideration to the cultures of the people involved. The practicalities of such a reading due to such as issues as distance between kingdoms, or other geographical or political situations.

Regardless of where the feast was held, the reading of the Covenant Laws was an imperative. It ensured that everyone understood their new laws, their responsibilities, the benefits of maintaining the Covenant and the penalties for breaking it. Without public declaration the people could not hope to keep the new laws.

Old Testament

The same principle is applied in the word of God. God does not want us to enter this relationship with him blindly or in ignorance. When God established his Covenant with Abraham he gave him explicit instruction on his Covenant in Genesis 15; 17; & 22:15-18.

These instructions are reasonably concise. No great demands were made due to the quality of the relationship between Abraham and God. The scripture makes it clear that they were friends.

> *and the Scripture was fulfilled which says, "AND ABRAHAM BELIEVED GOD, AND IT WAS RECKONED TO HIM AS RIGHTEOUSNESS," and he was called the friend of God. James 2:23*

Not only that, but the covenant was between Abraham and God not between a nation and a Great King.

The Covenant between Abraham and God was personal even though it was to benefit all his seed and many generations and nations for centuries to come.

When God cut a Covenant with Israel through Moses laws and regulations was needed due to the nature of the people and the nature of the Covenant. This new covenant is between God and approximately 3 million people.

> *Then Moses summoned all Israel and said to them: "Hear, O Israel, the statutes and the ordinances which I am speaking today in your hearing, that you may learn them and observe them carefully. "The LORD our God made a covenant with us at Horeb. "The LORD did not make this covenant with our fathers, but with us, with all those of us alive here today. Deuteronomy 5:1-3*

None of these people were counted as God's friend. They were his people and needed guidance and regulation on how to live. They were accustomed to slavery and the ways of the Egyptians rather than living for Jehovah. Instructions were required, not only to prevent the continued breach of the Covenant, but also for them to be able to live with each other and for God.

Most of these people knew no better than to act in an offensive manner toward God. Their hearts were hardened by slavery in spite of the many miracles they saw. Consequently, when God cut the Covenant with the children of Israel it became necessary to give more explicit details of the Covenant, its laws and expectations.

First God gave his law to Moses. Then Moses passed the law on to the people of Israel. They received the laws and the conditions of this Covenant. The elders came before God with Moses and they ate a feast with God. Following this God gave Moses the Laws on tablets of stone.

> *Then He said to Moses, "Come up to the LORD, you and Aaron, Nadab and Abihu and seventy of the elders of Israel, and you shall worship at a distance. "Moses alone, however, shall come near to the LORD, but they shall not come near, nor shall the people come up with him." Then Moses came and recounted to the people all the words of the LORD and all the ordinances; and all the people answered with one voice and said, "All the words which the LORD has spoken we will do!" Moses wrote down all the words of the LORD. Then he arose early in the morning, and built an altar at the foot of the mountain with twelve pillars for the twelve tribes of Israel. He sent young men of the sons of Israel, and they offered burnt offerings and sacrificed young bulls as peace offerings to the LORD. Moses took half of the blood and put it in basins, and the other half of the blood he sprinkled on the altar. Then he took the book of the covenant and read it in the hearing of the people; and they said, "All that the LORD has spoken we will*

do, and we will be obedient!" So Moses took the blood and sprinkled it on the people, and said, "Behold the blood of the covenant, which the LORD has made with you in accordance with all these words." Then Moses went up with Aaron, Nadab and Abihu, and seventy of the elders of Israel, and they saw the God of Israel; and under His feet there appeared to be a pavement of sapphire, as clear as the sky itself. Yet He did not stretch out His hand against the nobles of the sons of Israel; and they saw God, and they ate and drank. Exodus 24:1-11

The Covenant itself was complicated, however, the law of the Covenant was outlined, introduced, and received as theirs by all of the people.

These Covenant Laws covered every part of their lives and provided judicial, social, and religious laws, regulations and customs. To fully understand these Covenant Laws the reader is referred to the books of Exodus 19:1 to Exodus 40:33 with Deuteronomy 5:1 to 30:20. The books of Leviticus and Numbers also give a great deal of information about the Laws. The range of these laws is astounding in both detail and complexity. They show the extent that God was (and for that matter still is), involved in every area of human endeavour.

Whenever the Covenant was renewed in the Old Testament it came with the reading of the law. The Covenant was renewed yearly in several ways in the feasts of the Lord. These included:

The Weekly Sabbath	The Feast of the Passover
The Feast of Unleavened Bread	The Feast of First fruits
The Feast of Pentecost	The Feast of Trumpets
The Day of Atonement	The Feast of Tabernacles

At each of these feasts the reading and teaching of the word was an integral part of the feast day. The people were to read the law daily. They were commanded to read it as often as possible. However, God commanded every seven years, on the feast of tabernacles. The whole of the law was to be read.

> *So Moses wrote this law and gave it to the priests, the sons of Levi who carried the ark of the covenant of the LORD, and to all the elders of Israel. Then Moses commanded them, saying, "At the end of every seven years, at the time of the year of remission of debts, at the Feast of Booths, when all Israel comes to appear before the LORD your God at the place which He will choose, you shall read this law in front of all Israel in their hearing. "Assemble the people, the men and the women and children and the alien who is in your town, so that they may hear and learn and fear the LORD your God, and be careful to observe all the words of this law. "Their children, who have not known, will hear and learn to fear the LORD your God, as long as you live on the land which you are about to cross the Jordan to possess." Deuteronomy 31:9-13*

The book of Deuteronomy records more details of the Covenant and various other laws from God to the people than any other book in the Bible. An interesting law is found in Deuteronomy 17:15-20, note verses 18-19.

> *"Now it shall come about when he sits on the throne of his kingdom, he shall write for himself a copy of this law on a scroll in the presence of the Levitical priests. "It shall be with him and he shall read it all the days of his life, that he may learn to fear the LORD his God, by carefully observing all the words of this law and these statutes, Deuteronomy 17:18-19*

When the children of Israel were to take a king for themselves the Levites were to make him his own copy of the law. He must constantly read and keep it beside him. This would keep him right before God and his judgement would be consistent with the law of God. The king would directly represent the Vassal King and responsibility fell to him to keep the people right in God's sight.

When Joshua took over leadership of the children of Israel he was commanded to meditate on the word of God day and night for wisdom and understanding in God.

> *"No man will be able to stand before you all the days of your life. Just as I have been with Moses, I will be with you; I will not fail you or forsake you. "Be strong and courageous, for you shall give this people possession of the land which I swore to their fathers to give them. "Only be strong and very courageous; be careful to do according to all the law which Moses My servant commanded you; do not turn from it to the right or to the left, so that you may have success wherever you go. "This book of the law shall not depart from your mouth, but you shall meditate on it day and night, so that you may be careful to do according to all that is written in it; for then you will make your way prosperous, and then you will have success. "Have I not commanded you? Be strong and courageous! Do not tremble or be dismayed, for the LORD your God is with you wherever you go." Joshua 1:5-9*

Joshua's success was to be dependent upon his relationship with God. Without reading the word of God it was impossible for Joshua to be able to understand the will or the nature of God and so it was an imperative for Joshua to read and understand.

It was a further imperative that the people should have the law read to them on their feast days and explained in the tabernacle or temple on the Sabbath days. They were to frequently remind themselves of the commandments of God. Such consistent public reading caused an awareness of the word, and power of God, especially for those who had not seen the mighty miracles of God in Egypt or the wilderness. The awareness of the word developed an understanding and a relationship that was vital for the people of God even in those days.

> *For the LORD gives wisdom; From His mouth come knowledge and understanding. Proverbs 2:6*
>
> *The fear of the LORD is the beginning of wisdom, And the knowledge of the Holy One is understanding. Proverbs 9:10*

"The wise men are put to shame, They are dismayed and caught; Behold, they have rejected the word of the LORD, And what kind of wisdom do they have? Jeremiah 8:9

New Testament

It should be no surprise to learn that we are both encouraged and commanded to read the word of God to understand the New Covenant. The benefits of reading the word of God are incalculable.

First there is a clear command to read and study the word. Make no mistake, this is not an optional extra to our Christian experience. The language is clear and the imperative is quite absolute:

Be diligent to present yourself approved to God as a workman who does not need to be ashamed, accurately handling the word of truth. 2 Timothy 2:15

By reading of the word of God we are sanctified as we are "washed by the water of the word."

so that He might sanctify her, having cleansed her by the washing of water with the word, Ephesians 5:26

By the reading of the word of God we are guaranteed wisdom.

Let the word of Christ richly dwell within you, with all wisdom teaching and admonishing one another with psalms and hymns and spiritual songs, singing with thankfulness in your hearts to God. Colossians 3:16

As we read the word of God our faith is developed. Our capacity to hear God, to act on his word and to lead others to him, to witness and be a witness is also dependent upon our reading of the word of God.

How then will they call on Him in whom they have not believed? How will they believe in Him whom they have not heard? And how will they hear without a preacher? How will they preach unless they are sent? Just as it is written, "HOW

> BEAUTIFUL ARE THE FEET OF THOSE WHO BRING GOOD NEWS OF GOOD THINGS!" However, they did not all heed the good news; for Isaiah says, "LORD, WHO HAS BELIEVED OUR REPORT?" So faith comes from hearing, and hearing by the word of Christ. Romans 10:14-17
>
> "And now I commend you to God and to the word of His grace, which is able to build you up and to give you the inheritance among all those who are sanctified. Acts 20:32

Through the reading of the word of God we are changed into his likeness and are enabled more and more to meet the expectations that God has of us.

> But to this day whenever Moses is read, a veil lies over their heart; but whenever a person turns to the Lord, the veil is taken away. Now the Lord is the Spirit, and where the Spirit of the Lord is, there is liberty. But we all, with unveiled face, beholding as in a mirror the glory of the Lord, are being transformed into the same image from glory to glory, just as from the Lord, the Spirit. 2 Corinthians 3:15-18

Through the reading of the word of God we become more capable as ministers of God.

> and that from childhood you have known the sacred writings which are able to give you the wisdom that leads to salvation through faith which is in Christ Jesus. All Scripture is inspired by God and profitable for teaching, for reproof, for correction, for training in righteousness; so that the man of God may be adequate, equipped for every good work. 2 Timothy 3:15-17

Without the reading of the word of God, it is impossible for us to understand the will and purpose of God for our lives, in anything more than very broad terms. This New Covenant is written upon our hearts (Jeremiah 31:31-34, Hebrews 8:7-13), but this does not do away with the teaching or preaching of the word of God. Although we all become aware of God and his law through our conscience, we still need the ministry of the spirit of God in our lives.

God has given us the ministry gifts to guarantee our proper understanding, and perfection in him to enable us to get on with the work he has given us, as we represent him (Ephesians 4:7-16, note Vs. 11-12).

> *And He gave some as apostles, and some as prophets, and some as evangelists, and some as pastors and teachers, for the equipping of the saints for the work of service, to the building up of the body of Christ; Ephesians 4:11-12*

The list of benefits to us from reading the word of God is almost inexhaustible. Psalm 119:1-176 is one of the best lists of the benefits of understanding the word of God. The reading of the word of God guarantees peace, comfort, understanding, maturity, and a huge range of other benefits.

Sadly, because of our familiarity with the word of God, we often fail to see what is really happening, especially when we accept and agree with it without taking the time or effort to understand it. When we read the word of God we are affirming our acceptance of the Covenant with God. We are showing our willingness to participate in all that God is offering to us, or our acceptance of what he has said.

This book, the Bible, is not the work of a psychologist, nor of a single writer. It is not a novel, nor is it a simple piece of historical writing. It is a legally binding document in spiritual terms and must be understood in this manner[41], regardless of any other significance we may wish to place upon it.

The Bible must be accepted in total or rejected in total by all who read it. Our response to it will determine our relationship with God

---

[41] My comment, while true, is also contextual. The bible also has literary, historical, and poetical relevance, and in so many other disciplines that cannot be disregarded.

and the benefits we can enjoy at this present time. The penalties we will receive for our foolishness by rejecting the Covenant that God has offered us is truly severe.

The greatest benefit of reading the word of God comes to us when our reading is borne out of our relationship with Jesus. Without a relationship with him, the benefits of reading and sitting under the preaching or teaching of the word of God is almost pointless. Without a relationship with God the Bible will seem like just another book, and for many it is a dull, confusing, and boring book at that.

The only relationship that is open to us is that of the "NEW (COVENANT) TESTAMENT" relationship with him. This demands the frequent reading of the word of God. It begins with the reading of the word of God, the acceptance of the word and all the truths that it contains.

We must acknowledge our own sinfulness, and show a desire to enter a relationship with God. We need to see God our Father as the benevolent conquering Great King and ourselves as the Vassal King with Christ. To submit to him as such is the start of a wonderful relationship and the beginning of a spiritual development of the truths contained in The Covenant of God.

An Application

The reading of the word of God is not just a spiritual exercise, nor is it a matter of learning about Jesus, understanding doctrine or the exercise of self-discipline, good as all of those purposes are. Reading the word of God is a matter of understanding our rights and relationship with God.

The more we read the word of God, the more we are changed into his image, the more we are able to understand his will, the more we are able be what we are created to be, and the better we are able to enjoy the rights and responsibilities of the blood covenant relationship we have entered into.

Further the more we read the less likely we are to offend God and release His blessing into us.

There is nothing that a man or woman can study that is of more value than the study of the word of God.

With all due respect to the medical profession one can study for seven years to become a doctor and at best can do little more than diagnose symptoms and prescribe medication to alleviate the symptoms that sometimes heal the sick.

The Study of the word of God releases salvation, healing, deliverance and begins our relationship with God, change the present and future of those we come in contact as well as experiencing God's blessings for ourselves.

End Of Chapter Questions

1. List five benefits of reading the word of God in light of Blood Covenant principles. List them in order of personal preference and explain their value.

Chapter 11:

The Seal Of The Covenant

A Historical Perspective

Once the Covenant Ceremony is completed everyone goes home. The Covenant is a reality for everyone and it cannot be annulled.

All those involved in the Blood Covenant will remember their role in it.

The memorials will ensure that the people will remember the covenant for all time. The commemorative feast will provide an annual reminder to everyone of their covenant relationship along with the reading of the covenant conditions, laws, and blessings.

The memorial gifts will also serve as permanent reminder for the people of this new relationship and provide security for them.

The gifts exchanged between the Covenant Heads serve as personal reminders of the covenant. The clothing, the suit of armour and the weapons, will be hung on a wall in the palace as reminders to the Vassal of their Covenant. Other visiting Covenant Heads or other important visitors would see them daily.

The personal covenant gift as a prized possession of the covenant heads serves as a permanent reminder of their relationship and who they are in Covenant with.

The most important and personal reminder of the Covenant for the covenant heads was the Seal of the covenant. The Seal of the Covenant, the scar left on the arm of the covenant partners, formed from the "cut" when they cut the Covenant with each other. As they cut their flesh the wound was bound in such a way as to leave a permanent scar on their arms.

Whenever the Covenant partners see their scar, no matter where they are or what they are doing they are reminded of their Covenant.

Whenever they reach out their hand they will expose the scar on their wrist and be reminded of their Covenant. Whenever they bathe, they will see the scar and be reminded of their Covenant. As they reach for food or drink, they will see their scar and be reminded of their Covenant relationship. Whenever they change their clothing, retire at night, or rise in the morning, the first and last thing they will see is the Seal of the Covenant.

The scar itself served several purposes, as it was a permanent scar on the arms of the covenant partners. In part this was for identification. In many cases the scar was bound in a certain way leave a specific shaped scar. This was as effective in identifying the mark of the Great King as a mark from a branding iron is to identifying the owner of an animal. It was as effective as the Royal Seal on a parchment. Nothing and no-one would dare to break, erase or challenge a royal seal. In the same way, no-one would challenge the authority or rights of the Vassal of a Great King once they were identified as a Vassal of the king, the scar served this purpose. It was so specific that it would stand as the authority of the Great King.

Another of the many benefits of this seal was to grant access to places and people that would otherwise be forbidden to the Vassal King. As a Covenant partner, the Vassal has instant access to all the places, peoples, tribes, and countries that the Great King has access to. This access was granted simply by showing his scar, the Seal of the Covenant. For the Vassal King this was a major advantage, especially as he was the lesser king. His Covenant Seal opened doors to him that would otherwise be impossible to open.

It also helped to provide protection, as it would serve to advise strangers that this Vassal was in a covenant relationship with a Great King who was duty bound to protect him. In a foreign country this could be of great benefit if the Vassal found himself under attack, he would only need to show his seal. Instantly he is identified as a man in Covenant. At least two armies are at his disposal, his own and the armies of his Covenant partner. As the Great King would be a mighty king with powerful armies the Vassal King would often be left alone even if his attackers were not familiar with the Great King or his mark. The attackers would think twice before taking on so important and powerful a stranger with a seal of the covenant.

Occasionally the Vassal King was used as an emissary of the Great King in his dealings with his other Vassals or with kings or leaders of other nations. Although under other circumstances the Vassal may not be welcome and his life could be forfeit for entering the country. His Covenant Seal would serve to grant him immunity from harm in the foreign country. Failure to respect this seal was an act of war and punishable only by the death of the offender and often his entire family or tribe.

The covenant seal was, for the Vassal King, much the same as diplomatic envoy's passport, granting immunity in the nation to which he has been appointed an ambassador.

These laws were recognized in all the East and Middle Eastern countries. Amazingly similar principles apply in many African, North, and South American countries, particularly amongst the tribal groups. These principles appear to have a universal acceptance.

Old Testament

For the Jew there was a Seal of the Covenant. This seal was a physical scar that. This is not fanciful typology, it is quite clear that the scar of circumcision is the seal of the covenant in the Old Testament.

> *"And you shall be circumcised in the flesh of your foreskin, and it shall be the sign of the covenant between Me and you. Genesis 17:11*

For the Jew the covenant seal was the sign of circumcision in all the males of Israel. Circumcision provided a twofold application. Firstly the memorial gift to God as we have already seen and second, it provided the Seal of the Covenant.

> *God said further to Abraham, "Now as for you, you shall keep My covenant, you and your descendants after you throughout their generations. "This is My covenant, which you shall keep, between Me and you and your descendants after you: every male among you shall be circumcised. "And you shall be circumcised in the flesh of your foreskin, and it shall be the sign of the covenant between Me and you. "And every male among you who is eight days old shall be circumcised throughout your generations, a servant who is born in the house or who is bought with money from any foreigner, who is not of your descendants. "A servant who is born in your house or who is bought with your money shall surely be circumcised; thus shall My covenant be in your flesh for an everlasting covenant. "But an uncircumcised male who is not circumcised in the flesh of his foreskin, that person shall be cut off from his people; he has broken My covenant." Genesis 17:9-14*

As long as the Jew continued to circumcise the flesh of the fore-skin of the males, they had their own Seal of the Covenant and they enjoyed protection from God.

New Testament

As Christians we also have a Seal of the Covenant. It is as real as the Jews circumcision is. In fact it is called a circumcision, but it is very different. Our scar is "Seal of the Covenant." Our seal is invisible. It is not on our arms, nor has it been cut in our flesh, but we have a Seal of the Covenant that is as real and effective and as personal as the Jews "Seal of the Covenant." It is not just for men but also for men and women. Our circumcision is a circumcision of the heart.

> *For he is not a Jew who is one outwardly, nor is circumcision that which is outward in the flesh. But he is a Jew who is one inwardly; and circumcision is that which is of the heart, by the Spirit, not by the letter; and his praise is not from men, but from God. Romans 2:28-29*

Romans ch 4 gives us considerable detail of the circumcision of the heart. God makes it clear that it is the state of the heart and our faith in Jesus that makes us people of faith, people of God and as such, the children of Abraham.

We as people of faith, are the children of Abraham, we are Covenant heirs. We are also the heirs of a better Covenant. Just as Abraham was the Covenant Head and the male Jews all bore the mark of circumcision, Jesus is our Covenant Head and we also bear a mark of circumcision.

Our Identity

Our seal of the covenant is the Holy Spirit. Not a seal that will leave a scar, nor will there be any damage to any tissue. This scar will be physically invisible. Indeed rather than damage, this seal will bring healing and goodness with beauty and freedom. Yet this seal is as sure and effective as any visible seal can be.

> *In Him, you also, after listening to the message of truth, the gospel of your salvation--having also believed, you were sealed in Him with the Holy Spirit of promise, Ephesians 1:13*

> *Now He who establishes us with you in Christ and anointed us is God, who also sealed us and gave us the Spirit in our hearts as a pledge. 2 Corinthians 1:21-22*

Paul warns of the need to be careful because of the fact of the seal. The Seal of the Covenant, is God himself, He is sensitive to the things we do and the things we say. We are sealed by the Holy Spirit and we are cautioned not to offend him.

> *Do not grieve the Holy Spirit of God, by whom you were sealed for the day of redemption. Ephesians 4:30*

This seal is as effective for us as a Covenant Seal and serves the same purposes, whilst providing several other advantages over the physical scar of the Seal of the Covenant.

We need to recognize the Seal of the Covenant for who He is, the Holy Spirit himself. God no longer depends on the physical scarring of the human body. Now he looks to us, as temples of the Holy Spirit and he places within our being the Seal of the Covenant, the Spirit of God. God Himself, the Great King of the Covenant Heads, has also become the Seal of the Covenant.

> *Or do you not know that your body is a temple of the Holy Spirit who is in you, whom you have from God, and that you are not your own? 1 Corinthians 6:19*

This is worth considering for a moment. This is God's Covenant. He is the Covenant. He has exchanged himself for us in this Covenant. He is the Covenant sacrifice. He is the Covenant Gift. He is the armour of God and He is the clothing that is exchanged. He is the memorial meal and God is also the Covenant Seal.

Our whole Covenant relationship with God is totally dependent on Him for every part of the Covenant itself. He is the provider of every part of this covenant.

The Seal of the Covenant is the Holy Spirit. It is by this seal that we are recognized by God as His (Romans 8:16)

> *The Spirit Himself testifies with our spirit that we are children of God, Romans 8:16*

It is the very Holy Spirit who witnesses with our spirit that we are children of God (Note also Galatians 4:6; 1 John 3:24; 1 John 4:13; 1 John 5:6).

God is not the only one to recognize us by His Spirit. The fact is that very often our spirit "bears witness" also with the spirit of another who is also sealed with the Spirit of God. Without knowing anything about them somehow we are able to recognize that this person is a Christian.

Our Responsibility

It is by the Spirit of God that we have access to places that otherwise would be inaccessible to us. We have access to the very throne room of God itself. By the spirit of God, through the blood of Jesus we are able to enter the holiest of all that is the Holy of Holies, the very throne room of God in heaven itself.

> *And the Holy Spirit also testifies to us; for after saying, "THIS IS THE COVENANT THAT I WILL MAKE WITH THEM AFTER THOSE DAYS, SAYS THE LORD: I WILL PUT MY LAWS UPON THEIR HEART, AND ON THEIR MIND I WILL WRITE THEM," He then says, "AND THEIR SINS AND THEIR LAWLESS DEEDS I WILL REMEMBER NO MORE." Now where there is forgiveness of these things, there is no longer any offering for sin. Therefore, brethren, since we have confidence to enter the holy place by the blood of Jesus, Hebrews 10:15-19*

Note also Ephesians 2:11-22, and Ephesians 3:10-12, and Romans 5:1-5.

By the Spirit of God we have access to God at any time. Evidently we are free to come before God. No matter where we are, no matter what we are doing, we not only have access to the holy of holies, we have access to God himself.

This is not a one-way deal. Not only does Jesus have access to us at all times, but it is also our covenant right to have instant and free access to the Great King at all time. As much as Jesus has access to us, we also have access to Him.

> *teaching them to observe all that I commanded you; and lo, I am with you always, even to the end of the age." Matthew 28:20*

> *Make sure that your character is free from the love of money, being content with what you have; for He Himself has said, "I WILL NEVER DESERT YOU, NOR WILL I EVER FORSAKE YOU," Hebrews 13:5*

Jesus always has access to us. He is able to deal with us, as he requires, in blessing, direction, or correction. Whenever he wishes to speak with us he does, and he demands our attention at all times.

Not only do we have access to God at any time, but also, through the Spirit of God, we have access to people and places that would otherwise be inaccessible. The Holy Spirit send us to people and places as "Christ's ambassadors". As he does we will find that doors and opportunities will open to us.

> *Therefore, we are ambassadors for Christ, as though God were making an appeal through us; we beg you on behalf of Christ, be reconciled to God. 2 Corinthians 5:20*

In Acts 8:26-40. We read of Philip as he is sent to the Ethiopian eunuch, he converts and baptises him, and is sent and actually transported by the Spirit of God to Azotus and Caesarea.

In Acts 10:1 to Acts 11:18. We read of the conversion of Cornelius and his household. Peter is sent to them by the Spirit of God as an Ambassador. Without God's direct intervention, such an opportunity would never have been possible. Cornelius was a Gentile and as such not to be dealt with in religious matters. God saw things differently and used Peter to bring his Blood Covenant to the Gentile world through Peter and Cornelius.

Each of Paul's missionary journeys were made possible only because of the Spirit of God directed him. To have travelled as he did, to do the things he did without divine intervention in those days was impossible, yet, Paul was able to travel through much of the Roman Empire to bring the message of the Gospel to kings, soldiers, individuals and nations and finally to Rome and the throne of Caesar himself. He was able to go where God sent him in spite of shipwrecks, imprisonment, torture, pain, poverty, wealth and success. Paul was willing and God sent him.

Livingstone and Stanley

Both Dr. Livingstone and Henry Morton Stanley are reported to have cut covenants while Livingstone explored Africa. Later when Stanley searched for him, continued his work.

As Henry Morton Stanley attempted to make his way into Africa he found at first that he was not accepted. His bearers were killed or frightened off and he could make no advance into the country of Africa.

His chief bearer advised him of the Blood Covenant and told him about Blood Covenant, Stanley decided to enter a Covenant relationship with one of the Great Chiefs of Africa. As a result of this he was able to go into Africa and find Livingstone. Later when he retuned to Africa to follow in Dr. Livingstone's footsteps it was through blood covenant principles that he was able to take the gospel into the interior.

Unbeknown to Stanley, the chief he determined to enter Covenant with was the mightiest chief in all Africa and one of the most feared. Eventually, Stanley entered into Blood Covenant with him and found instant access to most of Africa.

As soon as the other tribes learnt who he was in Covenant with, Stanley found that their fear of his Covenant partner was great, that Stanley was seen as a great chief, thus he was held in absolute esteem. Since he was seen as worthy of being in Covenant with the mighty chief, and he was a mighty chief himself, not to be taken lightly.

Stanley is said to have cut over 50 Covenants with different chiefs in Africa. As a result of this he brought the Gospel to the "darkest continent," producing an unprecedented time of peace. Inadvertently he had, because of "Covenant Law," brought many warring tribes together as Covenant partners. They all became

"Covenant Brothers" through his relationship. They saw him as a great warrior chief and as such they had no choice but to accept his God as their God.

There are many records of people who have listened to the voice of the Spirit of God. Dr Livingstone and Stanley stand out as men who entered into blood covenant with man bringing there God with them, and probably inadvertently for the may not have understood the full impact of what they were doing. They enjoyed the benefits throughout their ministry in Africa bringing the Gospel and medicine to areas unexplored and undiscovered by man at that time.

There is potential to misunderstand a powerful truth here. While Livingstone and Stanley's covenants were physical, and there were clearly physical responses to their covenants, they had spiritual impact also.

The power and strength of Blood Covenant is spiritual. The spiritual strength of Blood Covenant is determined the spiritual empowerment of those entering into the covenant. In their case Almighty God Himself. They were his representatives. Both Livingstone and Stanley would have it no other way. In a real sense they saw staggering results from their exploits; so too can we, as seen in other historical leaders.

George Whitefield, an open air preacher from 1714-1770 was able to draw huge crowds. They were of such a size that they were measured by the acre that they covered rather than numbers. It is reported that he could be heard by up to 30,000 people at a time when it was not possible to magnify ones voice. He preached through England, Wales, and America and was a personal friend of Benjamin Franklin.

John Wesley travelled over 400,000 kilometres on horseback reaching men and women of all ages, races and stations in life. He brought the gospel to many, developing a new denomination that would shake Christendom and the political structure of the United Kingdom and the empire.

Finney, Calvin, Spurgeon and many others bringing revival to the world have been able to do so with a relative freedom that only comes when God is doing the bidding, not only revival but teaching that brought change to the church that continues unto today.

This same right is given, in the same measure, to women as to men. One of the most powerful female ministries was Aimee Semple McPherson. She was able, due to the Blood Covenant, to preach, teach and raise a church that became an international ministry, the International Church of the Foursquare Gospel.

Katherine Khulman an extravagant and effective minister operated effectively because of blood covenant relationship.

Billy Graham has travelled the world spreading the gospel of Jesus Christ and taking his crusades into nations where no other man could take it. He has brought Christianity to unnumbered hundreds and thousands and possibly millions through his crusades. His work and his ongoing ministry, like others, could not have reached the world in evangelism, raising churches and spreading the Gospel without Blood Covenant

Oral Roberts brought the message of Pentecost to many nations at a time when it was considered to be demonic by the established church. In spite of opposition he opened to the church the truths of the Pentecostal message, bring healing and deliverance to thousands and in his wake new churches sprang up while old churches found life,

Without his Seal of the Covenant, Brother Andrew could not have had access or opportunity to take Bibles to Russia and other Communist states.

The grand parade of saints and achievers in Hebrews ch. 11 are but a minute fraction of those who, because of the seal of the spirit of

God, have been able to defy all that man and Satan has used to hinder them.

Without the intervention of the Holy Spirit and the rights of the Blood Covenant of God, these men and women of God could not have achieved for God the things that they did.

Doubtless many of them new little of the underlying reason for their success, attributing it to the work of the Holy Spirit, and rightly so, but often not understanding that the reason for there success lay much more in the Blood Covenant relationship.

How much more could they have achieved if they, in ignorance, achieved so much. These are our examples, they illustrate to us how much more can we achieve in a world still desperately needing the Gospel.

An Application

Satan, the enemy of God and man, is powerless against the people of God when they are led by the Spirit of God. He realises that he is in opposition to the Holy Spirit. He recognizes the Seal of the Covenant, which is the Holy Ghost, in those people who have chosen to enter into a Covenant relationship with God.

Just as the great chiefs of Africa saw the seal of the covenant on David Livingstone and Henry Morton Stanley and had to respond to that seal so also does Satan. When he comes into contact with a Christian and sees the seal of God he knows that to interfere with this life is to interfere with God.

As in all biblical truths, blood covenant truths are absolute. However they are only as effective in our lives to the extent we understand them. As the more we understand the better we bring our lives into alignment with the word of God, principles, and the power of God. It is a matter of relationship.

Satan knows he is powerless to stop the Christian who understands his Covenant relationships, more importantly God knows that Satan is powerless to stop the Christian.

Nothing but our ignorance of truth is strong enough to stand between the Christian and the calling that God has for him. Sadly, it is often the Christian who fails to realise the truth of the matter. Consequently many Christians are deceived by Satan into believing that they are not good enough or that they cannot be what they were created for. Often defeat is seen at every turn in trying to fulfil God's will, although the defeat is a trick because we are tricked we fail.

Instead we should be *looking to Jesus the author and finisher of our faith* and grasp an understanding of who and what we are then we are able to rise above the difficulties that we face rather then fall under the weight of them.

I have had wonderful opportunities to minister the word of God as an ambassador for Christ in England, the United States, Kenya, India, Myanmar, Thailand, Nepal, China, Papua New Guinea, Fiji, New Zealand and Australia. This did not occur because I am a wonderful preacher. It is only in the last few years that I have realised that I am able to do such things because of my blood covenant seal. Where God will send me, I will go.

Indeed, I have made the same declaration as so many others in the past "if God will provide I will go". But now I go because God has said and if He commands He will provide from his blood covenant provision.

What ever God has called you to it is because He has created you to do it, to go, to achieve and He is with you to save and to deliver, and to bring to pass whatever He has spoken into your life.

You have the seal of God because your heart is circumcised. You have the seal of God, which is the Spirit of God and the Spirit of God can will, and shall strengthen, and enable us in all he asks us to do. As Christians it is our part to realise that He has called us to do greater things than He did. There is a vast resource open to us.

Paul tells us that we are able to do anything that Jesus asks of us.

> *I can do all things through Him who strengthens me. Philippians 4:13*

> *"Believe Me that I am in the Father and the Father is in Me; otherwise believe because of the works themselves. "Truly, truly, I say to you, he who believes in Me, the works that I do, he will do also; and greater works than these he will do; because I go to the Father. "Whatever you ask in My name, that will I do, so that the Father may be glorified in the Son. "If you ask Me anything in My name, I will do it. John 14:11-14*

> *from whom every family in heaven and on earth derives its name, that He would grant you, according to the riches of His glory, to be strengthened with power through His Spirit in the inner man, so that Christ may dwell in your hearts through faith; and that you, being rooted and grounded in love, may be able to comprehend with all the saints what is the breadth and length and height and depth, and to know the love of Christ which surpasses knowledge, that you may be filled up to all the fullness of God. Now to Him who is able to do far more abundantly beyond all that we ask or think, according to the power that works within us, to Him be the glory in the church and in Christ Jesus to all generations forever and ever. Amen. Ephesians 3:15-21*

Fellow Christian, you do not need to be defeated any more! Jesus has declared that we are over comers and indeed more than over comers. We can, we should be, and we are, successful in all that we do in him.

> *You are from God, little children, and have overcome them; because greater is He who is in you than he who is in the world. 1 John 4:4*

We can know where Jesus wants us to go. We can know what he wants us to do, simply because he tells us through the Holy Spirit. We are empowered to do his will, through the Holy Spirit, especially after the baptism in the Holy Spirit.

> *but you will receive power when the Holy Spirit has come upon you; and you shall be My witnesses both in Jerusalem, and in all Judea and Samaria, and even to the remotest part of the earth." Acts 1:8*

We are given all the ability and power to do anything that Jesus asks us to do. This was his last promise to us according to Matthew 28:18-20, Mark 16:15-19, Luke 24:46-49 and Acts 1:8. It is the evidence of the Seal of the Covenant of God.

End Of Chapter Questions

1. The seal of the covenant leaves a permanent scar on the wrist of the member. It served several purposes, discuss two of them.
2. What was the old testament Seal of the Covenant?
3. Discuss the value of the Covenant Seal to the modern day saint?

Chapter 12:

The Covenant Lawyer

Historical Perspective

When the kings of countries entered into blood covenant the lesser king and his people must accept the laws of the Great King as their law. These laws had been discussed and understood long before the ceremony took place. They were proclaimed and affirmed publicly during the ceremony. The Vassal king had a vested interest in understanding these laws, his continued role as a king, and his life, and the life of his family depended on his total acceptance of the new laws.

As already stated, the new laws applied not just to the king but to his people as well. Here a difficulty could arise. While the kings had a clear understanding of the new laws, often the people did not. Like us, thy relied on memory, familiarity and common sense and just as it is for us, this was not always reliable. People forgot, they made mistakes, sometimes they did not understand the consequences of their actions or out of ignorance people broke the law. But ignorance of the law is no excuse and in many cases people would break covenant law, at the cost of their life. Occasionally this would strain the relationship between the two kingdoms which could bring them close to war.

To resolve this situation people were appointed to become "expert" in Covenant Law. They were known as "Covenant Lawyers." It was their job to make sure that each of the Covenant partners knew of and understood their rights and responsibilities.

The laws were many and it was difficult to remember everything, especially if the Vassal was conquered by a significantly greater king. The new laws and ceremonial differences could be substantial and complicated. The process of educating the Vassal and his people to the new laws could be long and complicated. The new legal rights and responsibilities may be many and varied depending on the status of the Covenant Heads, the reason that they had entered the Covenant, and the culture they came from.

Differences in cultural values could easily complicate relationships between peoples. Unfamiliarity with the cultural differences could lead to a clash as easily then as it can today, for what is socially acceptable in one culture may be deeply offensive in another culture. Without realising it one could violate the Covenant, especially if the Vassal has to accept a new set of covenant standards.

Even after the public reading of the law, the Vassal or his leaders could be ignorant, or forgetful of their rights, or their benefits and responsibilities. This lack of knowledge could lead to unnecessary suffering or difficulty for the Vassal and/or his people.

Lack of knowledge could easily cause a violation of the Covenant simply out of ignorance. Such a violation could demand the life of the Covenant breaker. The Covenant Lawyer was in the best position to step in to prevent these misunderstandings and difficulties.

The Covenant Lawyer would move from partner to partner, explaining his rights and responsibilities and would be available to clear up any misunderstandings in the Covenant contract.

When the covenant incorporated two nations rather than tribes or families the covenant lawyer would take the dual role of both advising the king while moving from town to town, explaining the law and passing judgement as appropriate among the people.

Old Testament

God provided a Covenant Lawyer in the Old Testament days. A man was appointed to move from place to place as required by covenant law, reminding the people of their responsibilities, cautioning them of the consequences of their failures if they chose not to follow God's ways, advising them of the benefits available to them as the people chose to live in harmony with God's law.

The Old Testament prophet filled this role. He moved from town to town, village to village exhorting and warning the kings, priests and people to take heed of the word of God to their own lives. He would often issue fresh warnings and remind the people of the promises of God.

The messages of Jeremiah, Isaiah, Micah, indeed all of the Old Testament Prophets was a message to bring the Jews, the people of God to repentance and or blessing, reminding them of their standing with God and of their Covenant relationship.

> *"You gave Your good Spirit to instruct them, Your manna You did not withhold from their mouth, And You gave them water for their thirst. Nehemiah 9:20.*
>
> *"I will put My Spirit within you and cause you to walk in My statutes, and you will be careful to observe My ordinances. Ezekiel 36:27*
>
> *for no prophecy was ever made by an act of human will, but men moved by the Holy Spirit spoke from God. 2 Peter 1:21*

Most the Old Testament was written by these Covenant Lawyers. Most of their national prophecy had to do with the law and revealing the truths and consequences of the law

New Testament

As partners of the New Covenant we need a Covenant Lawyer. Perhaps as 21st century Christians we need one even more so than the Old Testament saints did. As with so many covenant partners in the past we are all too often quite unaware of all God has given to us.

Over the last 100 years so much change has occurred in our lives. Knowledge has increased exponentially. To think that until the end of the 19th Century travel, communication, and other developments had changed little since the time of Jesus. In less than a century we have placed a man on the moon, sent satellites to distant planets and galaxies, found cures for diseases, increased longevity for many, teach more to the average schoolchild than our forebears learned in a lifetime, technological advances exceed our wildest expectations in computerisation, robotics, communications, medicines and so on, but the process has had a devastating effect.

Rather than gaining better understanding, the choices offered seem to bring greater confusion. Our values are less clear, our boundaries are no longer well defined, thus making the need of the lawyer greater today than in the past. Our inclination to question authority permeates into the church and we find more excuses to evade responsibility.

Our need is indeed greater; God knew this and gave us a greater Covenant Lawyer, the Holy Spirit. Of course, He has always been the Covenant Lawyer; for it was the Holy Spirit who spoke through the Old Testament prophet; he used men then even as he uses men now.

> *for no prophecy was ever made by an act of human will, but men moved by the Holy Spirit spoke from God. 2 Peter 1:21*

The difference is that now he is our personal Covenant Lawyer rather than a "national" covenant lawyer.

Jesus could not have made the point clearer to us than He did in His major discourse on the role of the Holy Spirit in our lives in the Gospel of John chapters 14-16. It is especially helpful to note the use of the Greek word "*paraclete*[42]" and the way it is translated into English.

---

[42] G3875 parakletos par-ak'-lay-tos: An intercessor, consoler: - advocate, comforter. Strong's exhaustive Concordance by James Strong, S.T.D., LL.D., 1890.

The most correct is the term Advocate,[43] more commonly used in legal terms as a lawyer. Jesus explained to the disciples that one of the roles of the Holy Spirit in the lives of the believers after his crucifixion is that of an "Advocate[44]. "

It is the Holy Spirit who will be leading, guiding and teaching the apostles and all Christians.

> *John 16:7 WNT "Yet it is the truth that I am telling you--it is to your advantage that I go away. For unless I go away, the Advocate will not come to you; but if I go, I will send Him to you. 1912 Weymouth New Testament*
>
> *Some of His disciples then said to one another, "What is this thing He is telling us, 'A little while, and you will not see Me'; and again a little while, and you will see Me'; and, 'because I go to the Father'?" So they were saying, "What is this that He says, 'A little while'? We do not know what He is talking about." Jesus knew that they wished to question Him, and He said to them, "Are you deliberating together about this, that I said, 'A little while, and you will not see Me, and again a little while, and you will see Me'? "Truly, truly, I say to you, that you will weep and lament, but the world will rejoice; you will grieve, but your grief will be turned into joy. "Whenever a woman is in labor she has pain, because her hour has come; but when she gives birth to the child, she no longer remembers the anguish because of the joy that a child has been born into the world. "Therefore you too have grief now; but I will see*

---

[43] The following expressions are most commonly used in the translation of the word "paraklete" The Holy Spirit, Paraclete, Friend, Helper, Counselor, Advocate, Comforter.

[44] Advocate: AD'VOCATE, n. [L. advocatus, from advoco, to call for, to plead for; of ad and voco, to call.] Advocate, in its primary sense, signifies, one who pleads the cause of another in a court of civil law. Hence, One who pleads the cause of another before any tribunal or judicial court, as a barrister in the English courts. We say, a man is a learned lawyer and an able advocate. Noah Webster's 1828 Dictionary of American English

you again, and your heart will rejoice, and no one will take your joy away from you. "In that day you will not question Me about anything. Truly, truly, I say to you, if you ask the Father for anything in My name, He will give it to you. John 16:17-23

The major difference between the role of the Holy Spirit as the covenant lawyer in the Old Testament and the New Testament is that in the Old Testament His role was primarily to the nations rather than a personal ministry. In the New Testament His role is primarily to individuals, an intensely personal ministry.

The Holy Spirit has intimate knowledge of the saints even as Jesus had such a relationship and knowledge of His disciples.

This role of the Holy Spirit, as the adviser and guide, is to ensure that we are aware of our rights and privileges, to see that we accept our responsibilities and keep us aware of our relationship, with Jesus and each other.

This is further emphasised in the following scriptures.

> *for the Holy Spirit will teach you in that very hour what you ought to say." Luke 12:12*
>
> *"But the Helper, the Holy Spirit, whom the Father will send in My name, He will teach you all things, and bring to your remembrance all that I said to you. John 14:26*
>
> *"When the Helper comes, whom I will send to you from the Father, that is the Spirit of truth who proceeds from the Father, He will testify about Me, John 15:26*
>
> *"But when He, the Spirit of truth, comes, He will guide you into all the truth; for He will not speak on His own initiative, but whatever He hears, He will speak; and He will disclose to you what is to come. John 16:13*
>
> *The Spirit Himself testifies with our spirit that we are children of God, Romans 8:16*

which things we also speak, not in words taught by human wisdom, but in those taught by the Spirit, combining spiritual thoughts with spiritual words. 1 Corinthians 2:13

As for you, the anointing which you received from Him abides in you, and you have no need for anyone to teach you; but as His anointing teaches you about all things, and is true and is not a lie, and just as it has taught you, you abide in Him. 1 John 2:27

The Holy Spirit plays a major role in our life. However these verses, often taken in isolation, come together under the banner of the Covenant in a new dimension, presenting the Holy Spirit as our Blood Covenant Lawyer. This is clear to us from the scriptures, both from the Old[45] and the New Testament

While it is true that the Holy Spirit is our teacher who leads us into all truth and He does so both individually and corporately, for he never teaches the individual at the expense of the ministry gifts (as outlined in Ephesians 4:11-13). The roles of the pastor, teacher, evangelist, prophet and apostle are enabled through the Holy Spirit. This is further reinforced in 1 Corinthians 12:1-31, and in Romans 12:3-8 where the various ministries of the Spirit are presented and explained. Certainly, the primary place for the exercise of the ministry gifts is through the church, yet we must never limit the use of these gifts to church meetings. The apostles were free to exercise the gifts in public, we should be free to do so also.[46]

---

[45] Just two from the Old Testament:Nehemiah 9:20 You gave your good spirit to instruct them, and did not withhold your manna from their mouths, and gave them water for their thirst. Ezekiel 36:27 I will put my spirit within you, and make you follow my statutes and be careful to observe my ordinances.

[46] Note Peter and his "healing shadow" Acts 5:15-16; Peter and John at the temple healing the lame man, Acts 3; Pauls Lystra healing a lame man, Acts 14:8; and many others throughout the New Testament, not to mention the fact that Jesus almost always worked publically, all evidence of the use of the ministry gifts outside of the Church.

This role as Covenant Lawyer brings added dimension of His work to us and helps to explain why He is so involved with our daily lives, and not just our church lives. This role explains why it is that He is always present to teach us both simple and deep truths at any moment that we are prepared to receive it. It is His ministry to make sure that we understand our relationship with God to the best possible advantage to all concerned.

Our God wants us to understand his Covenant and our responsibilities to it and our benefits from it and the only person conversant enough with all the details of the Covenant is God himself. Therefore, it must fall to him to make sure that we do understand.

The Holy Spirit therefore will come and "teach us all things" that Jesus wants us to know.

> *John 14:26 But the Advocate, the Holy Spirit, whom the Father will send in my name, will teach you everything, and remind you of all that I have said to you.*
>
> *1 John 2:27 As for you, the anointing that you received from him abides in you, and so you do not need anyone to teach you. But as his anointing teaches you about all things, and is true and is not a lie, and just as it has taught you, abide in him.*

Our God wants us to understand the Covenant so that we will not violate the laws of the Covenant. The better we understand the less risk that we will shirk our responsibility to it, and therefore we will not incur His displeasure, or ultimately, if we do not respond to Him, find ourselves on the wrong end of his discipline[47]. Indeed

---

[47] and you have forgotten the exhortation which is addressed to you as sons, "MY SON, DO NOT REGARD LIGHTLY THE DISCIPLINE OF THE LORD, NOR FAINT WHEN YOU ARE REPROVED BY HIM; FOR THOSE WHOM THE LORD LOVES HE DISCIPLINES, AND HE SCOURGES EVERY SON WHOM HE RECEIVES." It is for discipline that you endure; God deals with you as with sons; for what son is there whom his father does not discipline? But if you are without discipline, of which all have become partakers, then you are illegitimate children and not sons. Hebrews 12:5-8

we will find ourselves walking in his blessing more and more as we are able to walk in understanding.

It is not simply a matter of meeting a set of rules and regulations just to keep a God somewhere up there happy. When we allow ourselves to become sensitive to the work of the Holy Spirit in our lives we will become increasingly more sensitive to the will of God and our own relationship with Him as our Covenant Head. We become much better equipped to fulfil the work that he has set out for us which is our life's calling.

The blessing of God upon us will be richer and fuller. We should realise that it is our best interest to see that we do not, in any way, violate the Covenant. The Holy Spirit wants us to receive the maximum possible blessing from God as well as be the best possible blessing to him that we can be.

It is indeed a matter of learning to live our lives as Jesus would live it.

> *Romans 15:29 and I know that when I come to you, I will come in the fullness of the blessing of Christ.*

An Application

Too often we miss the point that our God is involved with every area of our lives and relationships. He has advice on everything from our conduct at work, to our treatment of our families, the way husbands and wives treat each other and our relationship with people both within the church and outside the church. There is no area of legitimate human endeavour where God does not have advice, either directly, indirectly or in principle. As for illegitimate human endeavour he simply says, "Don't."

We cannot remember all of the issues of Blood Covenant, even though it has been written on our heart, nor indeed are we expected to. Instead, we find ourselves confronted, challenged, blessed, and surprised on every turn as our Blood Covenant Lawyer whispers to our heart the things we need to know, sometimes deep things of God.

I am reminded of a friend of mine, I will call him George, who once worked as an auctioneer. At the time of this incident he was a young Christian. Not so much a young man, but a young Christian, naive in the word and ways of God with little more biblical knowledge than the most basic understanding of the 10 commandments and his personal moral code.

Called upon, as he often was, to list and value the contents of an estate George found himself in the work-shed of the house he was evaluating and being challenged to secret away a drill-bit. The drill-bit was of little value to him, it was not something he needed, it was not valuable as it was worth only a few cents, but this was one of those momentary situations where temptation took over and without even thinking he slipped the object into his pocket and continued to work. . .

Quietly the Holy Spirit spoke to Him in the only version of the Word of God that he knew "Thou Shalt Not Steal". George continued to value and list the articles. Some of great value. Some small enough to secret away, of far greater value than the drill-bit. "Thou Shalt Not Steal". Echoed the voice. Moment after moment, time after time the echo came, "Thou Shalt Not Steal".

Finally, in frustration he threw down the drill-bit, listed the item, and declared aloud OK, I get it, I am sorry. George told me a great peace came upon Him, not just the peace of a silenced voice probing his conscience, but the peace that comes from knowing you have done what is right and your heavenly Father is pleased.

So many times the Holy Spirit has spoken to me in quietness, through the TV or in movie. Sometimes while listening to a sermon or song or listening to a conversation, but he speaks. Sometimes in revelation, sometimes in conviction, sometimes quietly and unexpectedly sometimes very loudly he speaks. Always for my good, he speaks.

The word of God declares to us the He will never leave us[48] and He does not. He is always there to speak and to share.

I am so often amazed as I read the word of God. I am suddenly aware of the truths of scripture that have been hidden to me before. We call it "inspiration" or "revelation" and indeed it is. It is also the blood Covenant Lawyer speaking to me.

I am sometimes astounded at a sudden knowledge of a principle of the word of God being opened to me as this Lawyer speaks to me, opening truth even before I have read it, only to find a few days or weeks later the scriptures open the same truths, reinforcing the principles I had been shown a little while before.

I am sure you too have found the same experience as your Covenant Lawyer opens truth to you. Sometimes he is warning against danger, sometimes encouraging towards an unrealised blessing, but always bringing me closer to Jesus. When I hear Him speaking[49] to me it is to change my life, to open a door of opportunity or to provide and entrance into a blessing or to re-direct me from an impending personal disaster.

My heart, like yours, if left unguarded or to its own devices, will prove to be "exceedingly[50] wicked" and yet my heavenly Father is so totally accepting of me. He will take personal interest in protecting me from myself by sending the Covenant Lawyer to deal with me, as much as he can, before the event.

---

[48] Hebrews 13:5

[49] I am using the term "speaking" rather loosely as this takes many forms for all of us, an impression, a thought, a conviction, the opening of scripture or even an audible voice from God. I do not wish to infer some special "spiritual value" on me.

[50] Jer 17:9 The heart *is* deceitful above all *things*, and desperately wicked: who can know it?

End of Chapter Questions

1. Discuss the need of the Blood Covenant lawyer.
2. Which persons in the Old Testament operated as covenant lawyers and how did they do so?
3. Who is the Blood covenant lawyer in the New Testament, and show references that explain his role?

Chapter 13:

The Forgiveness Of The Covenant

There are few places, if any, in the scriptures where the benefits of Blood Covenant are more graphically demonstrated to us than they are with the story of the relationship between David the son of Jesse and Jonathan the son of King Saul. The way this relationship works out between King David and Jonathan's son Mephibosheth is a profound example of the covenant in action.

From 1 Samuel 18:1-4 we can see that David and Jonathan entered into a Covenant to bind their relationship. The fact that Vs 3 says that there was a covenant between them is a part of the evidence. While the whole of the Covenant Ceremony was not demonstrated, we do see enough to know that they are fully committed to each other in a Blood Covenant.

The exchange of Clothing and weapons strongly indicate that it was a blood covenant. The little we know of their lives after this event shows that they had indeed entered into a Blood Covenant. They gave all that they possess to each other, not only in their present time, but also for their ill fated future.

> *Now it came about when he had finished speaking to Saul, that the soul of Jonathan was knit to the soul of David, and Jonathan loved him as himself. Saul took him that day and did not let him return to his father's house. Then Jonathan made a covenant with David because he loved him as himself. Jonathan stripped himself of the robe that was on him and gave it to David, with his armor, including his sword and his bow and his belt. 1 Samuel 18:1-4*

They exchanged their clothing and weapons. All that they owned they gave to the other. All their wealth, all the authority, all the social standing of Jonathan, the son and heir of the King of Israel became the possessions of David, a shepherd boy who became his blood brother.

While great speculation is often made of the few scriptures concerning David and Jonathan, very little is really known of them over the next few years. The few verses concerning them do show their care for each other and the depth of their personal integrity[51].

King Saul insisted that David remain with him. Later Saul became intent on killing David due to his demonic rages of jealousy. Eventually David was forced to go into hiding from Saul, and during this time Jonathan's loyalties were divided between his father and his blood brother, even so he remained faithful to David and their Covenant for the rest of his life.

Jonathan died, with his father, in battle against the Philistines at Gilboa (1 Samuel 31:1-13). As a result David was crowned King of Israel.

> *Then it came about afterwards that David inquired of the LORD, saying, "Shall I go up to one of the cities of Judah?" And the LORD said to him, "Go up." So David said, "Where shall I go up?" And He said, "To Hebron." So David went up there, and his two wives also, Ahinoam the Jezreelitess and Abigail the widow of Nabal the Carmelite. And David brought up his men who were with him, each with his household; and they lived in the cities of Hebron. Then the men of Judah came and there anointed David king over the house of Judah. And they told David, saying, "It was the men of Jabesh-gilead who buried Saul." 2 Samuel 2:1-4*

The announcement of his coronation would bring fear to the remainder of Saul's Family. For many years they had been taught that David was a usurper, he wanted to destroy the family of Saul,

---

[51] The relevant scriptural references concerning David and Jonathan are these: 1 Samuel 18:1-4, 1 Samuel 19:1-7, 1 Samuel 20:1-42, 1 Samuel 23:16-18.

so that he could take the throne for himself. When they heard that David was to become king they ran for their lives. This is an understandable re-action. It was typical in those days that the immediate family and chief advisers of a defeated, deposed or succeeded king should be killed to prevent them from rising up against the new king.

Jonathan's son Mephibosheth was only five years old when this event occurs and upon hearing that David is to be made king, the nurse picked him up by as she ran from the palace. She tripped on the stairs, fell, and crushed Mephibosheth's legs making him lame for the rest of his life (2 Samuel 4:4).

Mephibosheth lived in the plains of Palestine, in a village called Lodebar [52] (2 Samuel ch. 9). The name means "No Pasture"[53] or "A stony Place." It is an appropriate name for the area. Here he became a part of a gang of bandits. He spent his days and nights dreaming of how he could take the kingdom from David, who, he

---

[52] Lo-debar (lo dhebhar): A place in Gilead where dwelt Machir, son of Ammiel, who sheltered Mephibosheth, son of Saul, after that monarch's death (2Sa 9:4), until he was sent for by David. This same Machir met David with supplies when he fled to Gilead from Absalom (2Sa 17:27 f.). Possibly it is the same place as Lidebir in Jos 13:26 (Revised Version margin). No certain identification is possible; but Schumacher (Northern 'Ajlun, 101) found a site with the name Ibdar about 6 1/2 miles East of Umm Qeis, North of the great aqueduct, which may possibly represent the ancient city. Lidebir, at least, seems to be placed on the northern boundary of Gilead. The modern village stands on the southern shoulder of Wady Samar. There is a good spring to the East, a little lower down, while ancient remains are found in the neighborhood.

International Standard Bible Encyclopedia; James Orr, M.A., D.D. General Editor, John L. Nuelsen, D.D., LL.D. Assistant Editor, Edgar Y. Mullins, D.D., LL.D. Assistant Editor, Morris O. Evans, D.D., PhD. Managing Editor, Melvin Grove Kyle, D.D., JJ.D. Revising Editor, Copyright, 1939, by Wm. B. Eerdmans Publishing Co. (now in public domain)

[53] M.G. Easton M.A., D.D., Illustrated Bible Dictionary, Third Edition, published by Thomas Nelson, 1897.

believed, had stolen the kingdom from his father, Jonathan, and from himself.

Although he saw himself as the rightful king of Israel and David as the usurper who had stolen the kingdom from him, he was in fact a cripple, an outlaw both politically and legally. He was an outcast and was constantly hiding from the King's army. Only a very few people knew who Mephibosheth really was as he has been raised as little more than a beggar in a village of outcasts. The secret was very well kept.

Therefore, we take up the story from 2 Samuel 9:1-13. By this time, David had secured his throne and was the undisputed[54] King over Israel. The wars have finished, the country is enjoying peace and security, and now he has time to reflect and his mind turns to his deceased blood brother, Jonathan. Perhaps he longs for the past as he has time to contemplate the future. The king asks if any of Saul's family are still alive

To the best of David's knowledge, all of Saul and Jonathan's family had been killed when David became king. This was the custom of the time. The new king or the captains of his army, often killed off the old family to make sure that there would be no challenge to the authority of the new king. David did not know who Mephibosheth was. As we continue this story, we see that King David is intent on offering blessing on any of the remnant of the house of Saul. This was because of the Covenant he had made with Jonathan.

> *Then David said, "Is there yet anyone left of the house of Saul, that I may show him kindness for Jonathan's sake?" Now there was a servant of the house of Saul whose name was Ziba, and they called him to David; and the king said to him, "Are you Ziba?" And he said, "I am your servant." The king said, "Is*

---

[54] 2 Samuel 8:15 NASB So David reigned over all Israel; and David administered justice and righteousness for all his people.

there not yet anyone of the house of Saul to whom I may show the kindness of God?" And Ziba said to the king, "There is still a son of Jonathan who is crippled in both feet." So the king said to him, "Where is he?" And Ziba said to the king, "Behold, he is in the house of Machir the son of Ammiel in Lo-debar." Then King David sent and brought him from the house of Machir the son of Ammiel, from Lo-debar. Mephibosheth, the son of Jonathan the son of Saul, came to David and fell on his face and prostrated himself. And David said, "Mephibosheth." And he said, "Here is your servant!" David said to him, "Do not fear, for I will surely show kindness to you for the sake of your father Jonathan, and will restore to you all the land of your grandfather Saul; and you shall eat at my table regularly." Again he prostrated himself and said, "What is your servant, that you should regard a dead dog like me?" Then the king called Saul's servant Ziba and said to him, "All that belonged to Saul and to all his house I have given to your master's grandson. "You and your sons and your servants shall cultivate the land for him, and you shall bring in the produce so that your master's grandson may have food; nevertheless Mephibosheth your master's grandson shall eat at my table regularly." Now Ziba had fifteen sons and twenty servants. Then Ziba said to the king, "According to all that my lord the king commands his servant so your servant will do." So Mephibosheth ate at David's table as one of the king's sons. Mephibosheth had a young son whose name was Mica. And all who lived in the house of Ziba were servants to Mephibosheth. So Mephibosheth lived in Jerusalem, for he ate at the king's table regularly. Now he was lame in both feet. 2 Samuel 9:1-13

It is most interesting that many Bible commentators use the phrase "Covenant Kindness" when commenting on David's question.

Even today, as it was then, Covenant agreement affected all of the descendants of the families of the heads of the Covenant, regardless of their status or their crimes. In spite of the personal offences they may have committed, willingly or in ignorance, of the Covenant, they were still protected by the Covenant itself. David knew this and accepted it.

In all probability, Mephibosheth knew nothing of the Covenant between his father Jonathan and David.

In all probability he was spending his time angry, rejected, hurt, despairing of his lot in life, for he would be aware that his father was the king's son and he should be king. Instead, David is the king. In all probability, Mephibosheth is a man with a major chip on his shoulder. The place in which he lived was renowned for bandits, thieves and lawlessness he lives to fulfil his need for revenge.

In today's terms, he may well be considered a terrorist, attempting to overthrow the King, bent on revenge, in complete ignorance of the Covenant relationship he was in with the very person he was bent on destroying. Most likely he is guilty of some of the most terrible crimes including murder.

No-doubt there were those in the camp who know who he was, perhaps even harboured thoughts of overthrowing the king and bringing him to the thrown for there own purpose.

In all probability he was also living in fear of being discovered by the King. He knew that if he was discovered he would be killed as the son of Jonathan. He also knew that his criminal actions deserved the death penalty.

While Mephibosheth was living this terrible lifestyle, he was unaware that David was inquiring about the whereabouts of the relatives of King Saul. When Ziba told David of the existence and whereabouts of Mephibosheth, David commanded that Mephibosheth should be brought to him.

It should be easy to imagine the situation for Mephibosheth. One day he was dreaming and plotting the overthrow of the King. He was sleeping on a rough straw mattress on the floor, his clothes were rough, threadbare and patched. He ate crude food with barely enough nourishment to keep him in reasonable health. He must crawl from one location to another or hobble about on crutches; he is bitter, twisted, and angry at the world, the King, and himself. Mephibosheth is a picture of self-pity.

Mephibosheth was dependent on the kindness of some of the most vicious people of the time. They knew little of mercy even among friends. He was always looking over his shoulder for the King's men, afraid that at any moment they would come to arrest him.

One day he was woken to find that his worst nightmare had come true. The King's army, David's personal and elite troops, have surrounded the village of Lodebar in search of Mephibosheth. He was quickly handed over by his friends who, no doubt, were afraid for their lives.

The captain of the army would not know why Mephibosheth was wanted, he was simply told to bring him to the king. He would be thrown into the chariot and left to bounce around as they race back to the king. Mephibosheth's mind was no doubt racing, with why he was wanted by the king. Like a guilty man caught in a criminal act, his mind is racing, looking for an excuse, desperately seeking and praying for some shred of hope for himself. There is no doubt in his mind that the King was entitled to torture and kill him. It was nothing less than Mephibosheth expected and nothing less than he deserved.

He was brought before the king, fearful, defiant, so many emotions ran through his mind. As he began to plead for mercy he falls on his face and reveres David as the King.

Before Mephibosheth was able to say very much David called him by name and advised him that it was his intention to be kind to him. All his fathers' lands were to be restored to him. All his fathers' wealth would be returned to him. Mephibosheth was to be restored to his role as the grandson of the King. As the sole survivor of Jonathan's family, a blood brother of David due to the Covenant contract between Jonathan and David.

Mephibosheth was given his grandfathers servant, Ziba, who had fifteen sons and twenty servants to look after his land.

He was to be fed at David's own table. This was a sign that, despite his past, he was not only forgiven but he was now totally accepted by the Great King as his son, and an equal with his own sons.

At first Mephibosheth did not understand and asked why. He refers to himself as a dead dog a term that meant he was a person of no value.

> *Again he prostrated himself and said, "What is your servant, that you should regard a dead dog like me?" 2 Samuel 9:8*

A dead dog was fit only for burning on the rubbish dump. Most literally translated from the Hebrew he was referring to himself as a low-life, male prostitute fit only for burning on the garbage tip like a dead dog.

Mephibosheth came to realise that this honour was bestowed upon him because of the Covenant. Some of the things that would have helped him understand this would have been David's comment, "For thy father Jonathan's sake."

As Mephibosheth moved around the Kings castle he would see his father's suit of armour hanging on one of the walls of the great hall, where the armour of other Vassal Kings was kept.

He would have seen the scar on David's wrist that would also have spoken of a Covenant relationship, and he would have realised that this was the Covenant Seal between David and his father Jonathan.

Mephibosheth would have realised that all he had been told concerning David and the Kingdom was a lie. He must now make a decision. Turn his back on David and deny his Covenant privileges and be executed or accept the offer that David had made.

He chose to enter his Covenant relationship and enjoy its blessings. Because of his decision, Mephibosheth came into a Covenant relationship with David through his father. This included all its privileges and responsibilities.

The Covenant provided protection, guaranteed status and provided all he will ever need for his life. David was to Mephibosheth all that God had promised to be to Abraham, all that Jesus is to us.

> *After these things the word of the LORD came to Abram in a vision, saying, "Do not fear, Abram, I am a shield to you; Your reward shall be very great." Genesis 15:1*

Mephibosheth was a murderer a terrorist and a thief. A man destined to lead the life of a crippled thug and probably spend much of his lifetime in a dungeon. But the King was merciful, having totally forgiven him, and granted all that he ever needed for all his life. He moved from the status of pauper to prince.

Jesus illustrated this same level of forgiveness in the parable of the prodigal son (Luke 15:11-24.) In this parable Jesus demonstrates the willingness of the father (God) to forgive us, even though we, as his sons have moved out of relationship with him and we have broken the Covenant.

Like the prodigal son[55], regardless of his actions he was totally restored as he chose to return to his father. The father's acceptance of the son is absolute and so it is between God and us.

When we come to God in repentance, with a desire to establish our relationship with him, or if we have broken Covenant with him and we repent, and wish to return to him, we find that he is a forgiving Father, he is a "Great King."

The willingness of Jesus to forgive is most effectively demonstrated for us at Calvary, Luke 23:32-43, note verses 39-44

---

[55] Luke 15

> *One of the criminals who were hanged there was hurling abuse at Him, saying, "Are You not the Christ? Save Yourself and us!" But the other answered, and rebuking him said, "Do you not even fear God, since you are under the same sentence of condemnation? "And we indeed are suffering justly, for we are receiving what we deserve for our deeds; but this man has done nothing wrong." And he was saying, "Jesus, remember me when You come in Your kingdom!" And He said to him, "Truly I say to you, today you shall be with Me in Paradise." It was now about the sixth hour, and darkness fell over the whole land until the ninth hour, Luke 23:39-44*

Nowhere in scripture is the forgiveness of God better demonstrated than here. At the time of his torture, when it is at its cruellest, his body racked with pain, his spirit tortured with the ravages of the sin of all mankind. While he is fevered, grieved, and alone, a man, a malefactor, asks for forgiveness. In spite of his own suffering, Jesus has time to forgive. He probably weeps a little. Not just from the pain and suffering, but also, from the relief and joy that it is worthwhile. This request for forgiveness, the repentance of the thief, is a part of the joy that was set before him and the thing that makes it all worthwhile. Jesus forgives. God forgives. For one man, Covenant is restored.

In every sense, God is not concerned with WHAT our sin is. To him all sin is the same and is equally offensive to him. It is the violation of the sacredness of God, of all he is and a violation of what we are created to be. He is desires that we reach out to him and accept his offer of forgiveness and restoration.

His love to us is unlimited. The extent of this Covenant is absolute; it is the Everlasting Covenant of God that cannot be changed,

> *"My covenant I will not violate, Nor will I alter the utterance of My lips. Psalms 89:34*
>
> *"Thus says the LORD, 'If you can break My covenant for the day and My covenant for the night, so that day and night will*

not be at their appointed time, then My covenant may also be broken with David My servant so that he will not have a son to reign on his throne, and with the Levitical priests, My ministers. 'As the host of heaven cannot be counted and the sand of the sea cannot be measured, so I will multiply the descendants of David My servant and the Levites who minister to Me.'" And the word of the LORD came to Jeremiah, saying, "Have you not observed what this people have spoken, saying, 'The two families which the LORD chose, He has rejected them'? Thus they despise My people, no longer are they as a nation in their sight. "Thus says the LORD, 'If My covenant for day and night stand not, and the fixed patterns of heaven and earth I have not established, then I would reject the descendants of Jacob and David My servant, not taking from his descendants rulers over the descendants of Abraham, Isaac and Jacob. But I will restore their fortunes and will have mercy on them.'" Jeremiah 33:20-26

All that God is waiting for is for us to repent, (Acts 2:38), and allow him to bring us into our Covenant relationship with him, so that we may enjoy its many benefits.

Peter said to them, "Repent, and each of you be baptized in the name of Jesus Christ for the forgiveness of your sins; and you will receive the gift of the Holy Spirit. "For the promise is for you and your children and for all who are far off, as many as the Lord our God will call to Himself." Acts 2:38-39

We stand in the presence of God as Mephibosheth stood in the presence of David. The Blood Covenant stands between us and our Heavenly Father just as the Covenant with David and Jonathan stood between David and Mephibosheth.

The Covenant that David and Jonathan cut was to them as the Covenant that our Heavenly Father and Jesus cut. Our heavenly Father sees us no differently, than David saw Mephibosheth. No differently than the way the father saw his prodigal son and we are forgiven as easily and completely as Jesus forgave the penitent thief.

All that is required is the complete surrender of the individual to the will of God to accept the fact that God is greater than man, individually or collectively. We must accept the fact of our personal sin and our sincere appeal to him for forgiveness. This cannot come about until we accept, as individuals, the fact that without a right relationship with God man is doomed to an eternity in hell itself, a place never intended for man but for Satan and his angels.

We need to understand that this right relationship with God brings forgiveness, peace, healing, prosperity (the provision of my needs), security and eternal life, all these benefits and much more are the essence of Blood Covenant. It is all that God had promised to Abraham. It is all that he has promised to you and to me. It is all that he has given to us in Jesus.

Whether or not we will enter into and enjoy this relationship is left entirely to us.

> *"For God so loved the world, that He gave His only begotten Son, that whoever believes in Him shall not perish, but have eternal life. "For God did not send the Son into the world to judge the world, but that the world might be saved through Him. "He who believes in Him is not judged; he who does not believe has been judged already, because he has not believed in the name of the only begotten Son of God. John 3:16-18*

End of Chapter Questions

1. Discuss the relevance of David and Mephibosheth as a type of Jesus and the man in his unregenerate state,

Apendix I:

Ramsis II Hattusillis III

Ramsis the Great
The Pharaoh Who Made Peace with his Enemies
And the First Peace Treaty in History

By Dr. Sameh M. Arab[56]

Ramsis II", who reigned for 67 years during the 19th dynasty of the 12th century BC, was known as "Ramsis the Great". His glories surpassed all other Pharaohs, and Egypt reached an overwhelming state of prosperity during his reign. Not only is he known as one of Egypt's greatest warriors, but also as a peace-maker and for the monuments he left behind all over Egypt. He was the first king in history to sign a peace treaty[57] with his

---

[56] http://www.touregypt.net/featurestories/treaty.htm

[57] http://touregypt.net/peacetreaty.htm

enemies, the Hittites[58], ending long years of wars and hostility. The treaty can still be considered a conclusive model, even when applying today's standards.

Who are the Hittites? Their rise and hostility with Egypt:

The Hittites were a minor nation in Anatolia, who started to penetrate peacefully east and west through monopolizing political power in the Near East. By the second millennium BC, they became a great power that finally replaced the Babylonian state around 1530 BC. They started challenging the Egyptian Empire during its decline under the reign of Akhen-Aton (18th dynasty). International correspondence from the Asian princes in Palestine and Syria (known as the Amarna Letters) were sent to Akhen-Aton and his court requesting help, and warnings of the Hittites growing influence. The pharaoh unfortunately neglected them and never replied. This resulted in Egypt loosing control over considerable territory in Syria when aggressors, aided by the Hittites, invaded. After the death of Akhen-Aton, and the murder (or death) of his successor Tut-Ankh-Amon, his wife (and Akhenaton's daughter), "Ankh-Esenpa-Aton", attempted a diplomatic coup with the Hittites. In order to secure her position, she sent a secret letter to their king asking him for a son whom she could marry and make pharaoh. As this offer was astounding, the king suspected treachery and sent an ambassador to test the queen's true intentions. In response to her assurance, the king sent his son. However, he was captured and murdered by the Egyptian commander of the army, Horemheb (who later became pharaoh). Hostility between Egypt and the Hittites was further augmented.

---

[58] http://touregypt.net/featurestories/hittites.htm

The war between Egypt and Hatti:

With the rise of the 19th dynasty in Egypt, "Seti I" began to reestablish Egypt's power in the Near East. Within the first two years of his reign, he was able to restore all of Palestine and the city of Kadesh to Egyptian control. Afterwards, a short-lived truce was signed between the two empires.

During the reign of Seti Is son, "Ramsis II", advances were made against Syria that reached Kadesh one more. The resulting battle is one of the most famous in Egyptian history. It lasted four days, and initially Ramsis was losing the battle. However, his army managed to fight bravely until reinforcements arrived, turning the defeat into victory. The Hittites asked for a cease-fire, and Ramsis" officers advised him to make peace, saying,

"There is no reproach in reconciliation when you make it."

After the death of the Hittite king, "Hattusili III" usurped the throne from the legitimate prince who fled to Egypt and was granted political asylum by "Ramsis II". Hittite documents record Hattusili's complaint:

"When I wrote to him: send me my enemy, he didn't extradite him. Therefore there was anger between me and the King of Egypt."

While another round of war was on the horizon, both empires were under pressure with the Hittites were facing the reemerging Assyria in Mesopotamia, and Egypt was facing a threat from the Libyans in the west. Diplomatic negotiations took place for two years until a peace treaty was concluded in the 21st regal year of Ramsis" reign with "Hattusilis III" in 1280 BC.

The peace treaty:

Egypt's acceptance of a peace treaty that would end the war in Syria meant that there would be no chance to restore Kadesh and Amuru. However in return for this sacrifice, the dispute between the two countries would end with a clear line of demarcation between the Egyptian and the Syrian territories. Moreover, Egypt guaranteed the Syrians the right to use their Phenecian harbors, while the Hittites agreed to allow Egyptians free passage to the north as far as Ugarit without interference. This was a privilege lost for more than a century.

Two copies of the treaty were recorded, one in hieroglyph and the other Akaddian, and both still survive. Both copies are identical except for the overture, in which the Egyptian version stated that it was the Hittite king who demanded peace, whereas in the Hittite version, it was Ramsis who sent them emissaries. The Egyptian version was recorded on a silver plaque presented by Hattusili to Ramsis, then copied on stone at the Karnak and Ramesseum temples.

Akaddian Version of Treaty

The treaty was composed of 18 articles. After a long introduction recording the kings" titles and referring to establishment of good fraternity and peace, one article was included to exclude any further attacks on the other country's territories:

"Reamasesa, the Great King, the king of the country of Egypt, shall never attack the country of Hatti to take possession of a part (of this country). And Hattusili, the Great King, the king of the country of Hatti, shall never attack the country of Egypt to take possession of a part (of that country). "

Hattusili and his Wife, Puduhepa

Two articles follow that established the mutual alliance against any foreign attack on either country:

"If a foreign enemy marches against the country of Hatti and if Hattusili, the king of the country of Hatti, sends me this message: "Come to my help against him", Reamasesa, the Great King, the king of the Egyptian country, has to send his troops and his chariots to kill this enemy and to give satisfaction to the country of Hatti."

"If a foreigner marches against the country of Egypt and if Reamasesa, the Great King, the king of the country of Egypt, your brother, sends to Hattusili, the king of the country of Hatti, his brother, the following message: "Come to my help against him", then Hattusili, king of the country of Hatti, shall send his troops and his chariots and kill my enemy."

The treaty then included three articles establishing mutual collaboration against any internal mutiny or coups in either country:

"If Hattusili, the Great King, the king of the country of Hatti, rises in anger against his citizens after they have committed a crime against him and if, for this reason, you send to Reamasesa the Great King, the king of the country of Egypt, then Reamasesa has to send his troops and his chariots and these should exterminate all those that he has risen in anger against."

"If Reamasesa, king of the country of Egypt, rises in anger against his citizens after they have committed a wrong against him and by reason of this he sends (a message) to Hattusili, the Great King, the king of the country of Hatti, my brother, has to send his troops and his chariots and they have to exterminate all those against whom I have risen in anger."

"Look, the son of Hattusili, king of the country of Hatti, has to assure his sovereignty of the country of Hatti instead of Hattusili, his father, after the numerous years of Hattusili, king of the country of Hatti. If the children of the country of Hatti transgress

against him, then Reamasesa has to send to his help troops and chariots and to give him support."

To avoid any further dispute, if a refugee flees to the other country, ten articles were dedicated to their extradition. This was the first extradition agreement in history between two nations. The treaty did not exclude any person, and regardless of whether they were "great men", nobles or "unknown persons":

"If a great person flees from the country of Hatti and if he comes to Reamasesa, the Great King, king of the country of Egypt, then Reamasesa, the Great King, the king of the country of Egypt, has to take hold of him and deliver him into hands of Hattusili, the Great King, the king of the country of Hatti. "

"If a great person flees from the country of Egypt and he escapes to the country of Amurru or a city and he comes to the king of Amurru, then Benteshina, king of the country of Amurru, has to take hold of him and take him to the king of the country of Hatti; and Hattusili, the Great King, the king of the country of Hatti, shall have him to be taken to Reamasesa, the Great King, the king of the country of Egypt."

"If a nobleman flees from the country of Hatti, or two men, and if they don't want to serve the king of Hatti, and if they flee from the Great King's country, the king of the land of Hatti, in order not to serve him, then Reamasesa has to take hold of them and order them be taken to Hattusili, the Great King, king of the land of Hatti, his brother, and he shall not allow them to reside in the country of Egypt."

"If a nobleman or two flee from the country of Egypt and if they leave for the Land of Hatti, then Hattusili, the Great King, the king of the country of Hatti, has to take hold of them and make them be taken to Reamasesa, the Great King, the king of the country of Egypt, his brother. "

"If a man or two men who are unknown flee, and if they come to Reamasesa, to serve him, then Reamasesa has to take hold of them

and deliver them into the hands of Hattusili, king of the country of Hatti."

"If a man or two men who are unknown flee, and if they escape from the country of Egypt and if they don't want to serve him, then Hattusili, the Great King, the king of the country of Hatti, has to deliver them into his brother's hands and he shall not allow them to inhabit the country of Hatti."

"If a man flees from the country of Hatti, or two people, and if they flee from the country of Hatti, and if they come to the country of Egypt, and if a nobleman flees from the country of Hatti or of a city and they flee from the country of Hatti to go to the country of Egypt, then Reamasesa has to order them to be taken to his brother. Look, the sons of the country of Hatti and the children of the country of Egypt are at peace."

"If some people flee from the country of Egypt to go to the country of Hatti, then Hattusili, the Great King, the king of the country of Hatti, has to order them to be taken to his brother. Look, Hattusili the Great King, the king of the country of Hatti, and Reamasesa, the Great King, the king of the country of Egypt, your brother, are at peace."

Fugitives were to be treated with dignity and returned without being punished.

"If a man flees from the country of Hatti, or two men, or three men, and if they come to Reamasesa, the Great King, the king of the country of Egypt, his brother, then Reamasesa, the Great King, the king of the country of Egypt, has to take hold of them and to order them to be taken to Hattusili, his brother, since they are brothers. As for their crime, it should not be imputed; their language and their eyes are not to be pulled out; their ears and their feet are not to be cut off; their houses with their wives and their children are not to be destroyed."

"If a (man flees from the country of Reamasesa, the Great King, king of the country of Egypt), or two men, or three men, and if they come (to Hattusili, the Great King), the king of the country of Hatti, my brother, then Hattusili, the Great King, king of the country of Hatti, my brother, has to take hold of them and to order them to be taken to Reamasesa, the Great King, the king of the country of Egypt, because Reamasesa, the Great King, king of the country of Egypt, and Hattusili are brothers. As for their crime, it should not be imputed; their language and their eyes are not to be pulled out; their ears and their feet are not to cut off; their houses with their wives and their children are not to be destroyed."

The 1000 gods of either land were invoked as witnesses and guarantors of this peace in the remaining two articles. Only some of the gods were named, including Ra of Egypt and Teshub of Hatti:

"If Reamasesa and the children of the country of Egypt don't observe this treaty, then the gods and the goddesses of the country of Egypt and the gods and goddesses of the country of Hatti shall exterminate the descendants of Reamasesa, the Great King, the king of the country of Egypt.

If Reamasesa and the children of the country of Egypt observe this treaty, then the gods of the oath shall protect them and their ...."

"They who observe the words that are in the silver tablet the great gods of the country of Egypt and the great gods of the country of Hatti shall allow them to live and prosper in their houses, their country and with their servants.

They who do not observe the words that are in this silver tablet, the great gods of the country of Egypt as well as the great gods of the country of Hatti will exterminate their houses, their country and their servants."

The borders of the two countries were not laid out in this treaty but were in other documents. A papyrus enumerates the Phoenician coastal towns under Egyptian control, with the harbor town of Sumur being the northern-most town belonging to Egypt.

As soon as the treaty became effectiveness, greetings were exchanged between the two courts, particularly form the two queens, Nefertari of Egypt and the Hittite "Budu-Khebi". Nefertari wrote:

"I hear, my sister, that you have written to ask after my peace and the relations of good peace and fraternity that exist between the Great King of Egypt and the Great King of Hatti, his brother. Ra and Teshub will deal with this so you can raise your look, may Ra assure the peace and strengthen the good fraternity between the Great King of Egypt and the Great King of Hatti, his brother, for ever."

The tension after the treaty:

Despite the readiness of both courts to abide by the treaty, some tension persisted owing to the presence of the deposed Hittite prince who remained in political asylum in Egypt for 10 years after the treaty. Though Hattusili requested his surrender, Ramsis refused to apply the treaty in retrospect. This was probably due to the Hittites" refusal to re-adjust the borders between Egypt and Syria to their pre-treaty positions. This, together with the bitterness Hattusili felt due to the arrogant tone in Ramsis" messages, continued to create tension between the two courts. In letters, Ramsis had to remind Hattusili of their fraternity, and reproached him on their exchange of gifts. Hattusili had send but one handicapped slave as a gift, while Ramsis had sent a number of physicians who were in high demand worldwide, along with a substantial quantity of herbs.

As Babel began to establish diplomatic relations with Egypt, Ramsis accepted a Babylonian princess among his harem. Jealousy of the relationship between these two kingdoms, Hattusili cemented the treaty 13 years later by offering his daughter to

Ramsis. The royal wedding was depicted on the temples of Karnak, Elephentine and Abu-Simbel.

Tension started to fade gradually after the marriage, and later diplomatic missions came to include more elite personnel. A visit by the Hittite crown prince was arranged to Egypt, and upon his return with gifts, Hattusili himself accepted Ramsis" invitation to visit Egypt. Ramsis greeted him at Canaan and escorted him to Pi-Ramsis, where perhaps the world first summit meeting took place. Later, another princess was sent to the Egyptian court.

During the next 46 regal years of Ramsis II, peace continued and the treaty was respected until the fall of the Hittite Empire. When the king of Mira in Asia Minor attempted to form a coalition with Egypt against the Hittites, Ramsis refused saying:

"Today there is fraternity between the Great King of Egypt and the king of Hatti, between Ra and Teshub."

Appendix II:

The Mari Tablets

Mari or Tell Hariri is situated on the Euphrates River about fifteen miles north of the present Syria-Iraq border about midway between Babylon and Haran.

André Parrot, the chief archaeologist at Mari, conducted digging seasons from 1933-38 and 1951-56. Further work was done by Jean Margueron in 1979.

The city's ruins cover more than 245 ha (600 acres). Near the west wall is a series of temples

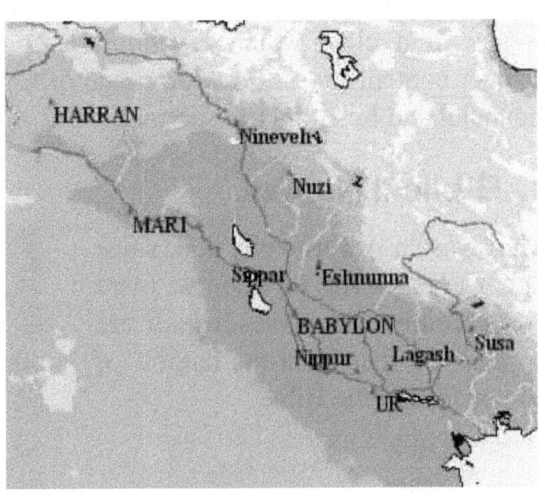

dedicated to the goddess Ishtar, which date from before 2500 to 1800 BC; more temples stood near the ziggurat at the centre of the site.

Votive statues from the mid-3d-millennium BC shrines show stylistic links with the southern Mesopotamian art of Sumer. In the northeast part of the city lies the 18th-century BC palace of Zimri-lim (1779-1761 BC); measuring, in its latest phase, approximately 24,000 sq m (260,000 sq ft), it contained nearly 300 rooms and courtyards, some of which were decorated with wall paintings including that of the famous Investiture of Zimri-lim (Louvre, Paris). The vast palace was not only the royal residence but also the administrative centre of the kingdom; it contained many thousands of cuneiform tablets, which form a key Near Eastern archive. In particular, the correspondence between Shamshi-Adad and his vice-regal sons gives a lively and detailed picture of the state administration, politics, and everyday life of the period.

Over twenty thousand tablets and a number of inscriptions on objects have been unearthed. The language of the texts is Akkadian. The period of the texts covers from 1800-1750 B.C. and comes to a close when Hammurabi conquered the city. Their subject content crosses a wide range of topics, but most deal with financial and business transactions.

1. Biblical Names.

Mari was an Amorite city and, since Amorite is similar to Hebrew, there are a number of names which are similar to the Hebrew names of personages in the Bible.

Tablet of King Zimri-Lim of Mari, ca. 1780 BC, Louvre Museum

  Terah
  Nahor
  Haran
  Nahor
  Ishmael
  Serug
  Variations of Abraham and Jacob

These names formed by a verb in the imperfect form are very numerous and very typical of Amorite names found at Mari, but are very rare for Canaanite-Phoenician names.

2. Travel and Commerce.

One tablet at Mari entailed a wagon contract. The contract stated that as a condition of rental the wagon must not be driven to the Mediterranean sea. This serves as an indication that such long-distance travel as Abraham undertook was normative.

3. Covenants and Sacrifices.

The Mari tablets describe the sacrifice of a young donkey as part of the ritual for concluding a treaty. The traditional language of "entering into a covenant" was "to kill a young ass" in the Mari texts.

Cuneiform Writing

Cuneiform means "wedged shaped" in Latin. This refers to ancient writings that had a wedged shaped appearance. The writing is usually made with a wedge stylus on soft clay tablets. Baking the tablets preserves them. A number of different ancient languages are written in cuneiform. The most widely used language was

Cuneiform Writing

Akkadian. Cuneiform is also chiseled on to stones and rocks. One famous carving on a cliff three hundred feet up is the Rock of Behistun in ancient Persia, now modern day Iran southwest of Tehran.

The man most responsible for the decipherment of cuneiform is Henry Rawlinson. Henry started to work for the East India Company in 1827 at the age of seventeen where he learned Indian languages and Persian. In 1835 he was sent to Persia as a military adviser. Near the city of Kermanshah he found two inscriptions on rocks which he figured out the names of Darius and Xerxes. He then started to copy the inscriptions on the Rock of Behistun some three hundred feet up on very shaky wooden ladders. In 1849 he completed his book *Memoir on the Persian Version of the Behistun Inscriptions*.

There were two other unknown ancient languages on the Rock of Behistun that said the same thing in Old Persian so Rawlinson turn his attention to their decipherment. In 1855 he published a book with notes and translation of the second language named Elamite.

Finally Rawlinson turned to the last language Babylonian cuneiform, or today called Akkadian. Edward Hincks, a Anglican clergyman had devoted himself to the decipherment of Akkadian. By 1847 he published a list of their signs and meanings. With the writings of Rawlinson and Hincks the Akkadian language was deciphered. Hincks was right in observing the signs stand for syllables. The final test came in 1857 when four scholars, Rawlinson, Hincks, Henry Talbot, and Jules Oppert independently translated the same script and came up with virtually the same translation.

Appendix III:

The Sacredness Of The Blood Covenant

These few comments are taken from Mr. Kenyon's notes on Blood Covenant to help illustrate its strength and power:

Mr. Stanley said he never knew this covenant to be broken in Africa, no matter what the provocation.

Dr. Livingstone also bears witness saying that he never knew it to be broken.

In Africa, if one was to break the covenant, his own mother or wife, or his nearest relatives would seek his death, would turn him over to the hands of the avenger for destruction. No man can live in Africa who breaks the covenant . . . he curses the very ground he walks on.

The vilest enemies become trusted friends as soon as the covenant is cut." page 10 Blood Covenant

One illustration of Stanley's might help us to grasp the significance. page 11 Blood Covenant

When Stanley was seeking Livingstone, he was on his first trip to Africa. He came in contact with a powerful equatorial tribe. (Tribe on the equator) They were very war like.

Stanley was not in any condition to fight them. Finally, his interpreter asked him why he didn't make a strong covenant with them? (The tribal chieftain, who was an older man, had taken a liking to Stanley)

Stanley asked what it meant and was told that it meant drinking each other's blood.

Stanley revolted from such a rite, but conditions kept getting worse, until finally, Stanley's lead bearer asked again; why do you not cut covenant with the chief of the tribe?

Stanley asked what the results of such a covenant would be, and was told "Everything the chief has will be yours if you need it!" This appealed to Stanley and he investigated. After several days of negotiation, they arrived at the terms of the covenant.

First there was a parley in which the chieftain questioned Stanley as to his motives and standing, and his ability to keep the covenant. The next step was an exchange of gifts. The old chieftain wanted Stanley's new white milk goat. Stanley's heath had slipped on his journey, and the only thing that would stay in his stomach was goats milk, so it was very hard to give this up, but Stanley had nothing else the chief wanted. (Stanley had questioned his interpreter and was assured the old chief only wanted to be the source of Stanley's blessing and had no intention of with holding the milk from him.)

Stanley gave the chief the goat, and the chieftain gave Stanley a seven foot tall spear that had the top portion wound in copper wire in a very intricate pattern. Originally, Stanley had no idea what that spear meant. Later on as Stanley continued with his journey, right out to the coast of Africa, as soon as anyone saw that spear they would immediately ask if he needed anything, people would fall all over themselves trying to help Stanley in any way.

The old chieftain then brought in one of his princes. Stanley led forth one of his men from England. (Kenyon leaves out the path of blood between the animal parts but in his book Stanley describes it, after each man had walked through the path and now stood facing each other.) Then the priest came forward with a cup of wine, made an incision in the young black prince's wrist, and let the blood drip into the wine. He then cut an incision in the wrist of the young Englishman, and let his blood drip into the wine. page 12 Blood Covenant, The wine was stirred and the bloods were mixed.

The priest handed the cup to the Englishman and he drank part of it and then handed the cup to the black prince and he drank the rest of it.

Next, they rubbed their wrists together so that their bloods mingled.

Now they had become blood brothers.

These two men were only substitutes, but they had bound Stanley and the chieftain, Stanley's men and the chieftain's soldiers into a blood brotherhood that was indissoluble.

Then gun-power was rubbed into the wound, so that when it healed there would be a black mark to indicate that they were covenant men.

The next step of the ceremony was the planting of trees, trees that were known for their long life.

After the planting of the trees the chieftain stepped forward and told his people "Come trade with Stanley, for he is our blood brother!".

Appendix IV:

Covenants Around The World

This appendix is offered to show the similarity, and diversity of covenants around the worlt over time. The customs we have seen are outlined below is a startling array of diversity and similarity at the same time

Evidence of Blood Covenant are found in almost every society and nation around the world.

The following passages are from the book "The Blood Covenant" by H Trumbull, a gentleman and scholar who has researched Blood Covenant in great detail. The following passages are but a few of the evidences of Blood Covenant from around the world and are presented to give a brief overview of these evidences. I refer you to his work for a much more comprehensive view of the impact of blood covenant around the world from the pen a respected scholar. The footnotes and endnotes relate to the work by H. Trumbal.

Europe

Different methods of observing this primitive rite of blood-covenanting are indicated in the legendary lore of the Norseland peoples; and these methods, in all their variety, give added proof of the ever underlying idea of an inter-commingling of lives through an inter-commingling of blood. Odin was the beneficent god of light and knowledge, the promoter of heroism, and the protector of sacred covenants, in the mythology of the North. Loke, or Lok, on the other hand, was the discordant and corrupting divinity; symbolizing, in his personality, " sin, shrewdness, deceitfulness, treachery, malice," and other phases of evil.[59] In the poetic myths of the Norseland, it is claimed that at the beginning Odin and Loke were in close union instead of being at variance[60] just as the Egyptian cosmogony made Osiris and Set in original accord, although in subsequent hostility[61], and as the Zoroastrians claimed that Ormuzd and Ahriman were at one, before they were in conflict.[62] Odin and Loke are, indeed, said to have been, at one time, in the close and sacred union of blood-friendship; having coven-anted in that union by mingling their blood in a bowl, and drinking therefrom together.

The Elder Edda[63], or the earliest collection of Scandinavian songs, makes reference to this confraternity of Odin and Loke. At a banquet of the gods, Loke, who had not been invited, found an entrance, and there reproached his fellow divinities for their hostility to him. Recalling the indissoluble tie of blood-friendship, he said:

> " Father of Slaughter[64], Odin, say,
> Rememberest not the former day,
> When ruddy in the goblet stood,
> For mutual drink, our blended blood ?
> Rememberest not, thou then didst swear,
> The festive banquet ne'er to share,

---

[59] See Carlyle's Heroes and Hero-Worship, Lect. I.; also Anderson's Norse Mythology, pp. 215-220; 371-374.

[60] See Anderson's Norse Mythol., pp. 372, 408 f

[61] See Wilkinson's Ancient Egyptians, III., 142; Renouf s The Religion of Ancient Egypt, p. 118 f.; Ebers's Picturesque Egypt, I., 100 f.

[62] See De Wette's Biblische Dogmatik, 79

[63] See Carlyle's Hero Worship, Lect. I.

[64] Odin " is the author of war." He is called " Valfather (Father of the slain), because he chooses for his sons all who fall in combat." Anderson's Norse MythoL, p. 215

Unless thy brother Lok was there ?"

In citing this illustration of the ancient rite, a modern historian of chivalry has said: "Among barbarous people [the barbarians of Europe] the fraternity of arms [the sacred brotherhood of heroes] was established by the horrid custom of the new brothers drinking each other's blood; but if this practice was barbarous, nothing was farther from barbarism than the sentiment which inspired it.[65]"

Another of the methods by which the rite of blood-friendship was observed in the Norseland, was by causing the blood of the two covenanting persons to inter-flow from their pierced hands, while they lay together underneath a lifted sod. The idea involved seems to have been, the burial of the two individuals, in their separate personal lives, and the intermingling of those lives—by the intermingling of their blood—while in their temporary grave; in order to their rising again with a common life[66]—one life, one soul, in two bodies. Thus it is told, in one of the Icelandic Sagas, of Thorstein, the heroic son of Viking, proffering "foster-brotherhood," or blood-friendship, to the valiant Angantyr, Jarl of the Orkneys. "Then this was resolved upon, and secured by firm pledges on both sides. They opened a vein in the hollow of their hands, crept beneath the sod, and there [with clasped hands inter-blood-flowing] they solemnly swore that each of them should avenge the other if any one of them should be slain by weapons." This was, in fact, a three-fold covenant of blood; for King Bele, who had just been in combat with Angantyr, was already in blood-friendship with Thorstein.[67]

---

[65] Mills's History of Chivalry, chap. IV.

[66] Rom. 6 : 4-6; Col. 2:12

[67] Anderson's Viking Tales of the North, p. 59.

The rite of blood-friendship, in one form and another, finds frequent mention in the Norseland Sagas. Thus, in the Saga of Fridthjof the Bold, the son of Thorstein :

> *"Champions twelve, too, had he—gray-haired, and princes in exploits,—*
> *Comrades his father had loved, steel-breasted and scarred o'er the forehead.*
> *Last on the champions' bench, equal-aged with Fridthjof, a stripling*
> *Sat, like a rose among withered leaves; Bjorn called they the hero—*
> *Glad as a child, but firm like a man, and yet wise as a graybeard;*
> *Up with Fridthjof he'd grown; they had mingled blood with each other,*
> *Foster-brothers in Northman wise; and they swore to continue Steadfast in weal and woe, each other revenging in battle."*[68]

England

A vestige of this primitive rite, coming down to us trough European channels, is found, as are so many other traces of primitive rites, in the inherited folk-lore of English-speaking children on both sides of the Atlantic. An American clergyman's wife said recently, this point: " I remember, that while I was a school-it was the custom, when one of our companions pricked her finger, so that the blood came, for one or lother of us to say ' Oh, let me suck the blood; then e shall be friends.'" And that is but an illustration of the outreaching after this indissoluble bond, on the part of thirty generations of children of Norseland and Anglo-Saxon stock, since the days of Fridthjof and as that same yearning had been felt by those hundred generations before that time.

---

[68] Ibid., p. 191 f

China

Concerning traces of the rite of blood-covenanting in China, where there are to be found fewest resemblances to the primitive customs of the Asiatic Semites, Dr. Yung Wing, the eminent Chinese educationalist and diplomat, gives me the following illustration : " In the year 1674, when Kanhi was Emperor, of the present dynasty, we find that the Buddhist priests of Shanlin Dynstry in Fuhkin Province had rebelled against authorities on account of persecution. In their counters with the troops, they fought against great odds, and were finally defeated and scattered in different provinces, where they organized centres of the Triad Society, which claims an antiquity dated as far back as the Freemasons of the West. Five of these priests fled to the province of Hakwong, and there, Chin Kinnan, a member of the Hanlin College, who was degraded from office by his enemies, joined them; and it is said that they drank blood, and took the oath of brotherhood, to stand by each other in life or death."

Burmah

Mention is made, in the text of this volume[69], of the fact that the primitive rite of blood-covenanting is in practice all along the Chinese border of the Burman Empire. In illustration of this truth, the following description of the rite and its linkings, is given by the Rev. R. M. Luther, of Philadelphia, formerly a missionary among the Karens, in Burmah. This interesting sketch was received, in its present form, at too late a date for insertion in its place in the text; hence its appearance here.

"The blood-covenant is well known, and commonly practiced among the Karens of Burmah. There are three methods of making brotherhood, or truce, between members of one tribe and those of another.

---

[69] At page 44, *supra*

"The first is the common method of eating together. This, however, is of but little binding force, being a mere agreement to refrain from hostilities for a limited time, and the truce thus made is liable to be broken at the briefest notice.

"The second method is that of planting a tree. The parties to this covenant select a young and vigorous sapling, plant it with certain ceremonies, and covenant with each other to keep peace so long as the tree lives. A covenant thus made is regarded as of greater force than that effected or sealed by the first method.

"The third method is that of the blood-covenant, properly so called. In this covenant the chief stands as the representative of the tribe, if it be a tribal agreement; or the father as the representative of the family, if it be a more limited covenant. The ceremonies are public and solemn. The most important act is, of course, the mingling of the blood. Blood is drawn from the thigh of each of the covenanting parties, and' mingled together. Then each dips his finger into the blood and applies it to his lips. In some cases, it is said that the blood is actually drunk; but the more common method is that of touching the lips with the blood-stained finger[70].

"This covenant is of the utmost *force*. It covers not merely an agreement of peace, or truce, but also a promise of mutual assistance in peace and in war. It also conveys to the covenanting parties mutual tribal rites. If they are chiefs, the covenant embraces their entire tribes. If *one* is a private individual, his immediate family and direct descendants are included in the agreement.

"I never heard of the blood-covenant being broken. I do not remember to have inquired particularly on this point, because the way in which the blood-covenant was spoken *of,* always implied that its rupture was an unheard-of thing. It is regarded as a perfectly valid excuse for any amount of reckless devotion, or *of* unreasoning sacrifice on behalf of another, *for* a Karen to say: ' *Thui p'aw*

---

[70] See page '54, *supra*.

th'coh li,.' literally, 'The blood,-we have drunk it together.' An appeal *for* help on the basis of the blood-covenant is never disregarded.

"A *few* of our missionaries have entered into the blood-covenant with Karen tribes; though most have been deterred, either from never having visited the' debatable land' where the strong arm of British rule does not reach, or else, as in most instances, from a repugnance to the act by which the covenant is sealed. In one instance, at least, where a missionary did enter into covenant with *one* of these tribes, the agreement has been interpreted as covering not only his children, but *one* who was so happy as to marry his daughter. In an enforced absence *of* fifteen years from the scene of his early missionary labors nothing has been at once so touching and so painful to the writer as the frequent messages and letters asking 'When will you come back to *your people?'* Yet, mine is only the inherited right above mentioned.

"The blood-covenant gives even a foreigner every right which he would have if born a member *of* the tribe. As an instance, the writer once shot a hawk in a Karen village, just as it was swooping down upon a chicken. He was surprised to find, half an hour afterward, that his personal attendant, a straightforward Mountain Karen, had gone through the village and' collected' a fat hen from each house. 'When remonstrated with, the mountaineer replied, 'Why, Teacher, it is your right, - that is our custom,- you are one of us. These people wouldn't understand it if I did not ask for a chicken from each house, when you killed the hawk.'

"In the wilder Karen regions, it is almost impossible to travel unless one is in blood-covenant with the chiefs, while on the other hand one is perfectly safe, if in that covenant. The disregard - of this fact has cost valuable lives. When a stranger enters Karen territory, the chiefs order the paths closed. This is done by tying the long elephant grass across the paths. On reaching such a signal, the usual inquiry in the traveling party is, who is in blood-covenant with this tribe? 'If one is found, even among the lowest servants, his covenant covers the party, on the way, as far as to the principal village or hill fortress. The party goes into camp, and sends this man on as an ambassador. Usually, guides are sent back to conduct the party at once to the chief's house. If no one is in covenant with the tribe, and the wisp of grass is broken and the party passes on, the lives of the trespassers are forfeited. A sudden attack in some defile, or a night surprise, scatters the party and drives the survivors back the way they came.

"Notwithstanding the widespread prevalence of the blood-covenant, the ceremonies attendant upon its celebration, and even the existence of such a custom, are shrouded with a certain degree of secrecy, at least from outside nations. The writer has been surprised to find, on some occasions, those longer resident in Burmah than himself in total ignorance of the existence of such a custom; and even the Karens themselves would probably deny its existence to a casual inquirer. Apropos of this, the writer did not know of such a custom in any other country until his attention was called to the fact by Dr. Trumbull, while this treatise was in preparation."

Another account of the blood-covenant rite in Bumah is kindly furnished *to* me by the Rev. Dr. M. H. Bixby, of Providence, Rhode Island, who was also for some years a missionary among the Karens. He says:

"In my first journey over the mountains of Burmah, into Shanland, lowJ.nl Western China, I passed through several tribes of wild Karens among whom the practice of 'covenanting by blood' prevailed.

"'If *you* mean what *you* say,' said the old chief of the Gecho tribe *to* me, refining *to* my professions of friendship, 'you will drink truth with me.' 'Well, what is drinking truth?' I said. In reply, he said: 'This is our custom. Each chief pierces his arm-draws blood, - mingles it in a vessel with whisky, and drinks of it; both promising *to* be true and faithful *to* each other, down *to* the seventh generation.'

"After the chiefs had drunk of the mingled blood and whisky, each one of their followers drunk of it also, and were thereby included in the covenant of friendship.

"A company of Shans laid a plot to kill me and my company in Shanland, for the purpose of plunder. They entered into covenant with each other by drinking the blood of their leader mingled with whisky, or a kind of beer made from rice.

"Those wild mountain tribes have strange traditions which indicate that they once had the Old Testament Scriptures, although now they have no written language. Some of the Karen tribes have a written language, given them by the missionaries.

"The covenant, also, exists in modified forms, in which the blood is omitted."

Borneo

In his History of Madagascar, the Rev. William Ellis, tells of this rite as he observed it in that island, and as he learned of it from Borneo. He says:

"Another popular engagement in use among the Malagasy is that of forming brotherhoods, which though not peculiar to them, is one of the most remarkable usages of the country. . . . Its object is to cement two individuals in the bonds of most sacred friendship. . . . More than two may thus associate, if they please ; but the practice is usually limited to that number, and rarely embraces more than three or four individuals. It is called fatridd, i. e., 'dead blood,' either because the oath is taken over the blood of a fowl killed for the occasion, or because a small portion of blood is drawn from each individual, when thus pledging friendship, and drunk by those to whom friendship is pledged, with execrations of vengeance on each other in case of violating the sacred oath. To obtain the blood, a slight incision is made in the skin covering the centre of the bosom, significantly called ambavafo, 'the mouth of the heart.' Allusion is made to this, in the formula of this tragi-comical ceremony.

"When two or more persons have agreed on forming this bond of fraternity, a suitable place and hour are determined upon, and some gunpowder and a ball are brought, together with a small quantity of ginger, a spear, and two particular kinds of grass. A fowl also is procured; its head is nearly cut off; and it is left in this state to continue bleeding during the ceremony[71].

"The parties then pronounce a long form of imprecation, and [a] mutual vow, to this effect:—'Should either of us prove disloyal to the sovereign, or un-feithful to each other[72], then perish the day, and perish the night[73]. Awful is that, solemn is that, which we are now both about to perform! O the mouth of the heart! —this is to be cut, and we shall drink each other's blood. O this ball! O this powder! O this ginger! O this fowl weltering in its blood !—it shall be killed, it shall be put to excruciating agonies,—it shall be killed by us, it shall be speared at this corner of the hearth (Alakaforo or Adimizam, S. W.) And whoever would seek to kill or injure us, to injure our wives, or our children, to waste our money or our property; or if either of us should seek to do what would not be approved of by the king or by the people; should one of us deceive the other by making that which is unjust appear just; should one accuse the other falsely; should either of us with our wives and children be lost and reduced to slavery, (forbid that such should be our lot!)—then, that good may arise out of evil, we follow this custom of the people; and we do it for the purpose of assisting one

---

[71] Apparently these articles form a "heap of witness," or are the aggregated symbolic witnesses of the transaction; as something answering to this usage is found in connection with the rite in various parts of the world.

[72] He who would be true in friendship must be true in all things. The good friend is a good citizen. See I Peter 2: 17.

[73] See Job 3 : 2-9.

another with our families, if lost in slavery, by whatever property either of us may possess; for our wives are as one to us, and each other's children as his own[74], and our riches as common property, O the mouth of the heart! O the ball! O the powder! O the ginger! O this miserable fowl weltering in its blood !—thy liver do we eat, thy liver do we eat. And should either of us retract from the terms of this oath, let him instantly become a fool, let him instantly become blind, let this covenant prove a curse to him: let him not be a human being: let there be no heir to inherit after him, but let him be reduced, and float with the water never to see its source; let him never obtain ; what is out of doors, may it never enter ; and what is within may it never go out; the little obtained, may he be deprived of it;[75] and let him never obtain justice from the sovereign nor from the people! But if we keep and observe this covenant, let these things bear witness[76].. O mouth of the heart! (repeating as before),—may this cause us to live long and happy with our wives and our children ; may we be approved by the sovereign, and beloved by the people; may we get money, may we obtain property, cattle, &c.; may we marry wives, ••ady kely); may we have good robes, and wear a good piece of cloth on our bodies[77] ;3 since, amidst our toils and labor, these are the things we seek after[78].4 And this we do that we may with all fidelity assist each other to the last.'

"The incision is then made, as already mentioned; a small quantity of blood [is] extracted and drank by the covenanting parties

---

[74] Here is the idea of an absolute inter-merging of natures, by this rite.

[75] See Matt. 13: 12; 2$: 29.

[76] Here is an indication of the witness-bearing nature of these accessories of the rite

[77] Compare these blessings and cursings with those under Mosaic laws : Deut. 27: 9-26; 28: 1-68.

[78] See Matt. 6: 31, 32

respectively, [they] saying as they take it, ' These are our last words, We will be like rice and water[79] in town they do not separate, and in the fields they do not forsake one another; we will be as the right and left hand of the body; if one be injured, the other necessarily sympathizes and suffers with it[80]."

Speaking of the terms and the influence of this covenant, in Madagascar, Mr. Ellis says, that while absolute community of all worldly possessions is not a literal fact on the part of these blood-friends, " the engagement involves a sort of moral obligation for one to assist the other in every extremity." "However devoid of meaning," he adds, "some part of the ceremony of forming [this] brotherhood may appear, and whatever indications of barbarity of feeling may appear in others, it is less exceptionable than many [of the rites] that prevail among the people. ... So far as those who have resided in the country have observed its effects, they appear almost invariably to have been safe to the community, and beneficial to the individuals by whom the compact was formed."

Java

Yet again, this covenant of blood-friendship is found in different parts of Borneo. In the days of Mr. Ellis, the Rev. W. Medhurst, a missionary of the London Missionary Society, in Java, described it, in reporting a visit made to the Dayaks of Borneo, by one of his assistants, together with a missionary of the Rhenish Missionary Society[81].

---

[79] This is a natural, simple, and beautiful allusion in common use among the Malagasy, to denote an inseparable association. The rice is planted in water, grows in water, is boiled in water, and water is the universal beverage taken with it when eaten."

[80] Ellis's Hist, of Madagascar, I., 187-190

[81] Cited in Ellis's Hist, of Mad., I., 191, note

Telling of the kindly greeting given to these visitors at a place called Golong, he says that the natives wished "to establish a fraternal agreement with the missionaries, on condition that the latter should teach them the ways of God. The travelers replied, that if the Dayaks became the disciples of Christ, they would be constituted the brethren of Christ without any formal compact. The Dayaks, however, insisted that the travelers should enter into a compact [with them], according to the custom of the country, by means of blood. The missionaries were startled at this, thinking that the Dayaks meant to murder them, and committed themselves to their Heavenly Father, praying that, whether living or dying, they might lie at the feet of their Saviour. It appears, however, that it is the custom of the Dayaks, when they enter into a covenant, to draw a little blood from the arms of the covenanting parties, and, having mixed it with water, each to drink, in this way, the blood of the other.

"Mr. Barenstein [one of the missionaries] having consented [for both] to the ceremony, they all took off their coats, and two officers came forward with small knives, to take a little blood out of the arm of each of them [the two missionaries and two Dayak chiefs]. This being mixed together in four glasses of water, they drank, severally, each from the glass of the other; after which they joined hands and kissed. The people then came forward, and made obeisance to the missionaries, as the friends of the Dayak King, crying out with loud voices, 'Let us be friends and brethren forever; and may God help the Dayaks to obtain the knowledge of God from the missionaries!' The two chiefs then said, 'Brethren, be not afraid to dwell with us ; for we will do you no harm; and if others wish to hurt you, we will defend you with our life's blood, and die ourselves ere you be slain. God be witness, and this whole assembly be witness, that this is true.' Whereupon the whole company shouted, Balaak! or ' Good,' ' Be it so.' "

Yet another method of observing this rite, is reported from among the Kayans of Borneo—quite a different people from the Dayaks.

Its description is from the narrative of Mr. Spenser St. John, as follows: "Singauding [a Kayan chief] sent on board to request me to become his brother, by going through the sacred custom of imbibing each other's blood. I say imbibing, because it is either mixed with water and drunk, or else is placed within a native cigar, and drawn in with the smoke. I agreed to do so, and the following day was fixed for the ceremony. It is called Rcrbiang by the Kayans; Bersabibah, by the Borneans [the Dayaks], I landed with our party of Malays, and after a preliminary talk, to allow the population to assemble, the affair commenced. . . . Stripping my left arm, Kum Lia took a small piece of wood, shaped like a knife-blade, and, slightly piercing the skin, brought blood to the surface; this he carefully scraped off Then one of my Malays drew blood in the same way from Singauding; and, a small cigarette being produced, the blood on the wooden blade was spread on the tobacco. A chief then arose, and, walking to an open place, looked forth upon the river, and invoked their god and all the spirits of good and evil to be witness of this tie of brotherhood. The cigarette [blood-stained] was then lighted, and each of us took several puffs [receiving each other's blood by inhalation], and the ceremony was over[82]." This is a new method of smoking the "pipe of peace"—or, the cigarette of inter-union! Borneo, indeed, furnishes many illustrations of primitive customs, both social and religious.

One of the latest and most venturesome explorers of North Borneo was the gallant and lamented Frank Hatton, a son of the widely known international journalist, Joseph Hatton. In a sketch of his son's life-work, the father says[83]: "His was the first white foot in many of the hitherto unknown villages of Borneo; in him many of the wild tribes saw the first white man. . . . Speaking the language of the natives, and possessing that special faculty cf kindly firmness so necessary to the efficient control of uncivilized

---

[82] St. John's Life in the Forests of the Far East, I., II6 f.

[83] In "The Century Magazine" for July, 1885, p. 437.

peoples, he journeyed through the strange land not only unmolested, but frequently carrying away tokens of native affection. Several powerful chiefs made him their 'blood-brother'; and here and there the tribes prayed to him as if he were a god." It would seem from the description of Mr. Hatton, that, in some instances, in Borneo, the blood-covenanting is by the substitute blood of a fowl held by the two parties to the covenant, while its head is cut off by a third person—without any drinking of each other's blood by those who enter into the covenant. Yet, however this may be, the other method still prevails there.

Malaysia, Timor, Papua

Another recent traveler in the Malay Archipelago, who, also, is a trained and careful observer, tells of this rite, as he found it in Timor, and other islands of that region, among a people who represent the Malays, the Papuan, and the Polynesian races. His description is : "The ceremony of blood-brotherhood, . . . or the swearing of eternal friendship, is of an interesting nature, and is celebrated often by fearful orgies [excesses of the communion idea], especially when friendship is being made between families, or tribes, or kingdoms. The ceremony is the same in substance whether between two individuals, or [between] large companies. The contracting parties slash their arms, and collect the blood into a bamboo, into which kanipa coarse gin) or laru (palm wine) is poured. Having orovided themselves with a small fig-tree (haliK) they adjourn to some retired spot, taking with them the sword and spear from the Lull chamber [the sacred room] of their own houses if between private individuals, or from the Uma-Luli of their suku [the sacred building of their village] if between large companies. Planting there the fig-tree, flanked by the sacred sword and spear, they hang on it a bamboo-receptacle, into hich—after pledging each other in a portion of the mixed blood and gin—the remainder [of that mixture] is poured. Then each swears,' If I be false, and be not a true friend, may my blood issue from my mouth, ears, nose, as it does from this bamboo!'—the bottom of the receptacle being pricked at the same moment, to allow the blood and gin to escape. The [blood-stained] tree remains and grows as a witness of their contract."

Of the close and binding nature of this blood-compact, among the Timorese, the observer goes on to say: "It is one of their most sacred oaths, and [is] almost never, I am told, violated; at least between individuals." As to its limitless force and scope, he adds: "One brother [one of these brother-friends in the covenant of blood] coming to another brother's house, is in every respect regarded as free [to do as he pleases], and [is] as much at home as its owner. Nothing is withheld from him; even his friend's wife is not denied him, and a child born of such a union would be recognized by the husband as his; [for are not—as they reason—these brother-friends of one blood—of one and the same life ?] [84]"

North America

The covenant of blood-friendship has been noted also among the native races of both North and South America. A writer of three centuries ago, told of it as among the aborigines of Yucatan. "When the Indians of Pontonchan," he said, "receive new friends [covenant in a new friendship]. as a proof of [their] friendship, they [mutually, each], in the sight of the friend, draw some blood . . . from the tongue hand, or arm, or from some other part [of the body][85]." And this ceremony is said to have formed "a compact for life[86]."

A similar tie of adopted brotherhood, or of close and sacred friendship, is recognized among the North American Indians. Writing of the Dakotas, or the Sioux, Dr. Riggs, the veteran

---

[84] Forbes's A Naturalist's Wanderings in the Eastern Archipelago, p. 452.

[85] Peter Martyr's De Rebus Oceanicis et Novo Orbe, p. 338; cited in Spencer's Des. Soc. II., 34

[86] See Bancroft's Native Races of the Pacific Coast, I., 741

missionary and scholar, says: "Where one Dakota takes another as his k.oda, i. e., god, or friend, [Think of that, for sacredness of union—' god, or friend'!] they become brothers in each other's families, and are, as such, of course unable to intermarry[87]." And Burton, the famous traveler, who made this same tribe a study, says of the Dakotas: "They are fond of adoption, and of making brotherhoods like the Africans [Burton is familiar with the customs of African tribes]; and so strong is the tie that marriage with the sister of an adopted brother is within the prohibited degree[88]."

Brazil

In Brazil, the Indians were said to have a rite of brotherhood so close and sacred that, as in the case of the Bed'ween beyond the Jordan[89], its covenanting par-tics were counted as of one blood; so that marriage between those thus linked would be deemed incestuous. "There was a word in their language to express a friend who was loved like a brother; it is written Atourrassap ['erroneously, beyond a doubt,' adds Southey, 'because their speech is without the r']. They who called each other by this name, ht.d all things in common; the tie was held to be as sacred as that of consanguinity, and one could not marry the daughter or sister of the other[90]."

South Seas Islands

Among the people of the Society Islands, and perhaps also among those of other South Sea Islands, the term tayo is applied to an attached personal friend, in a peculiar relation of intimacy. The formal ceremony of brotherhood, whereby one becomes the tayo of

---

[87] Lynd's History of the Dakotas, p. 73, note.

[88] Burton's City of the Saints, p. 117

[89] See page 10, supra.

[90] Southey's Brazil, I., 240.

another, in these islands, I have not found described; but the closeness and sacredness of the relation, as it is held by many of the natives, would seem to indicate the inter-mingling of blood in the covenanting, now or in former times. The early missionaries to those islands, speaking of the prevalent unchastity there, make this exception: "If a person is a tayo of the husband, he must indulge in no liberties with the sisters or the daughters, because they are considered as his own sisters or daughters; and incest is held in abhorrence by them; nor will any temptations engage them to violate this bond of purity. The wife, however, is excepted, and considered as common property for the tayo[91]. Lieutenant Corner [a still earlier voyager] also added, that a tayo ship formed between different sexes put the most solemn barrier against all personal liberties[92]." Here is evidenced that same view of the absolute oneness of nature through a oneness of blood, which shows itself among the Semites of Syria[93], among the Malays of Timor[94]. and among the Indians of America[95].

And so this close and sacred covenant relation, this rite of blood-friendship, this inter-oneness of life by an inter-oneness of blood, shows itself in the primitive East, and in the wild and pre-historic West; in the frozen North, as in the torrid South. Its traces are everywhere. It is of old, and it is of to-day; as universal and as full of meaning as life itself.

It will be observed that we have already noted proofs of the independent existence of this rite of blood-brotherhood, or blood-friendship, among the three great primitive divisions of the race—

---

[91] See page 54, supra.

[92] Miss. Voyage to So. Pacif. Ocean, p. 360 f.

[93] See page 10, supra

[94] See page 54, supra

[95] See page 55 f., supra.

the Semitic, the Hamitic, and the Japhetic; and this in Asia, Africa, Europe, America, and the Islands of the Sea; again, among the five modern and more popular divisions of the human family: Caucasian, Mongolian, Ethiopian, Malay, and American. This fact in itself would seem to point to a common origin of its various manifestations, in the early Oriental home of the now scattered peoples of the world. Many references to this rite, in the pages of classic literature, seem have the same indicative bearing, as to its nature primitive source.

Bibliography

The Holy Bible: New Revised Standard Version/Division of Christian Education of The National Council of Churches of Christ in the United States of America. Nashville: Thomas Nelson Publishers, c 1989

The New Strong's Exhaustive Concordance

Encyclopaedia Britannica, 1990

M.G. Easton M.A., D.D., Illustrated Bible Dictionary, Third Edition, published by Thomas Nelson, 1897

McCarthy, D. J., Old Testament Covenant, 1978

Baltzer, K., The Covenant Formulary, 1971

Beyerlin, W., Origins and History of the Oldest Sinaitic Traditions, 1965

Fensgam, F. C., Covenant, Promise and Expectation, TZ 23, 1967, pp. 305 322

Fensgam, F. C., Common Trends in Curses of the Near Eastern Treaties and Kudurru-inscriptions compared with Maledictions of Amos and Isaiah, ZAW 75, 1963, pp. 155-175

Fensgam, F. C., The Treaty between the Israelites and the Tyrians, VT Supp 17, 1969, pp. 78ff.

Hillers, D. R. Treaty-curses and the Old Testament Prophets, 1964

Hillers, D. R., Covenant: The History of a Biblical Idea, 1968

Kenyon, E. W. The Blood Covenant.

Kitchen, K. A., Egypt, Ugarit, Qatna and Covenant, Ugarit Forschungen 11 (1979), pp. 453-464

Kline, M. G., Treaty of the Great King, 1963.

Lloyd, S., The Archaeology of Mesopotamia (1980); Saggs, H., Everyday Life in Babylonia and Assyria (1965)

McCarthy, D. J., Treaty and Covenant, 1963

M.G. Easton M.A., D.D., Illustrated Bible Dictionary, Third Edition, published by Thomas Nelson, 1897.

Mendenhall, G. E., Law and Covenant in Israel and the Ancient Near East, 1955

Muilenburg, J., The Form and Structure of the Covenantal Formulations, VT 9, 1959, pp. 74-79

Lloyd, S., The Archaeology of Mesopotamia, 1980

Saggs, H., Everyday Life in Babylonia and Assyria, 1965.

Holman's Bible Dictionary for Windows v 1.0, Parsons Technology, 1994

Illustrated Bible Dictionary, ISBN 0-865110-628-5)

The Software Toolworks Multimedia Encyclopedia 1.5, 1991 Grolier Inc.

www.ingramcontent.com/pod-product-compliance
Lightning Source LLC
Chambersburg PA
CBHW071704160426
43195CB00012B/1568